Available in Fontana by the same author

Send No More Roses
Passage of Arms
The Intercom Conspiracy
The Schirmer Inheritance
Journey into Fear
The Dark Frontier
Uncommon Danger
The Care of Time
The Levanter

HERE LIES

AN AUTOBIOGRAPHY

Eric Ambler

Fontana/Collins

First published by George Weidenfeld & Nicolson Ltd 1985
First issued in Fontana Paperbacks 1986

Copyright © Eric Ambler 1985

Made and printed in Great Britain by
William Collins Sons & Co. Ltd, Glasgow

ILLUSTRATIONS

ONE

A bearded man peered at me through the window for a moment and then said something that I did not understand. He saw that I was now conscious, however, and managed to open the door beside me. He held out a hand and I was able with his help to crawl on to the grass.

The car was at the bottom of the deep ditch that runs alongside that section of the Lausanne–Geneva autoroute and my helper was the German truck-driver who had seen me go off the road ahead of him. The car had rolled over twice before cartwheeling through a clump of young trees and landing back on its wheels facing the way it had come.

Autoroute traffic in Switzerland is policed by the gendarmerie and the sergeant who arrived a minute or two later was trained to deal patiently with those who bloodied themselves on his territory. When he had my Swiss driving licence and had radioed for an ambulance he squatted beside me on the grass and asked what had happened. The truck-driver had been a hundred or more metres behind me with nothing else on that side of the road. My car looked as if it had been new. Had I perhaps been experimenting with unfamiliar controls? Had I perhaps taken my eyes off the road for too long?

I tried to tell him but found it difficult to find the French words I needed. Yes, the car was new, less than a day old. The local dealer from whom I had taken delivery had mentioned that the manufacturers were using a new kind of chemical preservative on their engine assemblies. At first it would give off smoke and fumes. I should ignore them. So, I had ignored them. I had ignored them all the way along the lake road to Ouchy and then all the way along the autoroute nearly to Geneva airport. During that fifty-minute drive I had been gradually asphyxiated.

Only I could not think of the French word for asphyxiated. This

1

was, and is, *asphyxié*. I remembered hearing somewhere or other that concussion can play odd tricks. In an unwise attempt to seem calm, collected and in possession of all my faculties I used the participle *m'endormi* instead.

The sergeant was on to it instantly. 'You fell asleep while you were driving?'

'Certainly not. At one-thirty in the afternoon? No . . .'

'Where did you spend last night and how many hours of sleep did you have?' He was going by the book now. Those were the key questions he asked long-distance truck-drivers caught in traffic violations.

'I was at my home in Clarens. I went to bed as usual. I had plenty of sleep.'

'On this part of the autoroute, sir, drivers will go to sleep at all times of the day and night, and at all ages. Even young ones go to sleep.' He glanced again at my driving licence and his lips moved as he did the arithmetic. Seventy-two, pushing seventy-three. He looked me in the eyes. 'Were you wearing a seat-belt?'

'No.'

I should have lied to him. He did not tell me, as so many did during the next few days, that I was lucky to be alive. He was the kind of policeman who would know better than most the exceptional quality, to say nothing of the quantity, of the luck involved. It was only natural that he should want me to have deserved it. Had I been wearing a seat-belt some of that luck could have been attributed to prudence on my part and to a decent respect for the laws that he spent long hours trying to enforce. As it was, I had failed him. Too much had been asked of providence. Justice would have to be done. He took out a second notebook, wrote in it a short statement saying that I had fallen asleep while driving and invited me to sign it.

I should have tried again to explain about the fumes, or at least temporized. I was in pain and I could have found words to say so. Moreover, the ambulance from Geneva had arrived and the crew were at the side of the road above audibly debating the problem of getting a stretcher down to me. It was going to be easier for all concerned and quicker, they told one another *en clair*, if the injured person could manage to climb up the bank to the stretcher. This distraction alone should have been sufficient. However, I failed to take advantage of it, though I did try to do so. When I saw that the sergeant was paying no attention to the ambulance men I told him

2

that I thought I could crawl up to the road. He nodded, but when I got to my knees he again shoved the notebook at me and again asked me to sign his statement. So, having by then had enough of the ditch and of him, I signed.

At the hospital they undressed me, X-rayed me, put me in an intensive care unit and wired me up to various machines. Blood samples were taken and an anti-tetanus shot given. Then, both I and the strips of paper from the machines were examined by no less than three doctors in turn. The first spoke only French, the second spoke English most of the time and the third, who said he was a neurologist, spoke a little of each. All three concluded their examinations by shining lights into my eyes while I looked at the wall behind them or at the ceiling. I told the neurologist, in English, that there appeared to be a yellow flower floating in the air in front of my right eye. He said that the illusion was caused by a slight haemorrhage in the eye and was nothing to worry about. What they were looking for with their ophthalmoscopes were signs of cerebral haemorrhaging. So far there were none. That was very good.

At the time, I found the fact that so many doctors were available to give their attention to one casual patient surprising but not extraordinary. I knew, as everyone knew, that most public hospitals were understaffed; but all that I knew about casualty departments and emergency wards had been picked up from old feature films about them. In the films there had always seemed to be as many young doctors as there were nurses. The Cantonal in Geneva is a major teaching hospital, so I assumed that the first two to examine me had been interns fulfilling daily work quotas.

I did them, and the hospital, an injustice, though it was not until that evening that I realized it. At about seven o'clock a fourth doctor came to see me. He was the surgeon in charge, he said, and apologized for not seeing me earlier. It had been a busy day. However, colleagues had told him about my case. He looked through the strips of paper from the machines and then at me.

'How is your headache now?' he asked in English. 'Is it any better?'

'Oh yes, much better.'

He smiled as if he were really pleased to hear such nonsense after a hard day's work; but it was a marvellous charmer's smile that lit the whole face. For a moment he no longer looked tired, only very interested.

3

'How did the accident happen?' He had switched back to French.

I tried to answer in French and began to stammer. He waited politely for me to find the words I needed. When I simply continued to stammer he broke in, still speaking French.

'The police say that you admitted going to sleep while driving.'

'I tried to explain, but . . .' I could get no further.

'Yes, well, we don't think you had a heart attack or a stroke.' He glanced again at the paper strips. 'At least it doesn't look like it. But you did lose consciousness.'

'Only for seconds.'

'No. Longer, we think. Perhaps two or three minutes.'

'Well, doctor, I feel better now. In fact, if I can have my clothes back I'd like to order a taxi to take me home. It's near Montreux.'

'Would there be someone there to look after you? Your wife perhaps?'

Trick question.

'My wife is in London for a few days.'

'Ah yes, of course. You were asking if you could telephone her earlier. I will see what can be arranged about that.'

'Our *femme de ménage* comes in every morning. And I can telephone more easily from home. I'll be all right.'

'How long have you lived in French Switzerland?'

'Fourteen or fifteen years.'

'Have you always found it so difficult to speak French, to find the correct words and to say them?'

'Yes, I have,' I said firmly, and then when he did not respond I stammered on. 'You see, I always think in English. That is probably because writing in English is my profession.'

'But you understand quite easily when French is spoken to you.'

'Oh yes.'

'And one of my colleagues says that when you were speaking English to him you spoke without difficulty.'

'I probably did. The fact is that when I speak French I speak slowly because I have to search for every word.'

'Is it always so?'

'Always.'

He smiled again, but this time regretfully. We both knew now that I was being untruthful, in English as well as in French. We both knew, too, that there was something wrong. The difference between our thinking was that he had by then diagnosed the

4

trouble as amnesic aphasia, and knew what to do about it more or less, while I, with a lifelong dread of hospitals behind me, was trying to go home so that I could get at the forensic-medicine reference books and read about the incidental effects of concussion. Fortunately for me, however, he had decided that it was time to put a stop to my wild talk of taxis to Montreux.

'Brain-cell damage from concussion', he said, 'is like a bruise. And if all goes well it will gradually heal like a bruise. But it is a slow process. In the early stages the danger is a haemorrhage that will do more serious and permanent brain damage, perhaps cause death. You should stay here in hospital for at least twenty-four hours. I will see you again tomorrow. For tonight you can be moved into a bed. And I will leave orders that you may make a short telephone call. Goodnight.'

After a while I was disconnected from the machines, transferred to a bed and wheeled out of intensive care. In the corridor there was a staff telephone from which I could make a local call. I spoke to a neighbour who promised to tell my wife that I was all right. Then I was taken to a casualty ward.

The nursing night shift had just come on and the lights had already been dimmed. They were not yet out though, and I counted nine other beds. I was the last one in. My fellow casualties were there either for observation following an injury, as I was, or for emergency treatment requiring skilled supervision. During the night most of them slept; not well perhaps, certainly not peacefully, but they did sleep and I envied them. I could not even doze. All through the night, at regular intervals of about half an hour, the sister in charge would walk slowly round the ward seeing that all was well. There were two patients with intravenous drips going and she would check the bottles with the small flashlight she carried. When she came to me, though, she would exchange the flashlight for an ophthalmoscope. Then she would move to the bedside, switch on the light inside the instrument and peer through its lens into my eyes. She never said a word. She just peered, very carefully, first into the right eye and then into the left. Then she would give me a reassuring nod and switch off. A small hand movement as she turned away told me that she would be back shortly. There was no chance while she was on duty of a haemorrhage going unnoticed. I was in good hands.

So, I was obliged to think.

It soon became clear that, if I was going to be able in the morning

5

to tell the doctor with any truth or conviction that I felt better, I would have to stop trying to relive the accident. Even more important, since I could not remember exactly what had happened, I would have to stop trying to revise what I did know as if it were a story that would change course and end differently if I decided to write it another way. For once, there could be no more revision. I would have to think of other things, of pleasant and amusing things.

This proved impossible. I tried counting my blessings and soon found myself counting bruises instead; not the obvious ones on legs and hands, but the late-developers on arms, chest and shoulders which were just beginning to make themselves felt. The trouble was, I found, that the only other things to think of immediately available were far from amusing and distinctly unpleasant. In fact, some of them were worse than the imaginary accident replays.

My spoken French had never been better than passable. In French I could call a plumber to deal with a leak, argue about a typewriter service contract or make polite conversation with the grocer. It really did not matter very much if, because of a bang on the head, I did those things a bit less fluently in future, did it? No, not very much. Sure? Well, yes, but suppose that was only part of the story. How could I be sure that that was the only damage done? One of the doctors had said that I could not expect to remember much about what had happened immediately before the accident. That was a pity and the insurance company would think so too; but that blank was *immediately* before the accident. Why was it that I could not remember what I had been thinking about before I had got on to the autoroute? I had a feeling that it had been something to do with the United States. But what? Another thing: in the Taverne du Chateau at Vevey, where I had stopped for lunch, I had been reading a book. But what book? Why could I not remember that?

When I was a child, a man described as 'living by his wits' was either a sponger or a con-man. A woman so described was either 'kept' or a professional shop-lifter. Genteel, lower middle-class versions of upper-class attitudes towards bounders and upstarts of both sexes were common, but that one puzzled me even then. As I saw it, you lived by working with your hands, or you lived by using your wits, or you lived by using both wits and hands together to produce something saleable like a chest of drawers or a smoking-concert performance of Chaminade's *Autumn*. I always thought of professional writers as, in that sense, living by their wits, and of the wits they lived by as valuable natural resources that could be expected to run out before the owner died. When writers lost their wits prematurely the cause was always 'a nervous breakdown'.

Though based on the overheard conversations of adults who were talking about writers of songs, lyrics, jokes, music-hall sketches and comedians' patter, that account of the writer's situation was not altogether outlandish I think. 'Nervous breakdown', of course, was the Edwardian euphemism for any disease that involved mental incapacity or brain damage, including alcoholism. Although I knew that writers were not the only workers who needed to keep all their wits about them, I also knew that writers, and actors, had to be seen to be doing so. With writers, as with actors, any loss of wits showed instantly. It showed in the quality of their work.

What I feared from the concussion was not a simple loss of memory but a loss of wits that might be irreversible.

They had taken my watch with the rest of my things and there was no striking clock in the hospital area of the city. I promised myself that when the sister next did her rounds and came over to look in my eyes I would ask her the time. My guess at that point was that it was between one o'clock and half past one. The guess was based on my estimate of the time between rounds as thirty minutes; but I fully expected it to be hopelessly fast. I was quite prepared to be told that it was only just after midnight.

However, I never did get to ask the time that night. Just as she reached the bed directly opposite mine, one of those where she had to check a drip bottle, something strange happened. I remembered what I had been thinking about when I had driven on to the autoroute.

For those who write books there is in America these days an ordeal to be faced called 'the tour'. It has nothing to do with tourism or what used to be called travel. It is the name that has been given by the American publishing and bookselling trades to a marketing process which sends authors flying to and fro from city to city across the United States, usually at their hardcover publishers' expense, to promote the sales of their books. This they do by going on television and radio talk shows, by giving press interviews, by chatting to audiences of prospective bookbuyers and by auto-graphing copies of their books a hundred or two at a time. The tour is highly organized, with publishers and the media cooperating to spread the authors evenly over the more densely populated areas of the country. The old publishing seasons are things of the past. Some of the bigger cities are now blanketed pretty well all the year round by the tour. It is as pervasive as smog.

I had been on the tour just once, the year before. Now, I had started to write a new book. As I drove on to the autoroute I was wondering what I would do if I were asked by my American pub-lisher to go on the tour again. I would refuse of course, but I would have to give a reason for refusing.

As I recalled the tour it became clear that the simplest way would be to plead lack of stamina. By now, everyone to do with American publishing must know that, for all but the most seasoned troupers, the tour was what insurance assessors call a period of high risk.

The calls on stamina began on most days at five in the morning. That was either because a car would shortly be arriving to take you to a local television station for the breakfast show, or because it was a travelling day and you had to pack, check out and get to the air-port. If it was a television day you could, on the way to the studio, raise your spirits by making a bet with yourself that the anchor man who was to interview you about your book would not have read even a small part of it. You would win every time. As one of the more candid of them explained to me, authors who could talk sense for three minutes on camera in return for a close-up of a book jacket were cheap programming. In these days of rising costs we were therefore welcome. All the same, he had six of us coming through on the tour that week. If he tried to read all of our books what did I think would happen to his golf game? It would be shot to hell, right? So, he just read the blurbs. It was better really. If you wanted to look spontaneous the only way was to wing it. That way it *was* spontaneous.

The station he worked for was an ABC network affiliate with control of its own programming and a local morning audience of about half a million. No matter how well you winged it, the number of bookbuyers you reached would be small. However, an appearance on one of the nationwide network shows, such as NBC's *Today*, could have disconcerting results.

At an autographing session in a Chicago department store I was approached by a woman who had bought ten copies of my new book. She wanted me to write in all ten, inscribing each one to a different person. She produced a list from her bag and read the names out for me at dictation speed. As I wrote she explained that the books, 'personalized' by my writing in them, would make great stocking presents for Christmas. When I asked her which name on the list was hers, though, she seemed surprised. 'Oh, I never read books,' she said with a smile; 'I haven't read a book in years. I saw you on the *Today* show.'

Yes, television does sell books, especially when there are authors on tour to personalize them. In America, too, the signing of books has a strictly commercial significance. It is a trade custom that copies in a bookstore on sale or return cannot be returned as unsold if they have been signed by the author. By energetic signing authors on the tour can make themselves really useful to their long-suffering publishers. All that is needed is a good felt-tip pen and a helpful salesperson to stack the copies for you. Then, if you are prepared to put your mind to it, you should be able to sign as many as two hundred copies in an hour.

If necessary I could plead bursitis and writer's cramp as well as lack of stamina. Of one thing I was sure. The real reason for my not wanting to do the tour again would be too difficult to explain, too difficult in New York anyway. There, publishers are understanding about physical infirmities but easily lose patience with behavioural quirks and frailties. The quirk was my belief, long held but still firm, that the best and by far the safest place for readers and writers to meet was on the printed page. The frailty was my inability to deal efficiently and forthrightly with the local wise-acres, rogue literati and aha-school instant analysts I encountered on the tour. I came to think of them as 'buttonholers'.

Professional radio and television interviewers are usually easy to get on with, even when they are discussing books they have not read. Generally, both parties to the interview talk a lot of nonsense, but nonsense of an acceptably entertaining kind. Press inter-viewers deal less in nonsense but read more and can sometimes be drawn into gossiping about their work. I am not intimidated by audiences. I can give little talks and even deliver a lecture if I have been told well in advance what is expected of me. If I have had sufficient time to prepare I can even sound and seem spontaneous. But I like to have a screw of paper with notes on it in my pocket. Though I may never refer to it I feel safer with it there. Off the cuff I am likely to talk rubbish.

9

I found that buttonholers stayed away from the straight signing sessions; they preferred the bookstore wine-and-cheese parties, the book luncheons and the library club evenings. Quite soon I learned to distinguish them from those gentler readers who came just to say hello, to get old editions inscribed, to draw attention to a paperback misprint, to satisfy their curiosity about an author they had first read when they were young or to ask if he yet used a word processor. The buttonholers would usually wait until the readers and autograph seekers had had their fill. Then, with their considered opinions to voice, their critical insights to display and their soft-nosed questions to fire at the target figure with the empty wine glass in his hand, they would move in.

'Doctor Howard B. Gotlieb of Boston University has said that on a twentieth-century comparative scale based on nineteenth-century literary ratings, you come out as a contemporary Wilkie Collins. Mr Ambler, how do you react to that?'

'I don't think I . . .'

'You're not denying you've heard of Howard Gotlieb, are you?'

'No, no. I like him.'

'Then how do you feel about being rated with Wilkie Collins?'

'Well . . .'

'He was a friend of Charles Dickens. Sure he was. Now does that in fact influence you pro or con? I'm only asking. Maybe you reject the whole basis of the comparison.'

'I'm not sure I . . .'

'How long since you read *The Moonstone* or *The Woman in White*? Thirty years? Forty?'

'I'm not . . .'

'Exactly. You know what I'd be asking Gotlieb if I were in your shoes? "If I'm Wilkie Collins, who's Dickens when he's *chez lui*?" That's what I'd be asking. What's the betting he'd say Norman Mailer, hah?'

'Well . . .'

'Don't tell me you're a friend of Norman's!'

'I've never met him.'

'For God's sake! You don't have to meet a writer to be his friend, do you?'

'Well . . .'

He gave me an unpleasantly confidential grin. 'You've been a friend of mine for years,' he said.

Although many of the buttonholers, most perhaps, were

teachers of one sort or another, a surprisingly large number turned out to be dental or medical sub-specialists. I recall two periodontists, a chiropractor and several podiatrists. Some gave me their cards. If, among the teachers, I remember Mat and Tommy best, that is only partly because I met them early on in the tour.

The occasion was a book club dinner organized by a department store and staged in its lunch restaurant and coffee shop. After the *chicken-à-la-King*, talks were given by three tour authors: me, an actress with a book of memoirs and a political columnist plugging his latest book-length polemic. Following the talks, the store's book department moved in with trolleys bearing stacks of copies, hardback and paperback, to be signed and sold. Long trestle tables were set up for the purpose. While all this was being done I was introduced to two club members, Mat Something-or-Other and Thomasina Such-and-Such.

There were a handsome, healthy-looking pair, he in his early forties, she a few years younger. They both wore designer jeans that looked as if they had come from the same shop. I could not tell whether they were married to one another or sharing a bed, or just holding hands because they were colleagues. He was an associate professor of English Literature at the local state university. She taught a Creative Writing course there. Or it may have been the other way round. Both were pursuing their own writing careers on the side, of course. As Thomasina put it, they were buying creative time by hacking.

'I may as well tell you', Mat said pleasantly, 'that you used to be a big hero of mine at college.'

'Well, that can't be very long ago.'

'Oh, I still use you as a model. I use you as a model all the time.'

'Of what?'

'Place,' he said. 'You have a great sense of place.'

'It's good of you to say so.' To me a sense of place has always seemed one of the more mundane components of a writing talent, but it is obviously better to have one than not to have one. It is possible, however, that my tone was no more than polite and that it lacked the throb of gratitude they may have thought to be due.

Thomasina gave a little laugh. 'I didn't believe you existed,' she said and then suddenly seemed to fly into a cold rage. 'And I certainly didn't believe that you were British. Eric Ambler, the legend in his own lifetime, the generic term for intrigue? No way. Have I got it right? Generic? Or do you prefer to be eponymous?'

11

Her eyes and the fury in them appeared to be focused now on something or someone behind my left ear, and I even glanced over my shoulder to see who was there, but there was nothing but a trolleyload of books going by. I realized that she had a cast in one eye.

'My father used to read Eric Ambler,' she went on accusingly. 'That was when he was in the navy in World War Two. He said that you knew how fear smelt. He thought you must be some sort of refugee, someone who had discovered secrets and was telling them. Ambler had to be a pseudonym. It *still* has to be.'

Her voice was getting louder and heads were turning. Mat put a hand to one of her elbows. 'He has a great sense of place, Tommy,' he murmured softly. He made it sound as if he were the sober one persuading the party drunk that no insult had been intended and that it was time to go.

She brushed his hand away and returned to the attack. 'Listening to you just now,' she said to my ear, 'listening to you up there on the podium getting your easy laughs from the garden club set, I had a strange feeling about the great premature anti-fascist, crypto-lefty, quasi-liberal, genre-crap innovator from dear old England. Know what it was, Mr Ambler?'

'You're going to tell me.'

'You bet I am.' She contrived a smile with which to say it. '*If* you exist, which I very much doubt, you have to be full of one hundred per cent non-biodegradable garbage.'

'She's trying to figure what makes you tick,' Mat explained; 'she's into the eternal verities.'

Her eyes switched to him for a moment. 'What I'm into', she said with a little catch in her voice, 'is people and basic human emotions, the places of the heart.' The eyes switched back and she gave me another look at her smile. Then she delivered her final, end-of-semester opinion. 'You put nothing of yourself into your books,' she said, 'nothing at all.'

'How can you tell?' I asked, but she had already turned away and the publicity person wanted me to start work at one of the signing tables. Later, I asked about Tommy and her plain speaking. The publicity person was airily sympathetic.

'Tommy has hang-ups,' she said, 'as well as loads of talent. And she's certainly not against mystery and suspense. In fact, I've heard her say that that's where today's true writing is. Maybe it was your suit.'

'What's wrong with my suit?'

'Nothing. It's just that Tommy always teaches her classes that real writers never wear ties or bras or suits.'

'I don't know about bras, but I wasn't the only speaker wearing a suit. Why does she pick on me?'

'You're the author she particularly wanted to meet. Maybe you're the one she thought ought to look like a writer. Do you want to sign the rest of these books?'

The complaint that this or that writer looked nothing like his or her books used to be made constantly. To make it nowadays, however, calls for naivety of an old-fashioned kind that I could not associate with Tommy. The suit suggestion was no less absurd. Even in Hollywood, where the wearing of a tie can be a sign of depravity, there would be nothing remarkable about a writer wearing a suit in the evening. Tommy was a little old for the quaint bohemianism that was being attributed to her. Obviously, though, her tourist-baiting game had proved a source of embarrassment to publicity persons and tour organizers. The tie–bra–suit routine must have been dreamed up as a way of apologizing for her.

None of the buttonholers I met later had anything as aggressive to offer as Tommy's bloodshot critical invective and wall-eyed stare; and none had a straight man like Mat to cue the punch lines; but nearly all asked the same questions. How much fact is there in your fiction? What makes you tick?

They were not often put as simply as that, however. Most buttonholers went in for elegant variation. Their questions came dolled up with French (as in 'To what extent are your books *romans à clef*?'), or nonce words ('Would you describe your work as fiction or faction?') or (as in 'Does it please you that your books are said to be liked by the CIA?') dressed to kill. One or two of the more delicate questioners seemed to sidle furtively into the matter of my truthfulness as if they had just started dealing in an illegal drug of suspect strength and purity. There was nothing personal, they said, in what they were saying. All they wanted to know was how true my stories were. It was as simple as that. Nobody was accusing anyone of anything. Look at it from where they stood, or sat reading. Just because I wrote a little better than your average hack and had been well thought of by Jacques Barzun didn't make me valid, did it? It could be simply that I was a more expensive, slightly up-market hustler, couldn't it? A reasonable question? Okay, so how would I reply?

At first I tried answering all questions but soon found myself in difficulties. So, instead of answering questions directly, I tried fielding them. I tried, for instance, saying that the relationship between storytelling novelist and reader is, in its way, as collusive as the relationship between playwright and theatre audience. However, this was not well received. A proscenium arch, I was reminded, was not a book. In America, as I should know, it was expected that politicians and rabble-rousing preachers should rely for success on the public's readiness to suspend disbelief. Of writers, even if they were only novelists, better things were expected.

By then I had identified among the buttonholers two distinct groups: those who read novels but disapproved in their hearts of the habit, and those who saw novel-reading as a game in which the reader is challenged to find and describe the real live person hiding behind the portrait on the jacket. For the tour author this can be confusing only if he fails to see that although both groups are asking essentially the same questions they are loading them to elicit different answers. He learns to avoid the use of phrases like 'levels of reality' and words like 'imagination'. The only safe way of answering is the obliging way.

For some writers, of course – and especially for those whose lives are always there, thinly covered with fictitious characters, in the pages of their novels – the obliging way can come quite naturally, with modest talk of minor insights and the holding up of mirrors. Historical novelists, as long as they do not object too strenuously to being treated as if they were academic historians, have a fairly easy time, as do writers of soft-porn blockbusters whose readers only want to know about the size of their royalty earnings. For contemporary storytellers, however, and particularly for those who write thrillers, the tour can be an unnerving experience.

'Which of your books is the autobiographical one?'

The first time I was asked that I answered without thinking. 'None of them,' I said and for a moment or two had no second thoughts.

Both the young man who had spoken and the girl with him looked like college students. No doubt some English teacher had told them about the traditional ways in which novels are conceived and written. They could be thinking of becoming writers themselves. They could already be writers. I should be as helpful as possible.

Then came the doubts. How could any of my books reasonably be thought of as autobiographical? Either they had not read them or they were attempting to amuse themselves at my expense. I was already on the defensive when the girl struck.

'None at *all*?' It was a high, piercing voice. 'Some of your books could very well be autobiographical, judging from the publisher's publicity sheet. Are you seriously telling us that your books are all cut from whole cloth, that there is nothing of yourself in any of them?'

Although years younger than Tommy she already had the plonking speech rhythms of the natural scold.

'What I'm saying is that my books are novels and are therefore fiction.'

'And therefore also untrue?'

'They are as true or half-true or false as they were when you saw them as possibly autobiographical.'

The boy said, 'Hah!' and they both gave me baleful, just-another-mean-old-bullshitter looks. The girl had been holding a copy of a book for me to sign. With a glance at me to see that I was watching, she ostentatiously put it back on the bookstore pile before they walked away.

Once or twice I tried pretending to be amazed by the novelty of the question but found that I lacked the determination and the effrontery needed to support the pretence. I tried a sort of casual, unconcerned frankness – 'I've sometimes wondered that myself' – but had difficulty extricating myself from the discussions that would follow. As a last resort I worked out a reply that contained a pinch of truth; enough to taste but not enough to stimulate. When the time came to try it out, however, I was in Los Angeles.

I had lived in that city once and still had friends and acquaintances there. I should have known the risks I was running. The very way in which the question was put should have warned me.

'Did you ever think of any of your novels as having been partly autobiographical?'

He was middle aged, well nourished, clear eyed and tieless. He had begun by greeting me as if we were old friends from way back, but in Los Angeles that meant nothing. He looked like a dentist. In fact, I thought I recognized him as a root-canal man from Westwood who had once given me a bad time. After a thoughtful pause I gave him the new reply.

'In the sense that my books are all the products of one mind and one accumulation of experience, I suppose it could be said that they are all more or less autobiographical. I wouldn't like to over-simplify though. Writing fiction isn't at all a simple process. I don't find it so anyway.'

'That's great!' He beamed approval. 'You've really been think-ing. It's like the man said. For concentrating the mind the book tour must beat the prospect of a hanging every time. Been telling them all what makes you tick, huh?'

'Not exactly, no.'

'Of course not. You're wise. You're saving it. Do you have a second act?'

'For what?'

'For the autobiography you're planning to write, champ. What else would I mean?'

I remembered him then. He was not the root-canal man, but a screenwriter who had become a director and worked in television. We were in a bookstore on Wilshire Boulevard only a few blocks from Hollywood. I had no car of my own there. The publicity person was driving me. Escape would be difficult.

'There isn't even a first act,' I said.

'Nonsense.' He moved to pen me against a computer game dis-play. 'Everybody has a first act. That's the trouble with autobiogra-phy in this town. Too many one-acters. You have your childhood poverty, your early struggles, your first big break, your first hit and you're in the money. Then what? Nothing. If you're a performer all you can do is let the credits roll. Writers have more to say, but most have trouble saying it nicely. Do you still take care of yourself? Do you jog?'

'No.'

'When you lived here you used to go to Doc Mitchell and work out with Marvin Hart. That's taking care. Do you still have regular check-ups? I know that over in Europe some people don't.' He looked as if he really wanted to know.

'Am I suffering from an incurable disease, do you mean?'

He bridled. 'You know damned well what I mean. In this town, when a writer starts telling what makes him tick, or even starts *thinking* of telling, word gets around. Questions are always asked. You know.'

'I know. Is he gaga or over the hill? Has he anything worth saying?'

He looked startled for a moment. 'Well yes, there's all that too.'

He waved it away. 'The important thing to ask about is his sense of values and proportion *as a whole man*. These days people don't like dying-writer stuff. It's either mawkish or harrowing. It can be bitter, too, about the living. *You* know what I mean. When some writers get the nod from the grim reaper they seem to lose all sense of proportion. Of course, I don't say you would.'

'I'm glad.'

'But you *might*. For instance' – he glanced round to make sure that he was not overheard – 'you happen to know that during the first writers' strike a very dear friend of mine was a scab. Okay, that was twenty-odd years ago and who cares now about scabbing that old? In your right mind you'd never think of it, much less write about it. But how do we know, me and my old friend, that you're in your right mind? Who's to tell us? Who but you? So I'm asking, champ. Are you in your right mind?'

I looked thoughtful so as to give myself time to think. During the first Hollywood writers' strike against the studios in 1961 a few writers had defied their Guild and some of them had later been disciplined. It was possible that this particular Guild member (or the friend, if he existed), having got away with it at the time, had become more and more troubled over his years of prosperity by fears of exposure. But why on earth was he asking for my silence? Was he mistaking me for someone else? I could not even remember his name. Was either of us in his right mind?

'I'm all right most days,' I said unconvincingly; 'at least, I think so. But my memory's terrible. I don't believe I'd know this old friend of yours even if I saw him.'

He beamed again and patted my arm. 'Thanks. I'm glad.' But doubts lingered. 'You've had no brushes with death lately? No intimations of mortality at all?'

'Not lately, no.'

'Well then, you won't be getting mean and vengeful. That's not what the reading public wants anyway. You know that. They want side-splitting true stories about crazy producers and megalomaniac stars and quirky character actors, the blacker the humour the better. But who am I to tell you? You were here for ten years. You know where some of the bodies are buried. You must have had plenty of laughs.'

'Oh yes. And it's the laughs I'll remember.'

He still had doubts about me but I was there to sign books and his time as author's old friend was running out. Now he spoke for all to hear. 'And how's Joan? She here with you? No? But you're still married, you must be. Of course you are. We're out in the valley now beyond Encino. Call me at the studio if you have a free moment. And let's keep in touch, hah?'

He gave me the little splay-fingered wave that serves as a hail or farewell in those parts and was gone. Part of the mystery was solved. Almost certainly it had been my wife who had known about his cheating during the strike. I would wait before telling her of the encounter though. If I described him too well she might be able to remember his name.

For the rest of the tour I dealt with persistent buttonholers by referring them to my forthcoming autobiography. It would, I assured them, be brutally frank: the ideal handbook for anyone setting out to make a fast buck writing thrillers.

I knew that I could never do it. Only an idiot believes that he can write the truth about himself.

The night sister peered into my eyes for the last time and then wrote something on the case record at the foot of the bed. Dawn was beginning to show through the high windows. There was a subdued bustle as the nursing shifts changed. Soon, lights were switched on and a male nurse came round with a tray serving out thermometers. By each bed he did a little mime to show that the thermometers were for rectal, not oral, use. After the temperature taking, *vases de nuit* were collected and breakfast was served, in my case a mug of tea. An hour or so later my friend the surgeon arrived, accompanied by a train of students, to do the rounds.

Amnesic aphasia, according to a medical dictionary, is a 'loss of memory for specific words, with hesitant and fragmentary speech'. The lesions which cause this type of aphasia 'lie in the parietal at or near the angular gyrus'.

After the accident I had given, with my hesitant and fragmentary French, a good demonstration of the way aphasia can work. Now, as if to show versatility, I proceeded to give an even better demonstration of paraphasia, which you can get from the same crack on the head that gives you aphasia. 'Sometimes,' the dictionary says, 'words are uttered fluently but inappropriately, as in jargon.'

As the surgeon approached my bed he gave me a friendly nod, glanced at my case record and then murmured something to the students behind him.

It could very well have been: 'This is the English writer who has a headache from driving off the autoroute at a hundred and then wonders why he can no longer speak French easily.'

Turning to me, he then said in French: 'And what do you think has happened to your car, Mr Ambler?'

Clearly, it was a test question. I decided to reply in English that I thought my car would be a total write-off. Instead, I found myself saying, without a moment's hesitation: 'Je crois qu'elle soit totalisée.'

It just slipped out. I was horrified as well as surprised. I had never before used *totaliser* in its slang sense. A French surgeon, I think, would have at once ceased to care what happened to me. The Swiss one seemed amused rather than offended. After another look at the case record, he wrote something on it (*paraphasie*?) and said that if, after his colleagues had examined me, all was found to be well I could go home.

The last of the colleagues was another neurologist, this time a woman. She thought that I might have a cracked bone in my neck and sent me off for more X-rays. When nothing new showed up she shook her head in disbelief.

'So, all that you have is a little concussion. You could have had worse from a bathroom fall, much worse. I am told that you write novels that are published in French.'

'Not my French, doctor. Translated from the English.'

'If you wrote in a novel about such an accident and stated that so little damage was done, nobody who knew anything would believe you.'

I asked if she was going to let me go home.

'Oh yes, I think you can go. All we ask is that you take care. You will not feel like driving for a while.'

'I'm sure I won't.'

She shook her head again as if in wonderment. 'Do you really understand how fortunate you have been?'

'Yes, doctor, I really think I do.'

TWO

Grandpa Ambler came from Preston in Lancashire and was a printer's proof-reader. Emma Rimmer, his wife, was Manchester born and had worked in a cotton mill. After their marriage they moved to Salford where their four children were born.

Occasionally, when she thought no children were listening, she would call him by his middle name, Fred. At all other times she called him Pa as the children did. His first name, William, no one ever used. He was an imposing man with fierce eyes, a sharply pointed beard and a habit of uttering an explosive 'Bah!' when he was displeased or effectively opposed in argument. He was also something of a dandy. At a time when other wage-earning men of his class had best suits of navy-blue or black serge and usually wore bowler hats, he would wear sponge-bag grey with a pearl stickpin in his tie and a curly-brimmed grey Homburg. When he went to church Granny Ambler used to carry the prayer books for both of them while he sauntered along beside her swinging a silver-knobbed walking stick. His lifelong weaknesses were chronic asthma, a sweet tooth that favoured Turkish delight and a recurring belief that the reams of commemorative doggerel he wrote would one day become publishable. In politics he was on the radical side of Liberal.

My father, the eldest child, was born in 1882 and christened Alfred Percy. Within the Salford family he was always known as Alf. By everyone else who knew him well, including my mother, he was called Reg. He grew up with two lives. As Alf he attended a Salford board school, sang solos in the church choir and left school at the age of twelve to work in the offices of a local brewery. Over those same years, thanks to a helpful Church of England vicar, a choirmaster trained in Manchester and a professional organist who enjoyed teaching, he was able to study music. In his late teens he was sufficiently known as an organist to be called on by other

20

churches when they needed a locum. Soon he was earning half-guineas as a piano accompanist and phono-fiddle duettist at club and smoking concerts in the Manchester area. After a while he began experimenting with marionettes; not the kind with whole puppets worked by strings from above, but what used to be called 'living' marionettes; that is, puppet arms, torsos and legs joined at the collar line to live performers' heads. In those days conjurors often doubled as living marionettists; the skills involved were to some extent those of a magic-box illusionist. From where he sat upstage at the piano Alf had no trouble seeing how marionettes worked or thinking of ways in which they could be made to work better. Although when playing the organ he was still A.P. Ambler, at concerts he had begun to call himself Reg Ambler or Reg Ambrose.

In 1903 most of the Salford Amblers moved to London. Only Charles, the second son who had a good job in Manchester, stayed behind. The reason for the move was that Fred Ambler was going to work in Fleet Street for Labouchere's *Truth*. The girls, Cis and Dot, went to sea as stewardesses with the Union Castle Line. In the Walworth Road my father found a church with a vicar who had a place for an organist. From digs in Camberwell he then set out to acquire a London accent and to make his mark in the old semi-pro concert world of the inner London suburbs. The job in the brewery was replaced by a better one in the advertising department of the Westinghouse Company. Later, about the time of his marriage, he left Westinghouse for the resoundingly named Indiarubber, Gutta-Percha and Telegraph Works Limited, which were across the river from Woolwich in Silvertown.

I know what my mother looked like when she and my father met because a photograph was taken soon after the meeting. How they came to meet, though, was never quite made clear. My mother had a tight-lipped smile with which to forbid 'personal' questions from children. My father was always readier with answers. But when he said once that the occasion of their meeting had been a smoker in Finsbury, my mother quickly corrected him. It had been a choral-society affair, she said sharply. How could he have forgotten? Her mother had been there in the audience that evening and in those days ladies had never gone to smoking concerts.

Even without my father's instant but slightly comic admission of error I would have known which version was the right one. Smoking concerts had long been mixed affairs. The people next

21

door went to them. It was possible that ladies and gentlemen of the upper classes still did not mix in places where men might smoke pipes; but that was because their ladies were very frail and wore tulle all the time. Our sort of ladies and gentlemen with clean faces and tidy clothes mixed where there was entertainment to be had: in theatre pits and galleries, in music halls and, more cheaply still, in the municipal halls and assembly rooms where most smoking concerts were given. The word 'smoking' had by then, and in that context, more to do with informality and the wearing or not-wearing of full evening dress than with tobacco.

What I think happened at the Finsbury smoker was that my father, engaged for the evening as a paid accompanist, took a fancy to Amy Andrews, the pretty nineteen-year-old soprano with the try-out close-harmony group. The choral society was probably the organization that paid for the hall and the semi-pro performers and sold the tickets through its members at a profit. I also think that my parents got to know one another without being formally introduced and that the delinquent chaperone had been Grandad, not Granny, Andrews.

Charles Butler Andrews was a cabinet-maker by trade and a Londoner. Though he lived in Tottenham he was always most at home, I think, in the pubs and coffee shops of the small factory and business area of Clerkenwell that used to lie between Farringdon Road and the City. There he had old friends, mostly grave, boozy men who wore dark clothes and bowlers and often smelt, as he did, of peppermint drops and mahogany dust. They were all men with whom he had worked. Some had been partners, some had been employers or employees, most had been all three. By the time I was old enough to wait for him by myself outside the pubs he had had a business career of several ups and downs.

The first up had been when, as a young craftsman not long out of his apprenticeship, he had started in the business of cabinet-making for scientific instrument makers and been awarded a contract to make hardwood wall cabinets for the early Bell telephones. However, commercial success never agreed with him. He soon drank away the business and went back to work as a journeyman. When he had enough saved he started up on his own again. This time he made small furniture, finely veneered boxes and table-top chests with fitted interiors. This time, too, he had a wife, Emmy, to support. She was the daughter of a solicitor named Wellbeloved who had worked all his professional life for the Corporation of the

22

City of London and who became a Corporation pensioner with rooms in the Charterhouse. He died there at the age of ninety-six.

'A nasty old man,' my mother said in later years. It was a rare confidence. She had been trying to explain – to herself perhaps as well as to me – how it could come about that her father, although a fine craftsman and the kindest of men greatly loved by all who knew him, could sometimes 'be a bit of an old rascal' and also be found wanting as a provider.

She was the eldest of his five children. The youngest of them was still a baby in arms when their mother became a chronic invalid. Daughter Amy had had to mother them all. She had mothered her father too. His pet name for her had been 'Charley' and the name had been a great comfort to her in bad times. Great-grandfather Wellbeloved had never comforted anyone. In the bad times *he* had even refused to acknowledge the Andrews' existence.

After they were married, my parents went to live in a rented terrace house in Wellington Road, Charlton. From there my father could cycle to Woolwich and then cross on the ferry to the Works in Silvertown. Evening and weekend travel about London was made easy for Reg and Amy Ambrose, entertainers at the piano, by the South-Eastern and Chatham Railway. My father's old marionette show, a cumbersome affair of conventional design with dolls bought ready made from a theatrical supplier, had been condemned. They were planning a new show with two dolls on stage and many costume changes as well as scenery and props.

I was born in 1909 at the Wellington Road house. Among the most peculiar memories of my childhood is that of discovering what was in the ottoman. This was a sofa with a hinged seat covering a trunk-like storage space. Inside, I found dozens of very small human hands and feet. They were beautifully shaped and delicately carved and had been made in beech and boxwood by Grandad Andrews in his Clerkenwell workshop. They were the hands and feet for the new marionettes.

I remember my first nose bleed. It was the result of a push-cart running away, with me in it, down a steep slope in Maryon Park. In charge of me at the time was Uncle Frank, the younger of mother's two brothers. He was then aged twelve. It was he, too, who later supplied me with the essential stuff and nonsense for years of bad dreams by telling me in secret what he had been able to find out about the mechanics of sex and childbirth from the other boys in his school playground.

In 1912 my brother Maurice was born. The midwife was a Nurse Black and she stayed with us for several weeks. A two-up, two-down, no-bathroom house can become cramped at such times. I slept in the kitchen, where I was able to hear too much and to see more than I could understand. One day, when the nurse's back was turned, I managed to get upstairs into the front bedroom and see the little stranger I had been told about below. For the time and circumstances, my infancy seems to have been no more than conventionally painful.

It was in Wellington Road, in the winter before the Great War, that I first heard the word 'refugee'. We had one there, living in the house opposite to us, the one with the laburnum tree. His name was Mr Peshik – that, anyway, was how it sounded – and he was, my father said, a Hungarian. He could, I suppose, have been a refugee Croatian nationalist, but we were not really interested in his past. For us, the important thing about Mr Peshik was that he was an inventor, a man of 'originality' – one of my father's favourite words – and that he had thought of a way of solving the back-cloth problem for the new show.

There is a picture* showing how living marionettes could look in front of Mr Peshik's back-cloth, and although my father had it retouched, that is more or less what an audience would see during a performance. In earlier shows the back-cloth had been a curtain of black material hanging from rings in vertical folds and weighted inside the bottom hem with lead pellets. To get on stage, the performer first put on a long black silk bib to cover his white shirt front and black gloves to conceal his hands. Then he would put his head through an upper slit in the back-cloth and his hands through two lower slits. He could now raise the marionette from the stage and fasten its collar round his own neck. Next, he would draw the operating rods for the small arms and legs back through the lower slits. The rods had shaped rings on the ends so that the performer's thumbs could work the hand rods and his forefingers those for the feet. He was now ready. Using a foot rope to ring up the front curtain, he could go straight into his act, usually a song and dance with a break for patter. An experienced performer could make costume and 'character' make-up changes in ten or twelve seconds. Variety was possible. Movement was more difficult.

With a good accompanist and a lot of rehearsal it had been

possible to contrive simple dance routines, but the old back-cloth had always restricted sideways movement. The material it was made of had to be opaque and it had to hang completely free of creases without being too heavily weighted. Velvet did not work because its folds caught the light. The best stuff was a very thin, fine, billiard-table quality, black felt. But even that would bunch up so that the audience could see it if the performer strayed too far from the centre of the stage. Some old pros would solve the problem of making a finale exit by decapitating the marionette on stage. They would then reappear to take their bows, still wearing their black bibs and with the headless marionette trunks dangling from their gloved hands like dead birds. Such men often doubled as ventriloquists.

The Peshik back-cloth had no folds and no lead weights, and it allowed the performer to use the whole width of the stage, including the wings. Before he met his neighbour Reg Ambler, Mr Peshik had invented an improved spring-blind roller for office and domestic use. He was a spring-blind man; so, naturally, his solution to the back-cloth problem utilized spring blinds. They worked horizontally. Two rollers were mounted vertically, one in each wing behind the proscenium arch uprights. Between was stretched a length of the back-cloth felt tacked on to and wrapped round the two rollers. The felt was held under tension by the roller springs. In this way, with a marionette in position, the back-cloth remained quite flat and smooth as it and the performer moved from side to side. It also permitted substantial forward movement down stage. After this success, a second, double-act back-cloth was made. This had four rollers and a vertical masking strip to conceal the gap between the two centre ones.

Grandad Andrews built the new show, and Billy Spinks, a comedy monologuist who lived nearby and doubled as an electrician, designed the lighting systems. There had to be two because in 1914 many of the buildings used to accommodate audiences were still lighted by gas and had no electricity. The second system had spotlights that worked on gas from an acetylene generator of the type used in those days for car headlamps. The whole thing had to be portable, of course. It was made in eight main sections which could be bolted together in ten minutes. Packed flat it all went into a coffin-like pine crate six feet long and two feet square with rope handles at each end. Two men were needed to handle it. It travelled mostly by Carter Paterson delivery service van and in the heavy-goods vans of trains.

The living marionette show was never comparable to a puppet theatre as a medium of dramatic expression. True puppets, no matter how they are manipulated, are essentially inanimate and their magic is a form of witchcraft. Living marionettes, even at their best, were never more than a seaside-pier, children's-party kind of trick that could be made to amuse grown-ups. During the war that began in 1914, the trick was sometimes used to take miniature variety entertainments into the wards of military hospitals.

All that the hospital had to provide was an upright piano; or, at a pinch, the chaplain's harmonium would do. Then, from their little stage, the marionettes would sing early Irving Berlin tunes like 'Everybody's Doin' It' and the sort of sentimental point numbers made popular by the American husband-and-wife act of Clay Smith and Lee White. A quick change and Reg would be in a kilt and tammy doing an impersonation of Harry Lauder. Amy would follow in a big feathered hat with Marie Lloyd and 'A Little of What You Fancy'. Reg would come back with a handlebar moustache and an excerpt from a Harry Tate sketch, 'Motoring' perhaps, or one of the other guaranteed laughter makers. The pair of them, in 'evening dress' again, would bring the show to a close with a tap-dance duet done to a nice bouncy 'Lily of Laguna'. Then would come the encores and requests, with the audience joining in the choruses of hits from *The Bing Boys*. The whole programme would last about an hour.

Later, when the audiences of wounded grew larger and those that were fit enough to be entertained were moved to auxiliary huts, life-size stages with lighting and curtains were put up in the hospital canteens. After a while, Reg and Amy Ambrose joined with others to become a concert party of six called The Harmoniques.

One Saturday afternoon in the spring of 1914 my father took me for a ride on a bus. This was not a horse bus, but the Number 75 petrol–electric Tilling that he had started using to go to the Woolwich ferry during the week. There was by then a regular service from Catford to Woolwich and back through Blackheath and Lee Green. We got off the bus that day just beyond Lee Station.

Most of Newstead Road then was lined with Victorian suburban houses of the kind with carriage drives that used to be called 'double-fronted'. There was middle-class money there. Two of the drives even had private cars standing in them. Then, two hundred yards from the end of what the council name plates said was still

26

Newstead Road, there was a sudden change. In what had recently been an open field a jerry-builder had been putting up rows of semi-detached houses. At the point where his houses started, the cambered road surface and the pavements abruptly ceased. The rest of Newstead Road was a slough of deeply rutted mud and vast puddles. The mud was of the yellow, extra-sticky kind that is produced by London clay. The only dry places were along by the new garden fences where the water mains and sewer pipes had been laid.

'This is where we're going to live, old chap,' said my father. He took my hand and we picked our way through the mud into one of the houses.

It was three up and two down, and there was something I had never seen before, a bathroom. There were also two lavatories, one upstairs and one in the back garden, and electric lighting. Everything smelt different. I did not believe that it was going to be ours. Grown-ups were always changing promises to 'We'll see.' Besides, I was used to the hills of Charlton and Maryon Park.

'Is there going to be a road?' I asked.

'As soon as we start paying the rent and rates,' my father said, 'then the council will do the road.'

It was not his fault that he was wrong. The war started; and although he always faithfully paid both the rent and the rates, the road remained undone for over five years. Among milkmen, dustmen, coalmen and Carter Paterson van drivers, the mud at the end of Newstead Road became a notorious nuisance. Carts stuck, horses fell, army lorries keeled over and shed their loads, dustmen refused to bring their carts to us and empty our dustbins. All the borough council ever did while the war lasted was to dump a few cartloads of road-sweepings into the deeper puddles and turn them into slush.

For a keen student of the war, as I soon was, the mud outside the house came to have a special importance. It was one thing to see pictures of army lorries battling through the mud of Flanders in the *Illustrated London News*; but to see an Army Service Corps three-tonner from Grove Park barracks trying to battle through Newstead Road, with a corporal bawling orders to push at two privates floundering up to their knees in London mud, was far more exciting and instructive. I knew how sticky that stuff was. Round the corner was even better. In Dallinger Road, there was, as well as plenty of wet clay, a whole row of roofless houses; roofless

27

because, when the war started, all speculative building had been brought to a halt. Although there was less traffic to get stuck in Dallinger Road, the half-built houses and the weed-covered builder's rubble made it fine country for small boys in search of adventure.

Only once during the war, when older men were reclassified, was there any serious possibility of my father being accepted by the army. However, he again failed the medical. In that war, eyesight defective enough to require the constant wearing of glasses was a disqualification for the armed forces. He enrolled eventually as a special constable and was pleased when he was given a uniform that fitted him. He did not, though, wear it much. During the day he was a manager at the Silvertown works which was now producing rubber tyres, electric cables and telegraph equipment for the army. In the evenings, he and my mother went off to entertain. At first they went mostly to the naval and military hospitals: the marionette show used to be shuttled on a roster basis from the Miller Hospital in Greenwich to the Herbert Hospital and then the Brook Hospital in Woolwich. Then, as The Harmoniques got into their stride and became known, the hospital chaplains and service staff began to get inquiries about them from entertainment officers and the YMCA in dockyards and army camps outside London.

By 1915, even the most senior British officers on the western front had come to realize that, for armies engaged in the new trench warfare, more was required to maintain soldierly attitudes than steady supplies of food, drink, sleep and church parades. It had been noticed, for instance, that periodic exposure to familiar light entertainment seemed to be good for the health of those who had to man the trenches. In France and Flanders the divisional concert party became a valued institution, and a refuge for much theatrical talent. In England, however, where threats to health and sanity were less immediate, 'singing to the troops' was left almost entirely to drawing-room amateurs and unemployable old pros. The employable pros outside the forces were all working full time in the theatres. If you were in Kitchener's army then, and in a remote camp in England, you could consider yourself lucky if you were assailed in the YMCA canteen hut on Saturday night by nothing worse than a programme from the local glee club or a colonel's lady rendering 'Pale Hands I Love'. The old pros could be deeply depressing. I remember my father complaining about an elderly north country comedian who used to enliven his act by waving his false teeth in the air and whinnying 'Ee . . . by gum!' whenever he felt he needed a laugh.

'It wouldn't be so bad', my father said, 'if he didn't stand there waiting for a big hand as if he'd earned it. *They* don't care if he's going it for love and a return ticket to Scarborough. The other night he nearly got the bird. I heard three or four raspberries, and not just from the back.'

'Disgraceful,' said my mother. 'The officers should have stopped them.'

'The officers knew better. Those troops were the kind who don't care who they blow raspberries at. There'll be more like them if the war goes on much longer.'

He was right. Army audiences became hard to please. While I think it unlikely that Reg and Amy ever got the bird themselves, other members of The Harmoniques did suffer indignities. In 1917 my father disbanded that party and formed a new one, with more talented people in it, called The Whatnots. There was never any risk of really good artistes* getting the bird. I once dared to ask my mother what sort of people they were who did get it, and what exactly happened.

Her lips tightened and she thought carefully before deciding that it was not a personal question. Then, she said that straight singers who sang out of tune would upset some audiences and get a bad reception. She thought that singing sharp was more irritating than singing flat. But little things could start it off, like one man in the audience who'd had too much to drink and was noisy. The worst times she knew of, though, had always been because of comedians who had got angry when they didn't go down well and then turned on the audience. It was stupid as well as nasty. Telling an audience that it had no sense of humour, or that it should be grateful for getting you without having to pay, could never make it like you. Some comedians could be awful. So could audiences. Once they really started they could get cruel.

'Blowing raspberries and booing?'

'It's not just raspberries and booing.'

'Do they throw things?'

---

* The word was pronounced by most members of the Concert Artistes' Association as if it had no *e* in it. The jargon of the profession always contained a lot of borrowed French, and in those days the classified advertisement pages of the *Stage* and the *Era* were full of references to *comediennes*, *siffleurs* (who often did animal impersonations as well as whistle popular songs), *danseuses*, *diseurs* (a kind of monologuist) and *soubrettes*.

'They might if they had anything to throw. No, it's the shouting and the catcalls and the jeering all together. You wouldn't understand. It's ghastly. When it happened to Mavis she came off shaking and as white as a sheet.'

Mavis had for a time sung mezzo-soprano ballads with the defunct Harmoniques. Her air of refined condescension had always seemed to me to invite dislike and abuse. If she had sung off-key too, that would have sealed her fate.

'What did they shout at her?'

'Oh, things like "get off" and "go home and tell your mother", and they blew very loud raspberries in a very rude way with their tongues out. Now stop talking about it, you little toad. Don't be so morbid.'

My first school was in Sandhurst Road, Catford. It was then one of the newer (1904) London County Council schools. The name of the headmaster could have been Crick, but I have always remembered him by his nickname, Mr Click. It was appropriate. When after morning prayers he conduced the singing with which the school began its day, everything about him, from the detachable celluloid cuffs on his waving arms to the ill-fitting teeth mouthing over the words of the hymn, made distinct clicking sounds. As the youngest boys' class in the school we stood nearest to him every morning, so we all knew that he clicked. He had a high colour, bulging eyes and a fearsome reputation as a thrasher of bad boys. He never came into our part of the school, but the sounds of his thrashings could occasionally be heard through the open windows. The lady teachers who dealt with us small fry had no trouble at all in maintaining discipline.

My parents called them 'mistresses'. I call them 'lady teachers' because that is what they called themselves when they told us that the proper and respectful way to address them, if we wished to be allowed to speak before we had been spoken to, was 'Please miss'. They were there to teach classes of thirty-two boys how to read and write and how to do the simple arithmetic of whole numbers and vulgar fractions. They did so patiently, cheerfully and, for the most part, successfully.

It was not easy for them. Ages in the junior class varied from five to twelve. Some of the older ones would be there simply because they were 'backward', others because they had long histories of absence through truancy. Most of the truants came from a slum area behind Lewisham Hippodrome and some came barefoot from families with no money in wartime for boys' boots. In cold weather, if they could find no one to give them cast-offs, the barefoot ones would again be forced to play truant, and their parents, if they could be found and served with summonses, would again be taken to court. Only those attending school with easily recognized infectious diseases of a serious kind, such as whooping cough, measles or mumps, were ever sent home or told to stay away. Sufferers from ailments like croup and tonsillitis were allowed to keep their flannel throat bandages on and suck cough pastilles in the classroom. There were often three or four of us at a time with heads shaved against nits, lice or ringworm.

The cleanest and most neatly dressed among us were three boys from an orphanage. They wore a uniform with old-fashioned knickerbockers which buttoned at the knees over long black stockings. The orphanage hob-nailed ankle boots were like the ones I wore, but my socks were calf-length with turn-down tops. I had a fear for a time of being made by my mother to wear long stockings and knickerbockers for their warmth in winter, but could not think of a good reason to give her for objecting to them. The reason I did give – that girls wore long stockings – was accepted, however, and I was spared. My real objection, I think, was to the knickerbocker uniform. Although Mr Click had said at prayers one day that everyone must always like and be specially kind to the orphanage boys because they did not have our family advantages, those of us who were smaller than they were loathed them from the start. They were spiteful and sly, playground bullies and masterly simulators of injured innocence. They smelt strongly of carbolic soap and joined in loudly when prayers were said. The rest of us smelt of less pleasant things, though not of piety.·Our teachers, dedicated women, never seemed to notice how any of us smelt. All they asked was that every member of a class had a handkerchief or piece of rag in which to cough or sneeze. Spitting in the classroom was strictly forbidden.

Reading was taught by a phonetic method to which I responded well. In 1916 Grandad Andrews went to work at Woolwich Arsenal and came to stay with us so as to be nearer the job. When he was on night shift he would have an early supper before he went to get the train. While he ate I was encouraged to read the evening paper aloud to him. My first successfully delivered polysyllabic word was Me-di-ter-ra-ne-an. He was delighted and at once taught me another dazzling word, ca-pi-tal-ism. He said that I should remember it carefully because the war would be its downfall.

Unwisely, I boasted of my new knowledge, and my father, who read the *Daily Mail*, called Grandad to account. 'The boy's not ready to start a revolution yet, Chas, but at least give him a chance to choose. What happens when all you Labour people at the Arsenal and in the munition factories convince the Great Unwashed that the Germans are our best friends? You'll all go on strike, I suppose, and they'll win the war because British gunners are short of shells again. Is that what the Labour Party wants?'

His tone of voice was mild enough, but my mother, always fussed by even a hint of discord between her men, imposed an instant peace. 'Don't answer, Dad. That's enough, Reg. Stop it, the pair of you.'

My father flung up his arms in mock surrender and that was it. Grandad giggled, but he would have done that anyway. He was always a bit of a giggler and rhetorical questions about the Labour Party coming from rabid new Conservatives were the sort of things he giggled at most. Later, I would hear him mutter to himself, 'Silly devils.' He would not mean my mother and father in particular, but people in general who did not share his views about the new Jerusalem and the brotherhood of man.

The first books I had of my own were Grimm's *Fairy Tales*, *Alice in Wonderland*, a Bible and R. M. Ballantyne's *Martin Rattler*. The only one of them I never read more than once was the Bible. Depressing typography, semi-transparent paper and a limp morocco binding may have contributed to my lack of interest in the spiritual nourishment that was there. Later, I came to think of it as a kind of reference book used by those who did not have Arthur Mee's *Children's Encyclopaedia*. *Martin Rattler* – the story of 'a remarkably bad boy' transformed by adventures in South America into 'a man of substance' – though not the best Ballantyne, introduced me to the titles of other books he had written and also the habit of scanning By-the-Same-Author lists. My mother complained that I was becoming a bookworm and said that I would ruin my eyes as my father had done.

The only book that I ever wanted to lose was *Eric or Little By Little*. I read it all, every page, because it was a Christmas present from Auntie Dora, my Godmother, who had been at Wellington Road when I was born and who liked to tease me gently with tales of how splendid I had looked wearing only a binder. She was, she would tell me, my first true love. She gave me the book, I am sure, without having read it and believing that the little by little of the title described the way in which the hero climbed up the ladder of fortune. And, of course, it had my name on it, like the christening mug she had given me. I had not then realized that some books could be treated like off-key mezzos and given the bird. I took *Eric* seriously as a cautionary tale written with me specifically in mind by a clergyman. Such a man, a dean, would be a more terrible threat to bad boys than Mr Click.

I was being taken to church on Sundays then and was trying to understand what the service was about. One of the things that baffled me was the way some of the words were said. Particularly worrying was the strangled, high-pitched singsong used to invite responses during the Litany. It reminded me of other things. Behind a butcher's shop at Lee Green there was a yard with a small slaughterhouse at the end. Carts would deliver sheep or pigs there and then the doors would be closed. There was not much sound from the sheep after that, but the screams and screeching of the pigs as their throats were cut could be heard for some distance. For me as I walked home those were the sounds of trench warfare and hand-to-hand fighting with bayonets. In church the sounds were translated into the voice of a clergyman trying to frighten the evildoers by impersonating a throat-cutting God. *Eric* showed me that I had been mistaken and that the impersonation voice was a code. By using that wailing falsetto the parson was telling all the *good* people there that if they joined in with him they would really be forgiven their trespasses, and at the same time distinguishing publicly between them and those dreadful, mother-killing sinners for whom there could never be any forgiveness. So, when the good people replied, 'Good Lord, deliver us,' they meant, 'All of us here except the likes of Eric the drinker, the smoker, the keeper of evil company and late hours, the anti-muff and corrupter, the liar and thief who causes unhappiness to all those who love him, the hateful and ungrateful Eric who refuses to join in the responses.'

All right then, I'll say it: 'We beseech thee to hear us, good Lord.'

'No, it's too late now. You had your chances and didn't take them.'

'But Eric wept and said he was sorry.'

'Eric is always weeping and saying he's sorry, the horrible little toad. Being sorry won't help a God-forgetting son who almost killed his mother. We're sending him with all the other little pigs to the slaughterhouse.'

So down went Eric, little by little, snivelling and screeching, the truly miserable sinner who always wept and begged for forgiveness instead of thumbing his nose at the good people, standing firm beside his friend the devil and fighting back. If there was a way of getting out of going to church I always took it, and I stopped trying to make sense of the service. That other Eric, the snotty-nosed one, might enjoy wallowing in tears of repentance while sanctimonious clergymen patted his head and said how sad it all was; but I wanted none of it.

Magic seemed a better thing to understand. In the weekly *Puck* there was a series about an amateur detective named Valentine Vox. He was a ventriloquist (a 'vent' in concert jargon) who dealt with his enemies by throwing his voice and ruining their plans by confusing them. I tried for a long time to achieve ventriloquial effects before I realized that they were all essentially visual tricks. That was when I began to ask myself why a clever man like Val Vox was not in the army and at the front confusing the Germans.

The war by then had come a bit closer to home. The Zeppelin raids had made people very indignant but had not done much damage. The German aeroplanes, the Taubes and Gothas, which raided us later dropped more bombs. There was a persistent local belief that the enemy was trying to hit the railway junction at Hither Green which was half a mile away on the other side of the allotments. The truth was that, coming in over the Kent coast from Belgian aerodromes, the German pilots found our corner of south-east London first. Several houses in the area were hit, including two halfway along Newstead Road. My brother and I shared a bedroom and that night our parents were with us. It can only have been a small bomb, no more than a hundred pounds, but the blast effect was impressive. Our beds bounced clear of the floor and my father, who thought the party wall was falling in on us, leapt to his feet and spread out his arms to support it. He could be funny at his own expense and his subsequent accounts of how, with only his bare hands and striped pyjamas, he saved the house from falling down were more entertaining than most bomb stories. The following morning at first light I was on the scene, along with a horde of fellow collectors, looking for 'shrapnel', but the police in charge were hostile. They had reason to be. What we were really collecting was not shrapnel but anti-aircraft shell fragments and there was not enough of the real stuff to go round. Boys like us digging such things as carriage bolts and other embedded old iron out of a road surface could do a lot of damage. My best real pieces were a wedge-shaped shell splinter six inches long with a fragment of copper driving-band attached to it and a lead shrapnel ball brought back from France by Uncle Sidney, another of mother's brothers, who was a sergeant in the Buffs.

The loudest bang I heard in that war was the Silvertown explosion. This happened one Friday in January 1917 when over fifty tons of TNT in a processing plant across the river from the Arsenal was accidentally detonated by a fire. The shock and sound waves set up by the explosion behaved oddly. It happened just before seven in the evening and my brother and I were getting ready for bed. First there was a vivid flash, then we saw a spreading yellow glow in the sky and the electric light slowly dimmed. Suddenly, a glass sky-light in the ceiling of the upstairs landing shattered. Then, as my mother hurried upstairs and crunched across the broken glass to see if we were all right, the sound of the explosion arrived as a succession of long, juddering claps of thunder. My mother's first thought, and mine too, was that the Arsenal had blown up taking Grandad Andrews with it. And why was Dad so late? When he eventually arrived home he and my mother had whiskies and sodas while he told us what had happened. He had been in the train. After the explosion, he had changed trains and gone back to see what had happened. Much of Silvertown had been demolished. Next day the papers said that sixty-nine people had been killed and four hundred injured. The Works, and the jam factory next door to it, were more or less all right.

Most air raids happened at night, but one afternoon I was on my way back to school after lunch when some German planes came over. The warning sound was a firing of three maroons, a kind of explosive rocket. When they went off I was halfway up Brownhill Road. For a minute or so I walked on. Then I realized that nobody else was walking and that everything had become still. Somewhere in the distance AA guns began to fire. I did not want to be hit by a shell splinter, with or without driving-band, so I did as I had been told to do in this emergency at school. I went to the front door of the nearest house and knocked. The lady who answered the door had two girls with her. They wore the uniform of a local private school. I raised my cap and gave the lady teachers' set speech for the occasion.

'Excuse me, madam, but I believe there is an air raid in progress. May I take refuge here until it is over, please?'

The lady stared, the girls giggled. Then the lady said, 'Of course. Come in.' She was a dark, pretty woman who smiled kindly but did not laugh at my pomposity. The girls, though, never stopped giggling. When I complained of this later to my mother she asked me what I had said. When I told her she said that in future perhaps I should write my own lines. She did not actually say that the lady teachers might not be infallible but the suggestion was in the air. It bothered me. I wished that I had walked on to school without stopping to take cover. The trouble was that I was timid as well as pompous, and that I knew what a shell-splinter wound looked like.

One Sunday my father had had to go to the Brook Hospital to set up the marionette show for an evening concert they were giving and to try out a new strip of lights. I had begged to be allowed to go with him and my mother had agreed. So, while he set up the show and tinkered with fuse boxes I talked to the patients. They did not mind showing their wounds. I took note of one of the shell-splinter cases particularly. He had a long ragged scar on one arm that ran from just below the shoulder all the way down to the wrist. That was all right, he said, but the same shell had taken half a leg off. It was the idea of having a peg leg that worried him.

The Brook Hospital, however, was friendly. The place I feared was a Victorian prison-style infirmary at Hither Green. It was a fever hospital and had an isolation ward with high, brown-brick walls and barred windows. When my brother went down with scarlet fever he was saved from going there, the doctor said, only by our mother's agreeing to isolate herself while nursing him and to do the things prescribed by the local health authority. My father had to go and stay with friends in Charlton. I was sent to Grandpa Ambler's in Balham where, instead of going to school, I helped Granny Ambler shop for food. It was a time of shortages and crude jokes about what went into a tin of Maconochie.* The only rationing was a rough-and-ready system worked by the shopkeepers of so much per person, first come, first served. At the greengrocer's, for example, when there were potatoes to be had, they would be doled out in fourteen-pound lots. So Granny and I would both stand in the queue, and when she had her fourteen pounds I would move forward and receive mine. Both lots were paid for from her purse, but no one objected that we were together.

* Canned stew made for the army.

It was one lot per person and I counted as a person. The hard part was lugging it all back to Yukon Road in string bags. Granny was a stocky little figure who always wore a bonnet and whose Manchester accent remained unmodified. At Christmas, when pressed, she would sing a comic song from the Salford days called 'Going to Pomona'.

> *We met in Albert Square*, [it began]
> *I never shall forget*,
> *Her eyes shone like the stars*,
> *The evening, IT WAS WET.*

The audience was expected to join in on IT WAS WET to show we all knew that Pomona was in Manchester. The story of the song is that, in the darkness and rain of the city, our amorous hero makes an embarrassing mistake.

> *Upon my LIFE*,
> *It was my WIFE*,
> *I was taking to Pomona.*

Granny Ambler remained loyal to Lancashire and took strongly against music-hall comedians who made ill-informed jokes about her people. Wilkie Bard was a notorious offender and if anyone dared to utter his name in her presence she would repeat it instantly in tones of withering contempt. She used the same snarling tones when speaking of another three-syllable man, the Tory politician Bonar Law. I understood her feelings about Wilkie Bard, but when I asked what Bonar Law had done that was wrong and mentioned that he was thought well of by the *Daily Mail* there was a glum silence. Then, Grandpa Ambler, who had overheard, said, 'Bah!' and Granny crushed a crab claw with a blow from a flat-iron.

She made the best dressed crab I have ever tasted. During those weeks in Balham I also learned to share Grandpa's fancy for Turkish delight. Auntie Cis used to bring home boxes of it for him from a shop in Durban, and her ship had just come in. Before she went back to sea that time she took me to a picture theatre in the Balham High Road. It was very crowded and we had to sit at the side very near the front. For several years, even after I had read Zane Grey, I continued to believe that all cowboys were narrow-shouldered men with elongated faces and that the chaps they wore were made of strips of plywood.

My brother recovered and went off to a convalescent home at the seaside. The house was fumigated. I returned to it and very soon started running a high temperature. I had scarlet fever, too, and my poor mother had to go through the isolation nursing routine all over again. This involved such things as bowls of disinfectant placed where it was easy to trip over them and doorways hung with sheets soaked in carbolic. The second fumigation, done when I got better, was devastatingly thorough. This time all my books had to go, together with some old telegraph equipment that my father had brought from Silvertown for me to examine and take to bits. Some of the books, the Bible and *Eric or* for example, were replaced at once in case I should miss them, but good things happened too. One of the engineers at the Silvertown works put together for me from bits and pieces a curious model electric motor designed so that the commutator and field coil circuits could be changed if I wanted to do my own experiments. The new books my father bought me were *Tom, Dick and Harry* by Talbot Baines Reed, *The Swiss Family Robinson* and *Treasure Island*. While they may just possibly have been chosen to shape my thinking about the future – thoughts on secondary education, thoughts on self-help and thoughts on the perils and delights of fortune-seeking – I think it more likely that they were happy accidents. In the local stationery shop, which also sold books, he would have explained that I was a little old for my age (the word 'precocious' was used then mainly to condemn sexual impertinence) and been directed to the Suitable-for-Boys-10–12 shelf. His own favourite novel was *The Card* by Arnold Bennett, but he said that I could get to that a little later on. His caution was understandable. To celebrate my recovery from the fever I had been taken by my mother to see a matinée of *Peter Pan* in the West End and had caused a disturbance by refusing noisily to join in with the other kids to save Tinkerbell by saying that I believed in fairies. 'Spoilt the show, the little fiend,' my mother reported over the small whiskies that evening. My father laughed. I left my hiding place on the stairs and went back to bed. All was well. No one now need know that I had believed in Captain Hook and been frightened by him. My idea of a good show was *Chu-Chin-Chow*.

In 1917 I sat for an entrance examination at Colfe's Grammar School and, thanks to the ladies of Sandhurst Road, was accepted and awarded a scholarship. The school was on Lewisham Hill then, and the only school uniform was a plain black cap with a metal shield badge of silver or silver plate. A big notice board outside said that the school had been founded in 1652 by Abraham Colfe and The Worshipful Company of Leathersellers 'for the Sons of Gentlemen'.

At about the same time in September that I took my place at Colfe's, Uncle Frank was called up for the army. He went most unwillingly and made no secret of his hopes for a quiet life somewhere far behind the lines. His brother Sidney, newly commissioned and bound for the campaign in Mesopotamia, was incensed by such unsoldierly talk. It was near Christmas and we had gone to Tottenham for the day to see Granny Andrews, so I witnessed the confrontation.

Frank was on a forty-eight-hour pass and due to report back for a draft going to France. He had slept the night before in the normally unused front sitting room and had all his army kit there with him. What Uncle Sidney did was to break off the argument about the rights and duties of free men and pick up Uncle Frank's rifle as if to inspect the breech. Then, suddenly, he threw it across the room with a jab of his right arm, straight and hard at his brother's body. It was an old drill-sergeant's trick, as I came to know later, a way of testing a recruit's reflexes or stating a parade ground relationship; and as he threw the rifle he gave an order. 'Play the game like a man,' he shouted.

Uncle Frank had caught the rifle, but only just, and I think he broke a fingernail. He licked his lips. Then he went pale with anger and for a moment or two looked ready to bash Uncle Sidney. My mother was upstairs with Granny Andrews. It was left to Grandad to save the day with a show of authority. 'Oh dear,' he giggled, 'oh dearie me. You silly devils.' To his sons' surprise they found themselves smiling at him.

In March 1918, when the German army launched their last big offensive on the Western front, Uncle Frank was in the trenches at St Quentin. Along with the rest of his unit he was taken prisoner.

We had other casualties. After the scarlet fever convalescence, my brother Maurice had pneumonia. Then, coming home from school, he was run over by a cart and kicked on the head by the horse. Six weeks after that accident he had a fall from the carrier of a bicycle and another spell in hospital. Influenza followed and he was left with a persistent chorea, the kind that used to be called St Vitus's Dance. 'He needs a break,' the doctor said. 'We all need a break.'

That summer, the last of the war, my father and Harry Roberts, our old neighbour in Charlton, shared the rent of a bungalow on Canvey Island in the Thames estuary. Both families spent the school holiday weeks there, with the two husbands joining us when they could get away.

In 1918 Canvey was separated from the mainland by a channel which at high tide could only be crossed by boat. The way to get there was to take a train from London to Benfleet, timing one's arrival to catch a low or ebbing tide. From the station one took a fly, which was a one-horse hackney with extra big wheels to keep the luggage and passengers' feet clear during the crossing of any seawater left in the channel. The island was surrounded by low sand dunes bordering mud beaches and criss-crossed by long reed-fringed dikes which drained the pastures between them for cows and sheep to graze. The holiday bungalows were perched at irregular intervals on the estuary side of the dunes and foreshore where marram grass had established itself, and most of them were built in the same way out of two old railway passenger coaches placed side by side with their bogeys removed and a corrugated iron roof over the space between. The old compartments made bedrooms and a kitchen, the space between became a living room. Fresh water was pumped by hand from a well, cooking was done on a paraffin stove and sanitation was by earth-closet in an outhouse.

Living on Canvey was cheap. Milk and vegetables came from the nearest farmhouse. A full-size shrimping net could be hired for a shilling a week and good big shrimps could be caught by the bucketful on the estuary flats. Clinging to the long breakwaters there were more mussels and winkles than the locals who fished for a living could be bothered to harvest. In the early morning there were always fresh mushrooms in the fields. On Canvey, then, it was possible, using the paths along the dikes and the wooden footbridges over them, to walk from one end of the island to the other. At the eastern tip there was the wreck of a big Dutch sailing barge. Although most of it was deep in the mud, the stern half was still accessible at low tide. While we were there that summer my brother and I made the wreck our own. The only reminders of the war in France were the periodic sounds of gunfire from the artillery proving range along the estuary beyond Shoeburyness.

The one snag was the Roberts' boy, Brian. He was about my age and size but in some respects backward. I had overheard conversations in which 'brain fever' had been mentioned. My mother had warned us that he was now 'a nervy child' and 'a bit babyish'. She had not exaggerated. If he hurt himself he yelled. If he saw one of us breaking a rule he instantly sneaked. When I called him a cry-baby he said that he would tell his father to bash me. He was still a bed-wetter. One of his most unacceptable habits was that of prefacing all his demands for food, drink and attention with a high, penetrating whine of 'I ain't got no . . .' and then waiting for someone to provide whatever it was he wanted. If the response was not prompt enough he would repeat the demand, raising his voice to give an edge to the whine. The whine conveyed an unmistakable threat and it succeeded every time. When I asked my mother why, she shrugged. 'The little monster's an only child of course, and spoilt because he's backward and been poorly. His father spoils him. I wouldn't put up with his nonsense myself, but then I'm not expected to. It's our holiday as well as theirs. Pretend he doesn't exist.'

However, that advice was not easy to take. Brian did exist, and all too noisily. Besides, with three exciting terms of Colfe's behind me, and having absorbed the somewhat eccentric disciplinary style of F. L. Lucas, that greatly loved headmaster known to generations of Colfeians as The Bird, I thought I knew how to deal with Brian. I would educate him. I would give him The Bird.

At tea that day we had winkles.

The moment we children sat down at our table Brian spoke up. 'I ain't got no winkle pin,' he announced.

There was a saucer of pins on the table. I at once offered it to my brother, took a pin and a handful of winkles for myself and then began addressing Brian in a parody of The Bird's manner.

'A pin shall be your reward, sir. But rewards must be earned. You are on your honour, sir, to answer truthfully. Is "I ain't got no winkle pin" a grammatical sentence? If it is, kindly analyse and parse it for us.'

Brian let out an extra loud whine.

'Come, sir,' I went on breezily, 'we trust but we also test. Trust and test. Subject, predicate, object. Go on, sir, parse! And as you do so kindly explain your use of the double negative. If you do not, I will ask you on your honour to give up margarine on your bread for a week.'

Brian's whine became a sort of muted shriek.

'A pauper spirit, sir, a pauper spirit,' I cried reproachfully and then added the Lucas watchword. 'Work, for the night cometh!'

41

Brian uttered a series of blood-curdling screams and began to throw things.

I had seen a temper tantrum before but never in a boy or girl of Brian's age. It was almost as violent and frightening as an epileptic fit. Mrs Roberts was there, of course, and knew how to hold him without anyone getting hurt, but we were all shaken. My mother spent a confusing evening trying to apologize to Mrs Roberts for my misbehaviour without quite understanding the nature of the crime. Was parse a dirty word?

'All I told him to do, Mum, was analyse and parse "I ain't got no winkle pin." I swear it.'

'Disgraceful. I don't know what your father will say.'

It was left to Mrs Roberts, who had been educated in Scotland and knew about parsing and double negatives, to put me in my place.

'Oh yes, I'll accept your apology,' she said; 'you're only a boy and you couldn't know. But I'll tell you something. You're getting to be stuck up and pleased with yourself. It's that school no doubt. I wouldn't send Brian there. They're snobs. What boys need is a school where they can learn to keep their minds clean and their mouths shut.'

THREE

When he registered my birth my father gave me a middle name, Clifford, after Clifford Grey, an actor who later became a successful musical-comedy lyricist. He gave his own occupation as 'Advertising Manager', and I can see why. In 1909 an advertising manager was a dashing thing to be for an up-and-coming young man from Salford. It sounded better and infinitely more respectable than Concert Artist, with or without an *e*. At the time, probably, he did not much care which of his two careers would eventually prove the more successful. His immediate tasks were to make the best of himself and his family and to keep moving up. Later on, he looked to his sons to follow his example.

The Colfe's I went to in 1917 was not a particularly snobbish school. It had a decent pride in its identity as an enduring institution and a school song with a Latin title, but it did not pretend to be anything that it was not. The notice outside which said that we were the sons of gentlemen was there not to be taken literally but to show that we were of good character, that we respected the gentility of our betters and that we looked forward to their continued patronage. We were, as the founder had intended, boys 'of good wit and capacity, and apt to learn' drawn from families living in Lewisham and the other parishes nearby. There were at that time about two hundred and fifty of us ranging in age from eight to sixteen. Colfe's saw its primary task as that of educating us to matriculation standard and seeing that we passed that examination as well as our individual abilities allowed. After that – well, yes, there was a sixth form. It consisted of ten or twelve exceptional boys who had matriculated and then gone on to read for the old Intermediate examinations of London University. From the sixth form boys had been known to win scholarships to Cambridge.

However, we were not much encouraged to emulate such feats. Colfe's ambitions for its sons were tempered by kindness and good sense. Higher education was not just for the few of us who could win scholarships; it was for the even more exceptional few who could win scholarships and who also had parents able and willing to support them for three more years. The rest of us were expected to set our sights on more accessible objectives. If we worked really hard, did our two hours of homework faithfully and got plenty of fresh air, we would end by matriculating, perhaps with honours. We would then be qualified to apply for a post as clerk in a bank or – nearly but not quite as good – an insurance company. All who failed matric would go downhill and end as roadsweepers.

The maker of this odd prediction was the second (senior) master, T.S.Simons, a tall, bluff, moon-faced man with a habit of chewing his moustache as he spoke and eliding his words that made him difficult to understand. He played the piano for morning prayers, often hammering out the tune of 'Deutschland uber Alles' so that we could do our bit for victory by singing patriotic English words to it. His main subject was physics which he taught with the sort of exuberant incoherence that boys like to amuse one another by imitating. His explanations of the principles of heat, light and sound using demonstration apparatus were almost totally incomprehensible. It did not matter because we could easily find out what he had been trying to tell us by reading the set book. Later, on the subject of electricity and magnetism, he became even better. His description of Ohm's Law, mumbled while writing at high speed on the blackboard, and his demonstration of the measurement of electrical resistance using a Wheatstone bridge were little masterpieces of nonsense talk and high confusion. He was not, I think, greatly loved. Boys do not mind eccentricity, but they do not like unconscious humorists. The novelist Henry Williamson, who left Colfe's in 1911, drew a recognizable portrait of Taffy Simons and also lampooned other masters in *Dandelion Days*. I was still at the school when it was first published. All we heard about the novel at the time, though, was that an old boy had done something discreditable. We were not told what he had done and were not encouraged to inquire. The police were not involved, it seemed, so we lost interest.

Many things at Colfe's were well taught, even in that wartime when the effective teaching staff, including the headmaster, numbered six. From F.W.Lucas, R.W.Creech and F.E.Bennett I learned to enjoy not only how to analyse and parse, but also to appreciate the beauties of algebra, Euclidean geometry, French grammar and Latin. There were, at the beginning, no organized games. There was no games master. I wanted to be a geometrician or, perhaps a Latin scholar. The world was good. Work, for the night cometh.

It all changed, of course. When the war ended and the young masters came back we had to wake up, buckle down, pull up our socks and jump to it. Not all of those who returned were in the best of health, or temper. When the man who now taught French had his attacks of malaria he went yellow and got the shakes. There was also a maths man who used to get the shakes, but without turning yellow, only a pasty white. We diagnosed shell-shock and were sorrier for him, perhaps, because he seemed only impatient with himself. He showed us how to work quadratic equations and explained clearly the kind of problems they could be used to solve. Then, one day, he gave us a time and motion problem that looked simple and soluble until we looked closer and found that our algebra could not do it. He was pleased. He told us that if we applied ourselves he would before long initiate us into the mysteries of the calculus. He made it sound as exciting as the map in Billy Bones' sea chest. Unhappily, he could not stay to keep his promise.

Most of what I knew or guessed about such things as shell-shock and the shakes came from listening to Uncle Frank; listening to his talk, of course, but also from listening to him having bad dreams. After the war ended he had been repatriated with other POWs and eventually sent home to Tottenham. He arrived there at the height of the great influenza epidemic in which his mother had just died. The Andrews aunts were taking care of Grandad. So, Frank came to stay in our spare room.

He had been skinny when he had gone to war. When he came back he was skeletal. He had been in a prison camp near Giessen and put to work there in a mine. He did not complain of his treatment. The prisoners had been no worse off for food than the German civilians; and when Red Cross parcels had got through the prisoners had been better off. It had been the mine, he said, that had ruined his nerves. He had been afraid all the time of a tunnel roof collapse and being buried as if in a dug-out that had taken a direct hit.

In his dreams the roof collapsed and the bodies were buried again and again. Although on some nights he only cried out or sobbed, on others he would scream or shout for help. He could become violent. On one occasion he fought the collapsing tunnel and, in fighting, swept the wash-stand clear of everything on it. The big jug and wash-basin were both smashed. My mother fussed and made suet puddings to fatten him up, but they did not improve his dreams.

The worst part of being taken prisoners, he said once, had been the three-day march to the German railhead. Then he thought again and corrected himself. He was my youngest uncle and he wanted me to understand. The worst part had been waiting in their trenches to be captured after they knew that they must be cut off; when they weren't being strafed any more, just left there without rations, mislaid in the fog and then forgotten about. They hadn't fired a shot. They had just manned forward-zone trenches and hoped to stay alive through the strafing. Then the battle had seemed to go away. They hadn't even seen the Jerries until a *feldwebel* came and told them through a megaphone to dump their equipment, pile arms and form up outside their trenches. Then the march began.

Uncle Frank had not liked his officers, not the young ones anyway. Out of the line they had been full of piss and wind. Under fire they had stayed in their dug-outs. They were immoral too. How did he mean, immoral? I might well ask. Filthy! He had been on guard duty one night before they went up to the line when two of the young officers had come back from an evening out in the local French town. They had come back arm-in-arm and drunk.

'I could smell what they'd been doing,' Uncle Frank added darkly. '*I* knew.'

'You mean they smelt of whisky?'

'No. In the estaminets they drank wine or beer. That's not what I meant.'

There was, I thought, only one other possibility. It might be an outlandish one but I had to try it.

'You mean they'd been with women and still smelt of scent?'

Uncle Frank became impatient. 'At this clever-dick school of yours, don't they teach you about nancies kissing each other?'

No, they did not; not for the Cambridge Locals; certainly not for the London matric. Of course, I knew as well as anyone else that nancy boys were effeminate men who walked and talked like panto dames; but I could not believe that infantry officers in uniform would be allowed to play the fool like that while on active service. There was something here that I did not understand. Or perhaps Uncle Frank had got things wrong. I had seen drunken navvies fighting in the street outside a pub at Lee Green and it had been just like a fall-about comedy act. Perhaps the officers had been even drunker than he had thought. I tried to suggest this, but Uncle Frank had gone quiet. When he had been fattened up a little he left us and went to work for a firm of scrap metal merchants who had a government contract to clear up the Somme battlefield.

Uncle Sidney's war reminiscences were more colourful. From Mesopotamia he had gone with his regiment right up into Turkey. 'Johnny Turk', he would say, 'is a gentleman,' and seemed to believe it. He may, of course, have been thinking of the Turkish army officers. His account of the detrainment of men and horses at Haydarpashá railway station showed what he thought of the Turkish *hoi polloi*. When an attempt had been made by hordes of Turkish porters to interfere with, and probably loot, the British officers' baggage he had immediately waded in, cracking heads with his loaded swagger stick, 'to teach the dirty buggers to keep hands off and mind their manners'.

I did not believe all Uncle Sidney's tales any more than I believed Uncle Frank's, but I liked the sound of Haydarpashá, pronounced with an accent on the last syllable, and looked it up. It proved to be near Scutari and Florence Nightingale's Crimean War hospital on the shores of the Bosphorus opposite Constantinople.

At school we were reading the essays of Addison, Steele and Lamb to show us how English should be written, and Milton's *Comus* because, I think, copies of a school edition happened to be available. The only French prose we read was *Le Roi des Montagnes*, also available. War shortages persisted. At home I was not short of books. My father used to ask those he knew whom he thought of as well-educated to send me their old school books. Several did so. I remember one batch in particular sent by that good actor, Henry Hewitt, whose wife Hilda had been a concert party pianist during the war. He had been a sixth-former at Highgate and had clearly enjoyed himself there. Green's *Short History of the English People* had been adorned by him in the margins with skilfully disrespectful drawings of the great men referred to in the text. Among his books, too, was a Skeat's *Etymological Dictionary* which was to become important to me. From another benefactor I received a broken-backed copy of Newth's *Inorganic Chemistry*. That I also came to know well.

On Sundays I read the *Sunday Pictorial* and discovered the *Nelson Lee* 'Library'. I had the library in bundles, borrowed from a boy whose father bought them for his own pleasure. Most fathers then liked the *Boys' Own Paper*, and one could see why; it was straight-laced and inoffensive. I liked the Nelson Lee stories. How an ex-private detective came to be a housemaster at St Frank's, and how his former assistant and henchman, Nipper, came to be one of the boys in his house were questions to which I did not really want answers. St Dominic's would have had nothing to do with either of them. Stalky & Co would have steered clear for social reasons. Even Greyfriars would have hedged. St Frank's was really a most peculiar place. States of siege rather like modern factory sit-ins occurred often, triggered generally by potty, cane-wielding, Latin-crazed martinets who believed that discipline was better imposed without the consent of the disciplined. St Frank's was, in effect, a school for delinquents of all ages, a sort of fee-paying, Eton-suited nick with Nelson Lee and Nipper there to monitor the rough stuff and act as what would now be called a 'crisis management team'. At St Frank's the boys were for ever behaving appallingly and for ever being allowed to get away with doing so. Snickery schoolboy justice was meted out by snickery kangaroo courts. Some of the revenges taken on the mad masters were, though occasionally funny, often cruel. The matric was never mentioned. Yet no one at St Frank's ever really worried; no one there had bad dreams about collapsing mine tunnels and the slaughterhouse at Lee Green; no one there was haunted by the accounts of atrocities – Bolshevik, White Russian and British–Indian – that I read in the papers. It was possible that at St Frank's they did not bother to read the papers; or that if they did, they simply did not mind much about what the Kurdish troops had done with their bayonets to Armenian women. Perhaps atrocities were not on the best boarding-school curricula; perhaps Nipper had said they were all rot. Who was to say? St Frank's might be a blood-and-thunder school (and the Nelson Lee Library might be trash), but it made soppy old St Dominic's seem like a school where that other Eric could have gone to weep.

In any quest for heroes, of course, there are bound to be disap-pointments. I read and reread several times a book by Guy Boothby called *Motor Scout*. It was about a boy who had a motorbike and led an adventurous life foiling South American bandits. The reason for this special interest was that Auntie Dot had married an adventur-ous man named Wilkinson and gone off to live high up in Bolivia at the mining town of Oruro where he managed the railway. For a while I was keen on South American lawlessness which I saw as possibly more exciting than the gloomy old Zane Grey stuff. It was a shortlived enthusiasm. We had seen photographs of Harry Wilkinson in which he looked very like the handsome white man on the jacket of Edgar Wallace's *Sanders of the River*. When they both came to England on leave, however, I thought he looked more like John Buchan's Richard Hannay. The disappointing thing was that he behaved like neither of them. Instead, he grinned broadly, snapped his fingers a lot and called everybody *che*.

In a school holiday after the war, Auntie Cis, home between voyages again, took me up to the printer's offices of *Truth* (no longer Labouchere's) from which Grandpa Ambler was shortly going to retire. He gave me a present from the composing room: my name set on a Monotype machine in 12-point Garamond and tied into a slug with twine. That was the last time I saw him. Within a few weeks of his retirement the influenza had killed him too. None of the verse he wrote has survived. His private jokes tended to be far-fetched. I remember only one. He always used to call the tea we drank 'bohea'. When I asked why I was given an elaborate explanation. It was a borrowed Chinese word that had started out in the eighteenth century meaning 'best black tea' and ended up a century later meaning 'worst black tea'. His considered belief was that, for the Chinese themselves, bohea had always been the low-grade stuff. It had been the natural arrogance and conceit of the white merchants that had originally led them to assume that the polite, respectful Chinese would sell them only the best of what they had. Did I know that when the Chinese laughed at us they always did so behind their hands? No wonder, eh? Tee-hee! Bohea! Bah!

For Reg and Amy Ambrose and The Whatnots 1921 was a make-or-break year. He had thought for some time that a concert party of quality with its own material and a well-directed cast of up-and-coming pros with experience in vaudeville (he used the word in its American sense) could make a West End hit. It would be like a traditional revue but have a smaller and more versatile cast. He set out to make The Whatnots good enough. It was an expensive task. In the end, he put the show on the market and financed it at the same time by giving a series of 'subscription' performances in West End concert halls.

The shows went down well and paid their way, but failed to interest a theatre management. However, his idea had been right.

Concert party did come to the London theatre that year. It came in the shape of *The Co-Optimists*, with a cast that included Stanley Holloway and Melville Gideon, and it ran for years. My father attributed a lot of the show's success to Melville Gideon's songs. 'So light and funny,' he said, 'so original. We never had material of our own to touch it.' He was probably right.

That was the end of The Whatnots and of thoughts of being real artistes. The choice of career had finally been made. Reg Ambrose had been discarded. A.P. (Reg) Ambler left Silvertown to become publicity manager of one of those old but still-enterprising companies which had suddenly become busy making 'everything electrical' for the British Empire. That, however, was only a first step in the chosen direction. Before long he had joined the London office of the American advertising agency that handled the Everything Electrical account.

The marionette show was almost the last bit of Reg and Amy Ambrose to go. It was advertised for sale in the classifieds of the *Era* and the *Stage* sandwiched between offers of Screaming Patter and cut-price band parts. It was bought by a new-rich, and eccentric, Canadian. I can still remember the tone of amused outrage in which my father reported completion of the sale. 'He wants to ship it back to Montreal as a present for his kids.' He managed a smile. 'He thinks it'll be a nice toy for them to play with.'

My mother said, 'Oh Reg, no!' and began to cry.

Have I been fair to them as entertainers? Have I done them justice?

Among the friends they accumulated during the war years was a man in the naval air service named Arthur Waters. His sisters, Elsie and Doris, were entertainers who, at the time, sang point numbers in close harmony and played, respectively, the violin and the piano. That summer, 1921, we went to Southwold on the Suffolk coast for a holiday and they were there in a Harry Pepper concert party called *The White Coons*. They were very ladylike on-stage and delightfully funny off. They had no thoughts then of the Gert and Daisy sketches that later made them stars on radio. For the Ambler and Waters families Southwold began a friendship.

I went to see Elsie Waters and asked her what she and Doris had thought of Reg and Amy as entertainers. Could they have made it professionally in the twenties?

'Oh yes,' she said; 'I think so. If they'd gone on their own. Songs at the piano. Your mother was so pretty. But it was for you boys

that they were giving it up, eh? That was what they said, I think.'
She chuckled. 'Did you know that your mother never read any of
your books?'

'I guessed.'

'She said she couldn't get on with them. You'd think she'd have
tried. She must have. She used to read a lot once. What did she
like?'

'Books from the tuppenny library. Maud Diver, Berta Ruck,
Marie Corelli, Warwick Deeping.'

'Maud Diver! Fancy remembering her. Marie Corelli wasn't bad.
Have another cup of tea.'

When my brother went to Colfe's his form master gave the new
boys a pep talk and some advice on how to succeed at the school.
One piece of the advice was: 'Don't be like Ambler's brother.' The
master, P. H. Rees, was a rugger-playing Welshman with a pawky
sense of humour and he was making one of his little jokes, but
when repeated at home it did not go down well.

My father's sporting ambitions for me were those of the
passionate spectator. He wanted me to be good at all games, but he
also dreamed of my excelling at one of them. He loved watching
rugby football. It was a game that he understood, though, of
course, he had never actually played it because of his bad eyes. He
wanted to be in the stand at Twickenham when I scored a winning
try for England.

I found football as boring to play as it was to watch. When Percy
Rees, persuaded by my father, put my name down for house
matches, I would simply fail to show up. As a player I would
certainly not be missed and I had a better use for those afternoons.
To cover up at home I used to muddy my boots and shorts in a ditch
before returning.

I liked cricket some of the time. Net practice on the hard asphalt
of the school playground, with wickets of sawn-off railway
sleepers and composition balls that could fragment like grenades
on impact, was good dangerous fun. More conventional play at the
Eltham Road field, on a shaggy pitch with one-strap pads, a ball
like a bag of bones and not enough stumps, soon palled. My father
gave me a bat signed by Jack Hobbs. I valued the bat; but my father
dreamed of my taking it to the Oval, where I would make a
gentlemanly century for Surrey against Lancashire.

He knew, of course, that he was going to be disappointed; but he had, as it were, written a part for me and, however badly miscast I was, wanted me to try out for it.

He was a cigarette smoker. One of his stage directions for me was that I should smoke a pipe. One Sunday he ran out of cigarettes. He could have gone to the machine outside the tobacconists near the station, but the machine only had Weights and Woodbines. He liked Three Castles. He gave me a careful smile.

'As a matter of interest, old chap,' he said, 'you wouldn't by any chance happen to have the odd packet of Players anywhere about, would you?'

I had been a secret smoker for some weeks, but this was the first time I had been challenged.

'No, Dad,' I said, 'but I've got half a packet of Goldflake. Would you like me to get them?'

'Thanks, old son. I would be grateful.'

No more was said about cigarettes until, two days later, he presented me with a sporty-looking briar and a pouch of tobacco.

'If you're going to smoke,' he said, 'you'll look better with a pipe than with those gaspers of yours. I'd have liked to be a pipe smoker myself but I came to it too late. You'll start off right and get used to it. That's a very mild tobacco I got for you there.'

I smoked the pipe, turned pale and had to go and throw up. My mother was very angry with him. He shrugged. 'You have to get used to a pipe,' he explained. 'He'll just have to persevere.'

I never again smoked the pipe and it was never again mentioned. He was not always so easygoing when I fluffed lines and misread or was careless with my part.

There had been a time, when we were on summer holidays, when he had liked to visit cathedrals and important churches in order to try out their organs. 'There's a five-manual Willis at Chichester,' he would say on a dull day in Bognor; 'let's go and see if they're taking care of it.' A shilling to a verger would usually get him to the organ and a second would open the door to the blowers' loft. Sometimes I would work the blowers' beam. 'Swell to Great!' my father would cry and glorious sounds would come forth. I enjoyed those days. He told me once of a voluntary he had written and played at the Church of the Lady Margaret when he had been organist there. It had been based on the melody of 'Stop Your Tickling Jock'. No one had ever noticed a thing.

When he became an advertising agent he took up golf and turned to sampling golf courses instead of church organs in the holidays. On these occasions I would caddy for him. He was not good at the game and we would spend most of the time in long grass looking for the repaints he had bought earlier in the pro's shop and then pulled or sliced into successive patches of out-of-bounds rough. Confronted on one of these occasions by a high hedge of bramble and bracken at the fifteenth and with no balls left to lose, we were on the point of giving up when a boy popped his head up over the hedge. He was in the farmer's field beyond.

'Excuse me, sir,' he said to my father; 'I think your ball may be just here. A Dunlop Dimple? Would that be yours?'

'Thank you very much indeed,' my father replied. 'Yes, I think that must be mine.' He glanced at me. 'Would you hop over and see, old chap?'

'Yep,' I said briskly.

At school that term pseudo-American turns of speech gleaned from pulp westerns and even more unreliable sources, such as John Buchan's terrible Mr Blenkiron, had coloured much of our conversation. For a while we had put 'I opine that' or 'I kinda guess and calculate' in front of everything. 'Yep', 'Nope' and 'Well, pardner, maybe' had been common currency.

When I reached the field the boy and I stared at one another. Same height, same weight, much the same clothes, but different accents and different expectations. He pointed to a ball lying under the hedge.

'Thanks,' I said. It did not, in fact, look much like one of ours but I picked it up and climbed back.

When I rejoined my father he took the ball and put it away in his golf bag. That, evidently, was the end of play for the day. I took the bag and we started back. When we had walked a little way he stopped and faced me.

'Did you notice the way that boy spoke?'

'Yes, Dad.'

'You said "yep" back there. *Yep!* Why can't you speak like he does? Why can't you speak like a gentleman?'

I started to reply and then shut up. What I had started to say was that if he had sent me to the same school as the boy in the field I would probably have spoken in the same way. I stopped myself because I did not want to hurt him and because I knew that, although I could not help letting him down at games, I did not have to let him down at everything. He had not really minded about the 'yep'. It had been my Lewisham accent that had suddenly bothered

53

him. For those who lived by their wits in England then a good ear for accents was essential. It was essential, too, to have good table manners and not to eat with your mouth open.

For speech my ear was not bad. For music I had an ear but no talent.

As a piano student at the Blackheath Conservatoire I managed to pass two Associated Board examinations but did not enjoy doing so. At one of them I was unnerved by the examiner, a stout man who sat on an air cushion with a slow leak which hissed at me steadily as I played a study by Burgmuller. Beatrice Howell, my teacher, refused to believe me when I told her about the air cushion. I must have been imagining it. If an Associated Board examiner used such a cushion, she said, it would certainly not hiss. I should not tell such tales.

She had in her room a collection of small ceramic busts of the composers. It stood on a bookcase full of bound German and French editions of their works. The oldest and most valuable of the busts were those of Beethoven, Mozart, Chopin, Schubert and Schumann. She never referred to any of them, though without the adjective 'poor'. It was always *poor* Beethoven and *poor* Schumann. I thought I knew what she meant. I had looked up all their sad case histories – deafness, pneumonia, TB, poverty, broken heart, broken fourth finger, madness and the rest – so when one day she referred to poor Mendelssohn I felt that I had to object.

'But Mendelssohn wasn't poor, Miss Howell. I read about him in the encyclopaedia. He was rich and happy and famous and he died young.'

She gave me her saddest smile. 'All composers are poor when they are badly played. And when pupils will not even play them as written they are even poorer. They turn in their graves.'

This was a reference to a habit I had developed of proposing changes. 'Don't you think, Miss Howell,' I would say, 'that it would be more original with an F-sharp there?'

She would take a deep breath. 'It would be different, but there would be nothing at all original about it. If poor Mendelssohn had wanted you to play an F-sharp he would have written it. Instead' – she would ring it firmly with her pencil – 'he has asked you for an F. We all like to hear music played as written, and examiners insist upon it. You will not please by playing wrong notes.'

In those days piano teachers had a reputation for being cruel to their pupils by standing over them with canes and whacking them on the knuckles when they made mistakes. Such things did not happen at the Blackheath Conservatoire. Though greatly provoked, Miss Howell never struck me with anything heavier than a sigh.

At school things were different. The paragon of Sandhurst Road had become the bad lad of Lewisham Hill. There, after some initial embarrassments, I got used to being beaten. The embarrassments were domestic. Until the onset of puberty, either my mother or Susan, our mother's help, would supervise our use of the geyser to run bath water and see that the soap was not wasted. When my mother saw the weals on my behind for the first time she was furious with me.

'What were you doing?'

'Talking in class.'

'Only talking? I don't believe it. Little fiend. I don't know what your father will say.'

He said nothing much. He seemed as pleased that I had committed the crime as he was pleased that I had been punished for it; it showed that I was manly.

The offences for which I was beaten derived mainly from failures to do homework. Some failures I could conceal or find ways to excuse. Most masters, I found, were more inclined to accept an interesting new excuse than a hackneyed one. When invention flagged I would fall back on half-truth. False frankness could disarm, but only if you knew your man. I once grew tired of lying elaborately to F. E. Bennett. I liked him. The next time he asked me where my history essay was I said that I had not done it.

'Why not?'

'I was lazy, sir.'

He thought for a moment, smiled faintly and then shrugged. No punishment was awarded. If I had told the truth – that I had not done the history essay because I had nothing to think or say about the Wars of the Roses that was not as boring as Stevenson's *The Black Arrow* – he would have had to punish. Laziness is a cosy, traditional schoolboy sin. A suggestion that the boy may not really be lazy but only, and understandably, bored is a reflection on the theory of education to which the teacher subscribes, and so inadmissible. Boredom with what is being taught is worse than a sin; it is a vice and the boy who admits to it is insolent. Sin is safer. So, keep a straight face and surprise the man; tell him what he wants to hear, something he thinks he knows already; tell him you're lazy.

For friendly masters simple lies were enough. For the others I planned more carefully. They were most vulnerable at exam times when professional pride made them look for success from their teaching efforts. That was the time to strike. The tactic was surprise, the weapon was disappointment. If you could succeed, fail. Top one term, bottom the next in the same subject: that was the way I chose to fight, and a very tiring way it was. I came to see punishment as useful. It strengthened resolve and nourished the hate an enemy of society needs when he is fighting a war.

Of course, I had allies. Their names were Edmond Dantès and A.J. Raffles, Arsène Lupin and Long John Silver, Rupert of Hentzau and Old Blind (God-if-I-had-eyes) Pew. There were others. Luckily, I had friends as well. The first was George Sims.

Before my father bought me a bicycle I used to get to school by the tram that ran between Lewisham and Lee Green. Although Sims and I were in the same form it was through using the tram and walking home together from Lee Green that we became friends. He was what was then described as 'delicate'. He had had rheumatic fever and at school was excused even the mild PT and gym periods that the rest of us had to attend. He was pale, frail and walked with a slight stoop. As he was also highly intelligent and a hard worker he was generally regarded as an inoffensive swot and left to himself. Only gradually did I discover that inside the swot there was a taste for crime and melodrama as keen as my own. His heroes were the great scientific detectives: Sherlock Holmes and Dr Thorndyke, of course, but also the less well-known Professor S.F.X. Van Dusen, the astonishing and all-powerful Thinking Machine created by Jacques Futrelle.

Mr Sims was a qualified mechanical engineer with a tool-room background and an important technical job in Woolwich Arsenal. The exact nature of it was never discussed. He was a tall, calm, very gentle man with the same rounded shoulders that his son had. Mrs Sims had been a schoolteacher before their marriage. My friend Sims – we always used our surnames or 'man', the school word, between ourselves – was their only child and they doted on him. At school he was meekly studious. At home he was a tyrant. 'Spoilt,' my mother said. She was quite wrong. He was indulged and he was worth indulging. Of course, I envied him.

The Sims had an old house with more rooms in it than they really needed. This was just as well. Sims had decided to be a polymath. One of the spare rooms became his engineering workshop. I was there when the lathe was delivered. It was a 3½-inch Drummond with backgear, and Sims Senior took personal charge of its installation. I enjoyed that day too. There were bookshelves full of books in the spare room, and they stayed even when it became a workshop. There were a great many novels, mostly in the old style hardcover 'series' editions, and Everyman classics. There were also Mr and Mrs Sims' college textbooks. Among these was Newth's *Inorganic Chemistry* in the edition that I had.

I cannot remember which of us it was who suggested that we might study chemistry with Newth as our guide, but I know how it arose. We had started going to the pictures on Saturday nights and one of the films we saw at the Lee Green flea pit that impressed us very much was *Dr Jekyll and Mr Hyde* with John Barrymore. When something impressed us very much it was natural that we should want to pick holes in it. We thought that the prop aparatus in Dr Jekyll's old laboratory had been highly unconvincing and probably designed by someone who thought of chemistry as 'stinks'. There were too many of those fellows at school. Although the labs had been opened up again after the war when Mr Kelland, the chemistry teacher, had returned from the army, they were too small for anything better than elementary teaching. Besides, both The Bird and his unhappy successor were classical scholars. Divinity was part of the syllabus but not biology. None of the physical sciences was a required matric subject. What hope had we of earning the approval of men like Holmes and Professor Van Dusen?

A few days later, Sims boldly commandeered the whole of one side of his mother's large kitchen for our use as a laboratory. To my amazement she submitted. On the following Saturday we began to work through the qualitative inorganic analysis tables from the beginning. We took rough notes as we went along and wrote them up properly later, as Mr Kelland had recommended, in special exercise books. For reagents we went to a friendly pharmacist in the Lee High Road who became faintly amused by and then interested in our project. The more dangerous substances he put up in blue poison bottles and he quoted us special prices for such things as filter papers and the pieces of laboratory glassware we could not make for ourselves. We had only one disagreement with him. There was a statement in one of our textbooks (not Newth) that we found it hard to believe: 'Lithium, a metal, is the lightest solid known.' We decided to ask our man to get us a gram of lithium so that we could work out its specific gravity. He failed to produce it. If he had explained that lithium was hard to handle, like sodium, and had to be kept floating in benzene away from atmospheric moisture, we would have understood. If he had said that wholesale druggists did not stock the stuff because doctors had no use for it, we would have believed him. Instead, he offered us a white powder which he said was lithium oxide and tried to charge us ninepence for it. We rejected the white powder haughtily. It was not what we had ordered. Besides, we did not have ninepence to spend that day.

For me, money troubles and puberty arrived together. At about the same time that I became a lecher I also became a thief.

The cost of our chemistry study programme had mounted steadily. Although Mr Sims continued to subsidize the work, even his generosity had limits. We had become ambitious. The inorganic field had been surveyed. Now the great world of organic hydrocarbons beckoned. Our eyes, too, were on quantitative analysis and calibrated precision apparatus of a kind that we could not make for ourselves even on Sims' precious lathe. We were also working, though independently, on wireless communication. I had an old WD spark transmitter, bought for me by Grandad Andrews off an army surplus barrow in the Farringdon Road market, that I used without a licence. I was also acquiring the components of a two-valve receiver with which I hoped to get KDKA Pittsburgh as well as 2MT, the Marconi station at Writtle. Mr Sims had invested in a readymade set, but my father did not believe that good music could ever be heard through earphones. If I wanted to listen to those quacking sounds I must make my own arrangements for doing so. However, he sanctioned the erection of an aerial mast in the back garden. It was made out of four ten-foot bamboo tent poles fastened end to end with iron clamps, but never braced with enough guy wires to stand upright for long. A stiff breeze would bring it all down. At its best it stood bowed like a huge fishing rod with a snagged line. In fair weather, though, it could support an aerial. The really difficult problem was the set.

This was during my Receding Chin period.

My search for a reliable way of making instant character and personality appraisals had been a long one. For a time I had thought that Lombroso might be the answer, but found his insistence on the theory of physical stigmata limiting. How was I to classify my certain belief that men who wore bicycle clips in the

58

house were not to be trusted? I knew why I had that belief. An insurance salesman named Harry Thorpe, who fancied himself as a teaser of small boys, had once fired a cap pistol in my face and a spark had hurt my right eye. He never, ever took off his bicycle clips. Who cared about his ear lobes? It was those clips and his fatuous grin that marked him down as dangerous. I moved on to phrenology. There, ear lobes did not matter. One had social characteristics to play with, solid things like philoprogenetiveness, approbativeness and amativeness, and quaint ones like sublimity. The trouble was that the bumps of, say, firmness, self-esteem and veneration were on some heads all in the same place. Until, a year or two later, I found Jung, I took up a sort of modified Lombroso position. Thanks to careful observation over a long period, and a steadfast unwillingness to accept evidence that did not fit the theory, I became convinced that all persons possessing exceptional talents of the kind I most envied had receding chins.

My first remarkable chin outside the Waters family, some of whose profiles may well have stimulated the chin idea, was a successful designer and manufacturer of time-switches whom we met on holiday. To impress him I pretended to invent the vernier scale, and made a good deceitful show of being abashed when he, while congratulating me, mentioned that the concept was not new. He told me a bit about becoming an engineer. I should aim for one of the science colleges of London University like City and Guilds. I was sure he was right. I tried to make my chin recede more and, with the unwitting help of our appalling local dentist, very nearly succeeded.

It was natural, then, that when I got into difficulties over the high cost of wireless components I should look for a chin to consult. Opposite us in Newstead Road there was a Member of the Institute of Electrical Engineers who looked just right. He was friendly and very helpful. When I complained that a small piece of ebonite panel cost a shilling, he said that with so many people building sets the wireless shop traders were making a fortune.

'Of course,' he went on casually, 'in the power generating business we don't have much use for ebonite as an insulator. On things like sub-station transformers we use ceramic and for power station switchboards we use polished slate.'

He did not actually turn and look in the direction of Dallinger Road as he said it, because, of course, no decent, respectable AMIEE would ever encourage a boy to steal; but there was no need for him to do so. I could take a hint. House-building had at last been resumed in Dallinger Road and there were big stacks of roofing slates no more than a minute's walk away.

'How do you drill and polish slate?' I asked.

It was not as easy as he made it sound and I had to steal a dozen or more before I got the knack of it. By passing the knack, and supplies of slate, on to others I was able to solve the component problem for the time being. When my father heard Melba's unmistakable voice coming through the earphones, even he had to admit that broadcasting might have a future.

After one Christmas, while I was still trying unsuccessfully to get KDKA, an unusual thing happened: I was sent to stay with Grandad Andrews in Tottenham. It was unusual because, although I had sometimes been sent away during the long school summer holiday, the Christmas and New Year break had generally been spent at home.

However, I did not ask questions. I liked staying with Grandad Andrews. He preferred back streets to main roads and our expeditions always ended up in interesting places like Clerkenwell and Shoreditch. On that occasion I had Christmas present money to spend. It was somewhere in Stoke Newington that I bought, from a box in a secondhand furniture shop, a copy of *John Halifax, Gentleman* by Mrs Craik. For a time that virtuous hero was someone with whom I could see eye to eye, and even envy. He was an orphan.

At the Andrews house in Sherringham Avenue I slept on a camp bed beside the piano in the unused front parlour. We always lived in the kitchen where the fire in the cooking range was kept going for warmth. Grandad's glasses were not very good, so in the evening I would read the paper aloud to him and drink strong tea while he smoked his pipe and had a bottle of stout. Then he would cook our supper of sausages and bubble-and-squeak.

One evening early in the New Year the frying pan was just beginning to sizzle when there was a knock at the front door. Before I could go to answer it, Grandad had dropped the pan with a clatter and was himself hurrying along the passage. To my astonishment I heard my father greeting him. When they came back into the kitchen they were both grinning broadly.

'Surprised to see me, old chap?' my father asked.

I was, a little. In those days of few telephones, unexpected callers were not necessarily surprising; but I was surprised that my father had come all the way across London to Sherringham Avenue on a cold night. I said so.

'Well, let's sit down, ' he said and produced half a bottle of whisky from his overcoat pocket. Grandad hastened to get glasses and a jug of water. We all sat down at the kitchen table.

'What would you say, old chap,' my father went on, 'if I were to tell you that you have a baby sister?'

'A sister, Dad?' It was a curiously formal, stilted conversation.

'Yes, old son, a sister. She weighs six pounds and she's beautiful.' He gave me a searching look. 'Your mother's been worrying about how you'd take it. What I mean is, not every boy of your age would want his friends to know that he had a baby sister. I hope you're as glad as we and your brother are.'

'Oh yes, I am glad. But it is a bit of a surprise.'

'Do you mean to say you didn't notice anything? Your mother was sure you would.'

Notice? See something I was not supposed to see? No, of course I wouldn't. True, with one bit of my mind I had noticed that for the last two months there had been, standing in the spare room at Newstead Road, a glossy, brand-new pram all wrapped up in corrugated paper. I had noticed that my mother had been getting fat and going to see Dr Park quite a lot. I had also searched the ottoman, in which secret things had always been kept, and found the layette. But most of my mind was absolutely innocent. About the other bit I thought it simpler to lie.

'No, Dad, I didn't notice anything. Why should I?'

He shook his head in amazement, pretending to believe me. We were both giving very bad performances. Grandad was smiling and sipping his whisky, pleased because his Charley had a daughter, but laughing at us too. He thought us silly devils, and we were. Later, when my father had gone, Grandad asked sympathetically if I would like a taste of whisky. I said no because I did not like the smell of it. He made me some cocoa instead.

My sister Joyce was indeed beautiful and I took a somewhat possessive interest in her. My mother viewed it with suspicion. 'When your brother was born,' she said, 'you were a perfect fiend.' She continued to believe, however, that I had failed to notice her pregnancy and I was suitably rewarded. 'You'll always be my first-born,' she assured me.

None of my friends seemed to mind that I had a baby sister, except Sims. He hoped that the event would not interfere with our

61

Saturday work programme. I think he felt that I was too easy-going with my parents. He cracked the whip. The ever-patient Mrs Sims was forced to surrender additional space in her kitchen so that we could use the sink more easily.

I tried to keep my friendships in separate compartments, as I kept myself, and usually I succeeded. Sims and Smith G. together would have been an unthinkable embarrassment. With Smith G. I used to go cycling in the country where we had long talks about sex. There was a boy in our form who liked showing us his penis during Mr Worthy's drawing classes. The boy was circumcized. We were not. How important was the difference? How could we find out? Did anyone really know? Were there no books on the subject? On these expeditions we became skilled fence climbers and orchard robbers. Fairly skilled anyway; once or twice we had to run very fast indeed to stay out of trouble. With Smith G., though, taking risks was fun.

With Hugo Cooke the risks were of a different kind and taken more deliberately. He was a member of the school rifle club and also played water polo. His elder brother was a rugger player. They did not appear to compete with one another so their mutual dislike always came as a surprise when it showed. They lived in an old house near the school. The Cooke basement contained a potter's wheel and a large kiln in which Mrs Cooke fired her artistic flower bowls and vases. Mr Cooke was a commercial traveller and often away in the provinces. He sold fire engines.

Hugh, as Hugo liked to be called, was a premature man of the world. A handsome boy and a natty dresser, he knew how a tie should be knotted to conceal an old food stain and what to wear to a Greenwich Town Hall dance. He knew how to ask a girl for a dance. Even more remarkable, he actually knew how to dance. His mother had sent him to a dancing class. His other social assets included an ability to play the banjolele and do an imitation of Jack Smith, The Whispering Baritone, singing 'I Can't Give You Any-thing But Love'. He taught me how to inhale cigarette smoke and how to buy beer in a pub without being spotted as an under-age schoolkid. He lived by commercial travellers' maxims learned at his father's knee. 'A clean shirt, a shit and a shave make a new man of you,' he would murmur contentedly as we sipped our illegal halves of bitter in the saloon bar of The Green Man. He became a junior member of the old, pre-Mosley British Fascists and when we went to dances he would wear his black and silver BF lapel badge.

Matric time came and most of us passed. Mr Sims had known about the virtues of City and Guilds for some time and had applied early on his son's behalf; but London University engineering degrees had become desirable and there were not enough places. To fill the gap, Northampton Polytechnic in Islington (now City University) had been upgraded to offer, as Northampton Engineering College, BSc degree courses in engineering. Sims secured a place there with Mr Sims paying the tuition fees. When I broached the subject at Newstead Road, however, my father sighed.

'I'm sorry, old chap, but we can't have everything. We're getting a car this year and there's our holiday to be paid for. Besides, you're not sixteen yet. It's a bit young for university.'

'Sims is going. He's only six months older than I am.'

'Sims doesn't have any brothers or sisters. I'll tell you what, old son. If you could get a scholarship to this college, I might just manage the exes. Otherwise, I'm afraid . . .'

There were four scholarships available. The best of the four was one which paid full tuition for a period of three years and all of them were awarded on the results of a competitive examination held at the college. My father entered my name and I was allowed to sit. When I arrived at Islington on the day of the exam there was hardly room to move. For the four scholarships there were nearly two hundred applicants, mostly sixth-formers from London area grammar schools. One or two had small moustaches. It was very depressing. The best part of the day for me was the meat pie I had for lunch at a tea shop near the Angel underground station.

It was weeks before the results of the exam came through and during them I lost some of my interest in engineering, and receding chins. For birthdays I was allowed by then to make out a list of the books I hoped for as presents; and Auntie Dora, the one who had given me *Eric*, that year redeemed herself by giving me William Archer's *Playmaking* which I had been wanting for a long time. When a letter arrived saying that I had won the top scholarship, I was pleased, naturally, but not perhaps as pleased as I should have been. I was already searching in secondhand bookshops for Everyman editions of the plays of Ibsen. Fired by William Archer and a London performance of Pirandello's *Six Characters in Search of an Author*, I had decided to become a playwright.

FOUR

When I gave my name to the head of the chemistry department he smiled at me.

'Ah yes,' he said; 'you're the one who did the one hundred per cent scholarship paper.'

'A *hundred* per cent?'

'I marked the paper so I know. You should have had a hundred per cent for your physics paper too, but the colleague who marked that doesn't believe in giving a student full marks. Bad for his soul, he thinks. He gave you ninety-five per cent. Five per cent off for bad writing. I hope you'll find some way of passing the time here.'

I stared. He smiled again, almost sympathetically.

'Nothing to worry about. It's just that you're already well up to or above intermediate standard. You won't have very much work to do here for the next few months.'

I should have taken him more seriously, but I had never before been warned against boredom. Sims was all right. He took easily to acquiring the polytechnic skills, such as those of the drawing office and the machine shop, that were still being taught at the college. I tried for a while to interest myself in a course of cable laying for telephone engineers. I also listened to a series of lectures on the phlogiston theory of combustion. They were delivered by a confused old man who seemed to want us to believe that phlogiston was the eighteenth-century word for oxygen and that Lavoisier's theory of combustion had been stolen from the honest English chemist Joseph Priestley. Soon, I became a truant.

At first the burden of guilt was tolerable. As a member of the university and an engineering student I was allowed to use the library of the Institute of Electrical Engineers. For a time I spent my mornings there with Steinmetz's *Theory and Calculation of Alternating Current Phenomena* or reading the latest scientific journals. Then I strayed. The Institute was on the Thames

Embankment only a few minutes walk from the Law Courts. Soon I was spend ng whole mornings in the public galleries of the King's Bench Division or the Criminal Division of the Court of Appeal.

There could have been worse places for an immature adolescent to pass the time. I learned a little about the rules of evidence and soon came to see everyone in a courtroom as a performer. Some of the acts offered, however, had long been curling at the edges. There was, for instance, Mr Justice Horridge in KB7 who would make a bad joke and then, when he got his laugh, threaten to clear the court. The best, as well as the worst, acting performances were usually given by witnesses.

One of the first trials I attended was an action for breach of promise of marriage. Unless there were aristocratic names or a rich man involved, such actions were by then becoming unusual in the high court, so it was odd to find Mr Norman Birkett, already an eminent and expensive KC, appearing for such a plaintiff. She was a seedy, pasty-faced spinster. Her seducer, the lodger, was a seedy, pasty-faced bachelor. The difference in their performances, though, was remarkable. She was able to shed a modest tear while giving her evidence. Her seducer was afflicted by a nervous twitch that several times looked disastrously like a smirk. Mr Birkett had only to purse his lips and ask quietly if there was something in the court or in the occasion that the defendant found amusing and it was all over. The jury gave the defendant the bird, and the importance of keeping a straight face for the world to see had been demonstrated to me yet again.

The case had interested me for another reason. If I had not heard the evidence I would have found the idea of that drab pair actually succeeding in the act of copulation hopelessly far-fetched. They were unmarried; that should have been an insuperable obstacle for such unattractive people. Yet, awful as they were, with none of the romantic advantages of a Pola Negri or a Ralph Ince to help them, they had somehow managed to do it; and to go on doing it; not just once, but several times. It made you think. Had I perhaps been over-estimating the difficulties? Or was lust as blind and all-conquering as love was said to be? If it was, then there was hope for fiends and horrors everywhere. There was hope for me.

I began to plan my truancy. On mid-week matinée days I would go to a West End theatre. On other afternoons, when there was no court case of interest to be seen through the day, I would go to a film. I took to carrying an attaché case with books and papers in it for all occasions. Some of the papers – a copy of the quarterly IEE Journal and things like student union notices – were for show in case of accidents. The copy of Jevons' *Logic* was only partly for show. I used to read a few pages of it every day over lunch or in the train to remind me that, even if I was going to end as a criminal, I still had a commitment to scientific method and rational thought. Jevons was my breviary. It was carried next to a foxed thirty-year-old copy of Winwood Reade's *Martyrdom of Man*. This was the book that Sherlock Holmes had casually recommended to Watson during their early days in Baker Street, and it was because of that recommendation that I had first been drawn to it. It had come as a revelation to me. 'Supernatural Christianity is false. Prayer is useless. The soul is not immortal. There are no rewards or punishments in a future state.' No wonder a conformist like Watson had not taken to it. That was the book I kept for serious reading on park benches. For the upper-circle queues outside the theatres I had pocket editions of Stevenson's shorter novels and stories.

I was stage-struck of course; but not stupidly so I think. Some plays I would go to often and jot down scenes that seemed to work particularly well so that I could see how they looked on paper. For a time I could rattle off Ben Travers' *A Cuckoo in the Nest* word for word as if I had a script, and I knew the mechanics and timing of every move and every bit of business in the Aldwych production. I haunted the tea shops, sandwich bars and pubs used by the stagehands and assistant stage-managers. I was an inveterate and shameless eavesdropper. Keith Prowse could tell me the seating capacity of a theatre. Only backstage shop talk could provide the titbits of local knowledge that I thought I needed. At the Criterion, for instance, no scenery at all could be flown; the Winter Garden stage had an irregular rake; the Embassy had no space under its stage. If I had been told that for a writer such information was irrelevant I would probably have agreed; but I would have gone on gathering it. I had by then sense enough to know that if ever I were to become a writer of plays worth performing I would have to earn a living while I learned how to write. The best sort of job, I thought, would be one that got me into the theatre. Stage management sounded too ambitious. The job for which I was at least partly qualified was surely that of an electrician.

The Coliseum was the London theatre with the biggest stage

area. That should mean that it had the most lighting equipment and the biggest need for electricians. They were rehearsing a Christmas pantomime production. I applied for a job.

My application was listened to absently by a fat man in a red pullover and a thin man in a suit of dungarees. We stood just outside the stage door. When I stopped listing my qualifications the fat one looked up at the patch of sky above the alleyway and cleared his throat.

'It's going to rain, Jack,' he said.

Jack grunted his agreement and then nodded in the direction of my attaché case. 'What you got there, son?' he asked. 'Your dinner? Samples?'

'Books.'

'Which union do you belong to? Not Theatrical Employees, I'll bet. Electrical? ETU? ACT? TGW?'

He was being a tease but I played it straight. 'Only the students' union so far. I haven't had a proper job.'

'Well, there's your answer, isn't it? You're at school, but you want to take the bread out of the mouth of a skilled man with a family to feed. Am I right?'

'I know a bit about switchboards and lighting cues.'

The fat man cleared his throat again. 'He's pulling our legs, Jack,' he said. 'Students are a randy lot. Young fellow like him probably fancies himself with the chorus. He just wants to dip his wick.'

Jack pretended to look deeply shocked. 'Well, I never! Is that right, son? Got a dirty mind, have we? Which is it? Come on, tell us. Boys or girls?'

'Neither,' I said foolishly.

'Instead of pulling his pud he wants to pull a few switches,' said the fat man. 'He knows we've got no work for his sort. He's only pulling our legs, Jack. I told you.'

'I don't know what the world's coming to,' Jack said and then suddenly tired of the game. 'All right, sonny. You heard what the gaffer said. No vacancies. Joke over. Piss off.'

I did so without further loss of dignity and received an amused nod from the gaffer as I went. He was the only skilled electrician there; Jack was one of the semi-skilled loudmouths. We both knew it. I had begun to develop an ear for the voices of experience and authority.

Some of them, however, had strange things to say. Among the books in my attaché case was *Infantry Training, Part 1*, an army manual. 'To do nothing', it told the young officer to whom it was addressed, 'is to do something definitely wrong.' That was the War Office speaking. It worried me. *Cogito, ergo sum.* How was it possible to do nothing? Or did the War Office not expect to be taken seriously? Ask no questions, mate, and you'll be told no lies. What the soldier said isn't evidence, Mr Birkett. If your Lordship pleases.

Hugh Cooke now had a job in the City and wore a bowler hat. It had been he who suggested that I join the Territorials. He had joined in order to keep up his school sport of rifle shooting; but there was a social side to it as well, he said. There were only two really decent regiments and both had their headquarters in the City. One was the Honourable Artillery Company and the other was the London Rifle Brigade. He was in the LRB and had ambitions to compete as a marksman for the King's Cup. One evening I went along with him to the old LRB drill hall in Bunhill Row, swore solemnly that I was eighteen and was duly enlisted.

The first camp I attended was at Shorncliffe. I went with the advance party and during the three weeks I was there found out a few things about myself. I found, for example, that I could never get drunk on bitter beer; because I invariably threw up after the third pint. I also had good night vision. These two qualities made me a useful man on a binge. I would be the sober one who could guide the party safely and secretly back to camp after lights out.

With a 303 rifle I was a fair shot but with a Lewis gun something of a menace. Platoons of us from the LRB used to go for weekends to the army ranges at Bisley to fire courses and to practise. The first time I got to be number one on a Lewis gun I distinguished myself by failing to spot the 'enemy silhouette' target and instead pouring an entire magazine of immaculate, stoppage-free bursts of five into the cut-out Kamerad figure raised in the butts to signal that we were to cease fire. The sergeant in charge of the butts party, who had been holding up the cut-out on the end of a pole, complained that the shocks of the bullets transmitted down his arms had been felt in his balls and could have damaged him for life. He was one of the Rifle Brigade regulars who nursemaided us on these weekends and to sooth his feelings I had to buy him beer. Of course, I also had to borrow money to pay for it.

In those truant days I was never out of debt. My legitimate income consisted of my father's allowance of two shillings a day and a season ticket. For anything extra I had to steal or scrounge.

Stealing was mostly by petty cheating. Book matches were then a novelty. I sold hundreds of them, printed with the name of a charity, for three times their cost price. However, I only gave the charity half. Scrounging was a mail order racket in horoscopes. I had a theory, based on my early studies in phrenology and a more recent reading of H. G. Wells's *Tono Bungay*, that most people were prepared to pay through the nose to be told what they wanted to hear. All the teller needed was a line of claptrap, steady nerves and a twinkle in the eye.

> Know Your Star Quality! Send birth date and
> PO for 2/6 to Mme Astra, Horoscopes, Box –

There was only one horoscope. 'Those born under your sign', it said, 'have only one thing to fear. That thing is diffidence. You underestimate your abilities and fail to see and cultivate your hidden gifts.'

It went on breezily in the same vein. For Mme Astra, her bright old eyes gleaming as she thumbed through the postal orders, there were no such words as 'failure' or 'can't'. Everyone had star quality, for everyone had stars. Yes? The whole effusion had been typed on a foolscap stencil by a girl I knew who worked in an office. She also ran off mimeograph copies for me in her lunch hour. My only overhead expenses were the costs of advertising, postage and envelopes. It was when the woman in charge of the classified section of the weekly I used began to give me unfriendly looks and ask if Mme Astra was my mother or just someone I worked for that I got cold feet. There must, I think, have been complaints. I tried using a different weekly, but the woman there was suspicious of me from the start. I learned to pawn a pair of cuff links that had been left to me by Grandpa Ambler.

In the spring of 1926 I began to take an interest in the way politicians behaved as well as in what they said about what they did. I had been on a Bisley range weekend with the LRB and, as usual, had taken my rifle home with me. Normally, we would return the rifles to Bunhill Row on the next drill evening we attended. With the General Strike threatened, however, the authorities suddenly became jittery. No doubt they feared a civil war. On the day before the General Strike telegrams were sent out to us saying that all rifles must be returned forthwith to the armoury. A telephone call to Bunhill Row to inquire about available military transport elicited a further order. Rifles must not be carried openly in a provocative manner through the streets. If you managed to get a lift in a car, the rifle was to be hidden in the boot.

My father, who had visions of his car being commandeered by Bolshevik strikers to build barricades, refused to let me have it. I tried to borrow Sims's motor bike, but he needed it himself as he was going off to drive a train on the Piccadilly underground. In the end I put the problem to the local bicycle dealer who had bought my bicycle when I left school. He had an old motor bike with a sidecar in which I could hide the rifle. The only trouble with the old thing, he said, was that she had a dicky clutch. If I promised to go easy on the clutch I could borrow her.

On the first day of the strike me and the old girl got as far as an impassable traffic jam in the Old Kent Road before the clutch seized up. From there I either pushed her or used the exhaust-valve lifter to change gear. When I eventually handed in the rifle at Bunhill Row I was told that we were being called up and that I should report back the following day. I would be able to get a lift on an army lorry from Lewisham.

That was a strange week. The word 'paramilitary' had not then been coined but it would have been useful. At the drill hall we were paraded by our own officers, including our highly-polished regular Rifle Brigade adjutant, and then addressed by a senior City of London policeman who said that from that moment we should consider ourselves technically to be special constables. We would be issued with police truncheons and striped police brassards. For dress, however, we should wear our army boots and khaki trousers with puttees and steel helmets. Our non-military status would be preserved by our wearing our ordinary shirts and ties and civilian overcoats. The police brassard would be worn on the left overcoat sleeve when on duty.

In this curious get-up companies of us were then marched about the City, mostly in the Fleet Street area. We marched well, as usual, at the brisk Rifle Brigade pace, but the attention we attracted was mostly for the oddity of our dress. Obviously we were troops; but troops disguised as special constables. Why? The stares were curious rather than hostile. Outside the offices of the *Morning Post*, where the presses were being used to print Winston Churchill's *British Gazette* for the government, we were even cheered. However, the cheers came not from the street but from a couple of comfortable-looking gentlemen in high stiff collars and swallow-tailed coats who were standing up to watch us in the back of a chauffeur-driven Crossley landaulet. 'Good boys!' they cried. 'That's the stuff to give 'em! Show the blighters what's what! Good boys!'

We all kept our eyes steadfastly to the front. There were no smiles. We took pride in marching well and looking disciplined, but none at all in being called good boys by politicos out for strikers' blood. Besides, nobody seriously believed that the *Morning Post* offices needed protection. The only threat of force in the Fleet Street area came from us and it was soon directed at the offices of the *Daily Herald* where the council of the TUC was trying to produce a strike sheet called *British Worker*. We 'protected' the *Herald* offices for three nights running and were forgivingly rewarded from inside with cups of tea.

When the strike was over I tried going back to college, but it did not work. By then it was working for only a few of the degree course engineers. Tales were being told of graduate engineers being offered three pounds a week in industry, and being glad to take it. The great depression was already looming. Some of those tales may have been true.

True or not, I used them to convince my father that he had been right all along, and that when I had left school I should have gone out to work and earned a proper living.

'Doing what?' he asked.

'Something with my hands.'

'Manual labour?'

He was trying to ease the situation by reminding me of an old Harmoniques gag. 'Alfonso lazy? What do you mean, lazy? Alfonso's just stupid. Alfonso's so stupid he thinks manual labour is the Spanish ambassador.'

But I refused to smile. 'I want to work with my hands in a factory,' I said. 'I'd like to do an apprenticeship as a machine-tool setter.'

It was a cruel thing to say to him. He could play several musical instruments and work marionettes and even do a few sleight-of-hand conjuring tricks. He had dextrous hands; but with tools he was hopeless, they defeated him. It may have been something to do with his poor eyesight. He was a bad driver too. He recognized these failings and did not much care about them. What he did care about was that his children should do well in the world according to his lights, that they should ascend the middle-class ladder and establish themselves among the well-dressed with decent underwear and clean nails. It was a cruel thing to say, too, because he was by this time ill with the first of a series of peptic ulcers. On a business trip to America he had gone down with pleurisy. The long strain of the climb was proving too much for him. He had not long to live. I think he already knew it.

But he was damned if he was going to let me end up on the shop floor of a factory getting my hands filthy and not caring if I wore cycle clips around the house. So, he spoke to some of his many friends and a job was contrived for me. At the Ponders End works of the Edison Swan Electric Company, the company that boasted of making Everything Electrical, there was a sturdy and forthright works manager who made a habit of referring to the company's world-wide sales force as 'those effing ignorant, bloody non-producers'. He had said this, and things like it, so often and so violently that official notice had eventually been taken. He had been asked to explain himself. What he said was that, since times had now changed, few, if any of the company's salesmen anywhere in the world knew very much about the products they sold. As the range of these products now included expensive components for radio transmitting stations, switchgear for generating stations, naval submarine storage batteries and power cables for collieries as well as ordinary household things like light bulbs and domestic appliances, they often made fools of themselves and the company. What he proposed was that suitable persons should be given technical training in the company's various factories and then sent out into the field to answer technical questions, or interpret them intelligently, when they were asked. In that way, he thought, it might be possible to reduce, at least marginally, the number of bloody silly answers that were given by the non-producers and counteract the impression of fucking ignorance they were spreading among the more serious customers. It was conceded that, although his language might be deplorable, there could be something in what he said.

I was the first of the technical trainees. We were called 'trainees' because calling us apprentices would have meant a legal contract with rights and obligations. As trainees we could be paid or not paid, depending on our immediate usefulness, and, if found wanting, sacked without fuss. Because I had been to college and could understand at least some of the chemistry of electric lamp and thermionic tube manufacture I was paid two pounds a week to learn more.

It was getting to Ponders End that was the trouble. Work there began at seven-thirty. To get there on time I had to leave the house at five to catch a train to London Bridge, then walk or trot to Liverpool Street station and one of the grimy Great Eastern locals that crawled out to Ponders End on their way to Enfield. The fares were not bad because at those hours I could buy cheap 'workmen's' return tickets. Lunch I ate at a good coffee shop near the works gate. The thing I dreaded was fog because it made me late clocking in. This happened several times that first winter and I spent petrified hours expecting to be called in, denounced as a bloody non-producer and sacked. At the time it did not occur to me that lateness because of fog might be understood and excused. For the first trainee, I thought, no delinquency would ever be forgiven or excused. When my father bought a house in Croydon and we at last left Newstead Road, the daily return journey to Ponders End became impossible. For a time the problem was solved by Auntie Ivy. She lived with her husband, Bob Barclay, only a short bus ride from Ponders End, and they agreed to have me as a lodger. Later, a second trainee, Alan Richardson, arrived. He drove from Norbury to Ponders End every day in his father's car and from Croydon it was usually possible for me to cadge a lift. He was a fast driver, even in fog.

Of course, the zeal of the reformed truant accounted for much of this anxiety about time-keeping; but not for all of it. I had become keenly interested in the work I was doing, and I wanted to do it better than well. I was there to gather facts and acquire know-how and those things I was doing; but I was also developing theories about the nature and quality of the skills employed in the works. I was doing private time-and-motion studies, though I did not call them that, and making unofficial job assessments. Going from task to task and shop-floor to shop-floor, I was in a peculiarly privileged position. Although I wore a brown work coat instead of overalls, as if I were a charge hand, I was a threat to no one. I gave no orders, signed no chits, had no power and told no tales. I did not even take notes. I only listened and looked and began to understand.

For instance, one of the things I soon learned was that when, in explaining the job he did, a man told me that there was 'an art in it' it would very likely turn out to be basically unskilled. I could probably learn to do it in half a day.

That statement looks so arrogant that I had better give an example of the sorts of skill I am discussing.

The manufacturing of ordinary domestic electric lamps was,

73

even in those days, a succession of processes that were to a great extent automated. The special machines came mostly from Holland where they had first been developed. There were, however, still a few unautomated processes. The blowing of non-standard glass bulbs was, of course, unmistakably skilful. In the making and drawing of some of the special wires needed, things were not so clear. One of these wires was called 'copper-clad' and was made up of layers of several different metals ingeniously combined to have the same coefficient of expansion as the glass pinch that supported the filament assembly and sealed it in. In the early lamps platinum had been used in the pinch. Copper-clad was cheaper.

It was called copper-clad because copper was the outside metal. Inside were four or five others, including nickel and zinc, and the stuff was made by taking a copper tube about a yard long and sliding smaller tubes and a centre rod of the other ingredient metals inside. The whole thing was then put through a series of rotary swaging machines which gradually made it longer and thinner. When it was thin enough to go through a die and be drawn, it quickly became thinner still and ended as a concentrically laminated wire only a few mils thick. It was ready then to be fed into a machine that would chop it up and spot-weld it to bits of molybdenum wire of the same diameter; ready, that is, if all the wire-drawing men and swaging-machine operators had done their jobs properly; and, even more important, as long as the die-cutters, who had a room of their own full of strange machines with swaying spindles that moved in unison like dancers, had worked patiently and watchfully to see that everything they did was up to standard. They did not think of their work as an art. They did not think of themselves as uniquely skilled. What they were paid for was to see that everything in their charge was done carefully and correctly so that costly materials such as copper, nickel and molybdenum were not wasted through inefficiency. Some of their jobs I learned to do; but not well. I lacked the needed care and patience, the love of exact measurement.

The man who had the softest job was very insistent on the art in it. He was the man who produced the bars of tungsten metal from which most lamp filaments were made then. Not all filaments were made of tungsten. At that time, the Royal Navy still insisted on having carbon filaments in the lamps it used on battleships because springy old carbon filaments were the only kind that would still work after a broadside had been fired. We kept this to ourselves as a quaint secret. We were of the tungsten generation.

It came to us as a greyish powder, tungsten oxide, and it was very expensive. The artist who handled it wore a white coat and worked alone in a large room without very much in it. The emptiness and his air of self-importance went well together. His working tools consisted of a laboratory-type balance, a small hydraulic press and an electric furnace. The first step in the process he operated was to measure a quantity of the oxide powder with the balance and then pour the powder into a narrow slot in the press. Then he closed the press and applied pressure. When he opened the press again what came out was a thin cake of tungsten oxide about half an inch square and a foot long. He put this in the furnace and switched on. After a time he switched off. His job was done. What came out was a bar of tungsten metal which duly went off to the swagers and wire-drawers.

Those were the early days of the coiled-coil filament lamp. Naturally, there were teething troubles. The engineer in charge of all lamp-making there was an American, Dr Hyatt. Encountering me on my second day of listening to the tungsten-bar fathead describing the weight of his responsibilities, Dr Hyatt gave me a compassionate smile and asked if I would like to assist him in doing some tests.

The small coil of the new filament was made by spinning a reel of tungsten wire around an iron wire mandrel. When this had been cut to the required filament lengths the iron was dissolved away in hydrochloric acid to leave the coiled tungsten. The trouble was that on recent batches of test lamps filament hot-spots were causing premature burn-outs. Microscopic examinations had shown that the hot-spots were caused by minute cracks in the coiled filaments. These faults had been traced to the use of some new high-speed coiling machines which had been put in to increase production without increasing labour. There were six of these machines and they were standing idle. Dr Hyatt believed that if the machines were run at less than full speed no hot-spots would be created. But at how much less than full speed? The only way to find out was to make a series of test runs on each machine and write the results down in the form of a report. I could make myself useful doing that.

What I found was that there was no high speed at which any of the machines would coil filaments free of hot-spots. My report concluded that this was probably due to a design fault. The radius of the spinning arms would have to be increased. However, any such increase would in effect reduce the speed of the coiling. Perhaps the tungsten wire could be partially annealed, or at least made more obliging, by heating the mandrel wire with a gas jet. In their present form the machines were useless. I received a friendly nod from Dr Hyatt for telling him something that he had undoubtedly suspected from the start.

In one of his labs I was allowed to be present at a discovery. Some very expensive new high-intensity lamps used for optical work were failing because, after only a few hours use, they leaked at the pinch and lost vacuum. No reason could be found for this until one of the scientists, a man named Parr, reminded his colleagues that glass was a liquid. When it became very hot why should it not behave like other liquids when an electric current is passed through them from an anode to a cathode? Why should glass not decompose by electrolysis? No reason at all, said Mr Parr. That was why those lamps had failed – electrolysis of the pinch. A glass with a higher melting point would have to be used. Science was a wonderful thing.

Less wonderful to me was the machine shop where most of the switchgear was made. The first job I was given there was drilling the busbars for a paper-mill switchboard. The busbars, which were to be used for making mains connections to some heavy circuit-breakers, were thick slabs of copper a foot long and weighing a couple of pounds or more. All I had to do was drill half-inch bolt holes at each end using an old drill press. They were an unfriendly lot in the machine shop; maybe because the foreman was a bastard who thought that he should really be the department manager; maybe because all the new machinery went to the tool room across the way. There were no apprentices in the machine shop. Trainees were naturally treated with suspicion. So, nobody bothered to warn me that drilling holes in copper was not as simple as it might look. The main difficulty was that, no matter how much or what kind of lubricant you used, a drill going into soft, high-grade copper would always, suddenly and when you least expected it, seize up. When that happened other misfortunes would follow. If the copper you were drilling was secured in any sort of vice, the drill would probably break in a way that would ruin the work piece by scoring the surface. If, to guard against spoiling the work, you were holding it in place with a block of wood or other material when it seized, it would whip round smartly and slice open your knuckles. Nobody liked working with soft copper. In the machine shop there were several jobs like that: jobs that nobody liked. I did them all. I had asked, self-righteously, to work with my hands and I was doing so. If my hands now suffered I had no one to blame but myself.

All the same, it was highly inconvenient. Bob Barclay, my land-lord, though a grainer and scumbler by trade, was a keen semi-pro concert artist and was busy booking our new act – Barclay and Ambrose (Original Humour and Songs at the Piano) – for dates at working-men's club concerts and socials. The original songs, 'Radio Romeo' and 'Why Won't You Give up the Blues?', had been written and composed by me and I had to supplement Bob's stran-gled baritone with flashy piano accompaniments. I was also supposed to cover one of his quick changes with thirty-two bars of Billy Mayerl's 'Jazz Mistress'. Since that had a left hand consisting almost entirely of tenths, I needed unbruised hands without open cuts in order to play it properly. Complaints from concert organizers of blood smears on the keys of their hired grand pianos were not infrequent at the time. I was glad when my spell in the machine shop ended.

My next stop was the storage battery department. There, the worst that my hands suffered was from 'acid corns'. That was what the men who worked there called them. They were a kind of ulcer caused by constant dabbling with sticks of cadmium in tanks of sulphuric acid. These were in long, open sheds where the larger battery plates were cured. We were supposed to wear protective clothing, but there was never enough of it to go round.

All the same, I enjoyed my time in that department. For one thing, I learned the real and rare skill of lead-burning. There were elements of suspense and danger in it. Without learning breath control and acquiring real delicacy of touch with the blow flame you were likely not only to waste a lot of very expensive lead, but also to poison yourself.

From that happy department, too, I was sent out on day trips with the men who serviced the many house-lighting battery plants the company had installed over the years. Most were in public institutions such as hospitals, but many were in country houses where they had been installed before electric power cables had reached outside the towns. I remember an estate somewhere west of Tunbridge Wells that had its own little generating station with a beautifully clean single-cylinder gas engine coupled by belt drive to an ancient Crompton dynamo. The engine made a soft, sooth-ing, chuffing sound and smelt of warm oil. Our 150-volt storage battery was used only in emergencies or when a lot of light was needed in the house for big parties of guests. It had a room to itself with the one hundred heavy glass cells arranged on two long varnished wood racks. The whole thing was in charge of an imposing man who looked like the owner of the estate but turned out to be the head gardener. He supervised every moment of our work and wrote down in a ledger the cadmium readings of each plate in each one of the cells as we called them out. Then, all three of us solemnly signed the book. I have no idea how good he was as a gardener but as a man of trust he was deeply impressive.

The only departments of the Ponders End works that I feared were the ones in which there were lots of women working to-gether. The dry-battery shop was particularly alarming because all the girls who worked there had exceptionally large breasts. That, at least, was what the men said who worked there, and the girls played up to them by claiming that the phenomenon was due to the manganese dioxide dust in the air they breathed. My theory was that their breasts looked bigger because of the loose working clothes and no underwear they wore so as to make washing the dust off quicker and easier at the end of the shift. They were a rough lot anyway. I was glad to be able to learn about dry-battery manufacture in the relative seclusion of the test-metering and in-spection bay.

In radio component assembly things were very different. In that shop there were no men at all. There was even a lady supervisor instead of a foreman and the charge hands were all women. I tried to persuade the works manager that I already knew enough about radio components, but he did not agree. What the bloody non-producers had to know about, he insisted, was the nature of re-petition work and what it entailed. The supervisor would have a lot to teach me.

He was right of course. The supervisor knew her job. During the stimulating month I spent there I learned about the importance of quality control; and I learned that, however finely and thoughtfully made they were, jigs and tools used for repetition work for days on end would raise blisters and sore places on the toughest hands. If the nature of the work ruled out gloves, all you could do was pray for callouses.

I also learned that the best way of hiding blushes was to laugh.

The girls with whom I worked on component assembly were mostly about my age, though some were even younger. Jenny, the dominant personality on the line who sat directly facing me, was sixteen. She was also one of several unmarried mothers in our group.

The others called her Creeping Jenny. I never knew why, but she seemed to like it. As a nickname it was quite unsuitable for her. Creeping Jenny was the old country name for moneywort, an attractive weed that grew as ground cover in many neglected London gardens. But it was a lowly, very green, apologetic little plant; Jenny was pink, buxom and outrageous. She also had a laugh with a leer in it that made the other girls laugh with her.

There was a lot of talk and laughter. We were assembling variable capacitors (called variable condensers in those days) and it was very tedious work. Talk and laughter helped and were encouraged by the supervisor. I was left out of it the first day, but when it was seen that I had the knack of the job and was not going to cause trouble by making mistakes, Jenny decided to include me in the talk. Her way of doing so was characteristic. She gave one of her mischievous chuckles, threw me a sly glance and turned to the girl next to her.

'How big do you think his prick is?' she asked.

'I hadn't given it any thought,' said her neighbour austerely.

'You said you thought he had a big Adam's apple. That meant you thought he had a big prick, didn't it? The two go together.'

'Ooh, I never said a word about his Adam's apple. Why should I? It looks like anyone else's to me.'

'I dare say it is, but if we're going to have a feller working with us we'll have to know what sort of a prick he's got. It stands to reason. One of us had better take him out on the bank and find out.'

'Oh Jenny, you are awful. Look, you've made him blush. Don't mind Jenny, mate. She's only joking.'

'Out on the bank' meant the bank of the River Lea that ran behind the works and was the boundary between the company's land and the marshy meadows beyond. On fine days those who brought sandwiches for the midday break would sit out on the grass of the bank to eat them. It was also used by those seeking privacy for other purposes. Some of the girls were said to earn substantial bonuses there when the shifts changed on pay days. I knew, of course, that Jenny was only joking; but all the same there was fear as well as embarrassment in my blushes. I went on being afraid of Jenny's jokes almost until the end of my stay on the assembly line. Then, something happened to make me see her differently.

In the field on the other side of the river there was a mare turned out to graze by the carter who rented the land. She was in foal and during one midday break the foal was born. Both mare and foal were all right, but when the mare stood up and moved round the foal the afterbirth still trailed from her down to the ground. One of the watching men seemed to find this amusing. Jenny, who was standing a yard or so away, turned on him in a rage.

'What's so funny?' she snarled. 'The poor old dear can't help it. I'd like to see you with your guts all trailing out. I'll bet you wouldn't be laughing, you sod. Poor old girl. Why weren't you over there helping her? Afraid of getting your feet wet?'

Her tone was so menacing that the man and his mates turned away looking sheepish. For the rest of the day she talked about her son, Patrick, who was looked after by his Grannie. After the tea break, though, her black mood went and the mischief returned. 'Perhaps he'll grow up to be a trainee,' she said, and when the other girls chuckled she winked at me.

A few days later the works manager called me in, said that head office were pleased with his reports on my progress and told me that I was shortly to go for six months to the company's new cable factory at Lydbrook in the Forest of Dean. 'It's colliery country,' he said; 'you'll learn a lot there. You'll be their first trainee.'

I was pleased to be going, but that was the end of Barclay and Ambrose, entertainers at the piano. We managed to do only two more shows before I had to leave. At one of them, a smoker in Edmonton, I found after the show that my father had been in the audience.

It was for me an awkward occasion; and not just because I did not want to be told that our act was lousy. The real trouble was that I was wearing his second-best dinner jacket which I had borrowed without asking permission some weeks previously.

About the show he had little to say; perhaps the fact that Bob was a brother-in-law by marriage imposed restraint. He had a suggestion or two to make. 'You'd be better if you could learn to take your bows and get off without taking so long about it,' he said; 'and never go off waving opera hats in the air as if they were real toppers. As you bow, fold them flat against the stomach' – he showed us how – 'before you start your move off together. If you've got a prop like that, use it.' About the dinner jacket, all he said was: 'It seems to fit you. You'd better keep it.'

Before I went to Lydbrook, however, he had things to say to me about the problems of going on the stage as well as those of getting off it with opera hats. 'It makes no difference,' he said; 'music hall, concert party or legit, it's a highly competitive profession. Don't let anyone kid you. It's only good if you're at the top, or always near it and in work like Harry Hewitt. For third-raters with no originality, like you and Bob Barclay, it's hopeless. I wouldn't like to see you try it. I sincerely hope that you don't seriously want to.'

'I'd like to write plays.'

'That's different. You don't have to be a performing artist to write plays. As an engineer you could have a safe job. That would let you be original in your spare time.'

When Uncle Frank and his first wife came to see us that summer it was clear that the scrap metal trade was being kind to him. His suit had been made to measure and he wore a silk shirt with a Sulka tie. He seemed to have made a complete recovery from the war. He had confidence in himself and had acquired important skills. We knew that because just a week ago he had been giving evidence at the Old Bailey. He had been called as an expert witness for the Prosecution. His expert field was the identification and valuation of non-ferrous scrap metal. He had clearly enjoyed the experience and spoke with kindly contempt of the ignorance and simplicity of those who had questioned him. The biggest nitwit of all had been counsel for the Prosecution.

It must have been at about that time, I think, that he began his remarkably long career as an embezzler.

FIVE

When the works manager had spoken of colliery country I had thought of a landscape of slag heaps and pit-heads once seen from the window of a train going north. I knew little of England outside the London area. After the war ended some friends, the Thompsons, had moved to Huddersfield and I had spent one glorious summer month staying with them there. Lou Thompson's demobilization idea had been to buy a fleet of cheap motor vehicles from army disposal and set up a transport service that would connect the wool industry mill towns around Huddersfield and Bradford. From the front seat of a Dennis three-ton lorry I had seen plenty of Victorian factory buildings and streets of back-to-back houses; but the only pit-head I had ever seen close-to had been in Kent.

Lydbrook is in one of the most beautiful of English river valleys, that of the Wye on the edge of the Forest of Dean. The cable works had been built during the war to house latex-processing mills and stranding machines imported from the United States. It stood on a bank of the river about two miles from a famous beauty spot, the gorge and rock of Symonds Yat. It was an outrageous place to put such a factory; I can see that now. At the time I was pleased to be working in such surroundings; they made a pleasant change from Ponders End and the muddy Lea.

Lydbrook itself was an extraordinary mixture of attractions. At the lower end of its main street, where it joined the road between Ross-on-Wye and Monmouth, was a broad, shallow stretch of the river where it ran fast and clear over a bottom of gravel and flat boulders. Across the river, standing on a hill above landscaped parkland, was a middle-sized country house named Courtfield. The owner of the Courtfield estate also owned the salmon fishing. On the Lydbrook bank, where all the poachers lived, there was an inn, The Courtfield Arms, and the local bus stop. From there the

Lydbrook main street climbed steeply with short side roads of cottage-like houses branching off on either side. I had digs in one of them. In Lydbrook then most families were in some way related to other Forest of Dean families. My landlady was, I think, a sister-in-law of the assistant works manager who was my mentor at the cable works. He was a Lydney man from the other side of the forest and lived in a house a couple of hundred yards higher up. Outside the houses, at night when there was little road traffic, the night shift working at the Waterloo could be heard plainly.

The Waterloo was at the very top of the main street, on the hillside off to the right, and was, as its name suggested, a fairly old pit. They worked three shifts there then. The company that owned it was a small one and meant, no doubt, to have the last ton of its coal out of the ground before some crackpot government finally rationalized or nationalized it out of existence. Walking back to my digs at night I often stopped to listen. The winding gear was steam driven and when starting or stopping made a quick, stammering huff-chuff-chuff sound like a locomotive leaving a station. The sound seemed to echo and reverberate down through the miles of old workings that were said to run deep beneath the hillside, and I sometimes fancied that I was listening to history. It was probably only fancy; the echoing surfaces of the valley would be mostly above ground. All the same, on a clear night I was glad to be able to look up and see the stars.

Although I asked several times for permission to go down the Waterloo I never managed to get it. I was not exactly refused, but at the cable works, I believe, it was felt that I should not waste my time exploring a pit that had so little use for electricity. More modern pits, such as Cannop, which had just bought miles of our most expensive armoured three-core, would be better for my morale and future usefulness to the company. At Cannop, they said, electrification was far advanced, perhaps very nearly complete. It showed what could be done using really modern methods.

According to those who worked there it was the deepest pit in England; and going down in the main shaft cage that is how it felt; if you did not hold on tight to the handrail, your feet left the cage floor. Yet that was only the start of the journey. From the main roads which radiated from the bottom of the shaft some of the men had an hour's walk or more to get to the coal faces at which they worked. Several of the older branch workings – 'dipples' they were called – went on down, thousands of yards beyond, with gradients of three-to-one and steeper. The coal tubs were hauled up to the main tramways by a system of electrically-driven steel hawsers to which the tubs were hooked. The hawsers sometimes whipped about dangerously and could take a man's foot off if given half a chance. In earlier times, presumably, the tubs had been winched up less efficiently by hand. However, I did not ask about this. The under manager who showed me the latest way was clearly pleased with it.

Most Forest of Dean pits had no methane gas to trouble them, but the deeper pits usually had drainage problems. The main roads of a pit like Cannop could look safe and sound, much like an old London Underground train tunnel, with runs of heavy-duty cable on hangers along the walls and steel rails under foot; but on the other side of the doors to the ventilation and drainage tunnels the picture was very different. On one occasion I was given a guided tour of this other underworld. Much of it consisted of old workings from which the coal had all been taken. They had never been more than five feet high and usually less. Their use as ducts had reduced the height still further. You shuffled along them, crouched-down almost to your knees, with water dripping down your neck. Three or four inches below your feet, which had to slither across a series of wooden plank bridges, roared a black torrent of water. This could be coming from an underground spring, from last month's rain, from a rotary pump somewhere below, or it could be falling from a trompe tower thousands of feet above and drawing in fresh air with it. At one point my guide showed me an upright post with markings on it. They indicated recorded depths of water just there. It was all too clear that, at times, that particular section of the ventilation system could flood and become impassable. He explained this not to scare me but in order to remind me of the stresses to which our cables would be subjected. He had sharp questions for me too. How thorough was our testing, how genuine our inspection processes? How long would a three-core cable with jute-wrapped bitumen insulation last under five feet of water? How long was it before lead sheathing became porous? How many years? Of what quality was the lead we normally used?

At the cable works I learned many of the answers to such questions, and something, too, about the pains and pleasures of starting businesses and being a manufacturer. Small can be beautiful, but how beautiful depends on where one is standing. At Ponders

End there had been a work force of over two thousand; at the company's Lydbrook subsidiary there were then under two hundred. The cable works had been built up by a local man who had originally earned his living more or less single-handed out of a one-bay workshop in which he had been drawing special-alloy wires for such things as resistances and rheostats. He had been a small man. The war and government subsidies had enabled him to grow suddenly into a bigger man with a cable works that for a time made him fat profits. With the profits he had built himself a large mock-Tudor house with a tennis court. Then, soon after the war ended, he went broke.

When he asked me to tea and tennis with his wife and daughters he was not well thought of in Lydbrook. It was possible that he was no longer absolutely *flat* broke; but that, they said, was only because he never paid his bills. Ask the local tradesmen. It was the company from London, not he, who had found the capital needed to save the cable works and the jobs of those who worked in it. They had not needed his help in any capacity. He was back in his old workshop again, drawing wire. If he was still living in that fine big house, that was because, although he couldn't afford to keep it up, he couldn't sell it. Why? Because nobody wanted to buy it. He had once looked down on his neighbours and given himself airs. Now they remembered that, and the unpaid tradesmen's bills, and meant to look down on him. There would be no forgiving and no forgetting. The assistant works manager advised me to decline the invitation to tea and tennis. I would not enjoy myself, he said.

I went anyway; not for the tea or the tennis, but because I was curious to see the house, and the daughters.

The best thing was the tea; I have always liked watercress sandwiches. The tennis was absurd. The court was ankle-deep in weeds; the rackets kept for guests to use all had broken strings; the net cord was spliced with lamp flex. The fact that I knew how to play the game only as a sort of pat-ball using ping-pong tactics went unnoticed. The girls, sturdy but square and slow-moving, could not play either. I did not see much of them or their father. I seemed to spend most of the afternoon talking to the mother. She was, I thought, unnaturally curious about my family and their friends. That evening, when I reported this to my mentor, he sniffed.

'She wanted to see if there was a smell of money anywhere.'

'Money? Me? You must be joking.'

'Her husband would borrow your last five bob if you'd let him. If you had more than five bob he'd marry you off to one of his daughters.'

I laughed dutifully but not heartily. I thought that I was being reproached, with that sly reminder about my trainee's wage, for having ignored his advice and accepted the invitation. I was quite wrong. On my way home from the cable works I had to pass the old wire-drawing workshop, and a few days later saw its owner, my host for tea and tennis, standing outside in his shirt-sleeves unloading wooden crates from a van. He waved and beckoned to me. I responded thinking that he wanted help with the crates.

He was a tall, broad-shouldered man with the mock-modest smile of the professional cricketer who has just brought off a spectacular catch. 'Thought you might like to see how the other half lives,' he said. He was offering to show me round his work-shop, 'a *real* works.'

I accepted promptly and was well rewarded. He was a bit of an engineer, a bit of a metallurgist, a bit of a technician, and highly skilled in the craft of drawing fine wire. He talked fascinatingly about the work. He was an enthusiast. Even I, though, could see why he had failed. He was vain, and also, I suspected, a bit of a twister.

'I hear your father's an advertising man,' he said suddenly as I was leaving; 'director of a London agency they tell me.'

'Yes, he is.' The 'they' who had told him could only have been his wife.

'Strange business that. Big turnover, piddling ten per cent returns. Does he ever think of investing in a business that shows a real profit?'

'I really don't know, sir.'

'With what you know you could wake his ideas up, lad. He could make a snug little thirty per cent on his money here.'

I thought of trying to explain that my father's only income now came from his salary, but then took what I thought would be an easier way out. 'He's not a technical man,' I said.

He gave me his cricketer's smile. 'I don't want technical men, lad. I'm the technical man. What I want here is capital for some new machines and one or two extra pairs of hands to help with the heavy work. With just a few hundred quid to prime the pump I could grow fast. As it is, I'm having to turn away work. I can show you the inquiries.' When I did not answer because I did not know what to say, he made me feel even clumsier. 'You know I built that place up the road where you work, don't you?'

'Oh yes, of course.'

'They don't like me there, do they?'

'Well . . .'

'You know why? Jealousy. I built it. I started it. I'm a local man. It's only the local men there who are jealous. You ask the others. You ask the rubber department men. I brought them in from outside, from the Midlands and up north. They're not against me like the locals.'

It was almost true. Those who took the raw latex and turned it into vulcanized rubber had mostly come from other parts of the country, and, although they now all lived locally near the works, tended to keep themselves to themselves. This was natural; they were an elite. Most of the processes of cable making – the wire-drawing, the tinning, the stranding, the sheathing – were plain and straightforward. There were machines to do the work and all that was needed apart from the materials was a work force that knew how to set the machines up to perform the tasks specified on the job sheets. The manufacture of different grades of vulcanized rubber (VIR) for electrical insulation and of 'cab-tyre' sheathing (CTS) to defend the insulation were processes of polymerization involving not only manual skills but also industrial secrets. For operating some of the new coal-cutting machines that were coming in, highly flexible trailing cables were needed to carry the power supplies. For work in the confined and potentially dangerous spaces near a coal face no ordinary steel wire or tape armour could be made flexible enough; only the highest quality CTS would be practical and safe. That quality was achieved by the use of secret catalysts as well as the better known vulcanizing agents, antioxidants and fillers. Understandably, those who did the compounding were a close-mouthed lot who would think twice before answering any question put by an outsider. When I asked about their former boss, however, they thought only briefly; then I got a grin or a shrug. They preferred the new management, they said. The new people could always be relied on to pay a man his wages. Things had not always been that way.

That summer in Lydbrook I wrote the first two chapters of a novel. It was called *The Comedian* and was about my father; or rather, about the way I thought he would have liked to have seen himself. He had once told me that as a boy in Salford he had heard of a music teacher who used to strap bells to her pupils' wrists and tell them to play 'Bells Across the Meadow' for practice so that the neighbours could hear them distinctly and know that she was responsible for all those richly artistic sounds. In the novel, which was never even half-finished, I made him one of her pupils; and, since I did not know what Salford looked like, I moved his boyhood south to Grandpa Ambler's house in Yukon Road.

I cannot recall the reasons I gave myself for starting to write such a book. My reading preferences at the time were for Aldous Huxley and Dornford Yates. The manner I was trying to write in was that of Arnold Bennett on one of his pawky, cloth-capped jaunts in the Five Towns. It is clear to me now that in a muddled way I was hoping to make amends for some of the disappointments I had caused. The title was an attempt at flattery, and a poor one. My father could be lightly comedic but he was not a true comedian, and he knew it. He would have liked, I believe, to be able to think of himself as another Denry Machin, the hero of Bennett's *The Card* and *The Regent*, who was 'identified with the great cause of cheering us all up', but he lacked Denry's impudence and audacity. He was a gentler humorist.

When I finished my time at Lydbrook it was decided that, during the reorganization of the company within the new Associated Electrical Industries group, I should make myself useful doing odd jobs in the publicity department at head office. My father was pleased. 'It'll be good experience,' he said; 'but don't you let me down with Miss Miller.'

In the twenties there were not many women executives in engineering companies. Because it was comparatively young, perhaps, the electrical industry had attracted some of the more able ones. Many, including Nora Miller, were members of the Electrical Association for Women, an organization that did pioneer work in persuading a public still largely at the mercy of the country's Gas, Light and Coke companies that the days of the gas-mantle and the carpet-beater were gone. Miss Miller was not only manager of the publicity department but also in charge of the company's advertising campaigns.

The first odd job she gave me was given, I think, partly to see if I was going to be of any use at all to her, and partly to show me the sort of thing she and the department had to put up with from the sales people upstairs.

A recent stock-taking had shown that the company had manufactured many thousands of a type of motor headlamp bulb that nobody wanted to buy. Upstairs were now asking for an advertising campaign to sell them. She had no money to spare for that kind of folly. She asked me to make non-violent suggestions for disposing of the unwanted bulbs. Was there, perhaps, some other use to which they could be put? Could they be used, for example, wired in series to make Christmas tree decorations? Or electric signs? Think about it and draft something for me to sign.

The reason that the bulbs were not wanted was that they had been made of 'daylight' glass. Whose idea this had been I never discovered. I was sure that Dr Hyatt had had nothing to do with it because I knew about 'daylight' glass. Its chief and most undesirable characteristic was that it absorbed over fifty per cent of the light emitted by the filament and converted it into heat. And the 'daylight' it gave was not daylight, only a bluish-white imitation.

Undeterred by my knowledge of the truth, however, I set about making a case for the daylight bulb. Almost without thought or hesitation I used a standard advertising ploy of the period: I described an invented disease and then said that I had the cure for it. The disease for which I condemned all ordinary headlamp bulbs was 'penumbra', the area of partial shadow at the edge of the central beam of a headlight. With the daylight bulb, I claimed, there was no penumbra and the edge of the beam was clean and sharp.

In the piece I wrote explaining all this I did not trouble to mention that the reason for the absence of a penumbra or partial shadow was that with daylight glass partial shadow became total; our daylight bulbs simply gave less light, and in doing so created a minor optical illusion. However, I knew that no one there wanted to listen to that sort of quibble. My piece went out, unaltered, as a press release to the motor trade journals and to motoring correspondents. A surprisingly large number of them ran it in their columns, or used bits of it. There was a sudden demand for daylight headlamp bulbs and stocks soon ran out.

Of course, there was at once foolish talk of making more of the stupid things to meet the demand. Luckily, the talk came to nothing; but the people upstairs were already casting about for other dud lines for me to dispose of by writing puff pieces. They called the pieces 'free advertising'. In the end Miss Miller had to speak firmly to them. She pointed out that puff publicity was not free; it was published because, and generally only because, the company was a big-budget advertiser. Editorial publicity was too valuable to squander on dud lines.

It was a pleasure to work for Miss Miller. She protected her people and she trusted them. She could delegate boldly. Who but Miss Miller would have sent a youth of nineteen off to Birmingham with a set of standfitters' blueprints, an expense account and orders to see that the company's stand at the British Industries Fair was finished and ready to receive a royal visitor on opening day? True, she had no one else available to send, and I was, after all, the odd job man; but still, she took a risk.

My main difficulty was with the Grand Hotel into which I had been booked. I was too scruffy for it. The waiters in the grill room were haughty. They recommended dishes like snipe, which I found uneatable, and wanted me to drink wine instead of beer. Out at the exhibition hall things were easier. I got over the moments of panic by modelling my behaviour on that of the LRB adjutant, a regular officer from the Rifle Brigade who managed to combine beautiful manners with an unyielding intolerance of the slapdash or inefficient.

After the mission to Birmingham, I was given the same sort of job at other trade exhibitions. Chivvying standfitters became a regular duty. Standfitting contractors always tended to take on more work than they could handle and had to be coaxed and watched over if the company's work was to receive its proper priority. The fact that the company was a Royal Warrant holder could be a handicap rather than a help; some of the carpenters who did the work, which called for long hours in an atmosphere of strain and, often, bad temper, were said to be militant left-wingers. 'Bolshie' was the word usually applied, but for standfitters 'bloody-minded' would have been nearer the mark. At my age, and with my small capacity for drink, it was no use my attempting to jolly the foreman along. The only way I could be sure of getting action was by going over the foreman's head to the contractor's representative who had costed the job and who was going to get paid a commission on it. Men more used in business to dealing with other men rather than with women were always curious about Miss Miller. I satisfied their curiosity with fairy tales. In the same breath that I spoke of her kindness and consideration to those who worked for her I would speak of a vindictive streak and of the retribution visited on those who let her down. There was a printer, one of the very biggest – I would breathe a name in confidence – who would never again get a print order from the company. His offence was a broken delivery promise. Not entirely his fault, perhaps, but that made no difference. He had failed, so he was out. Personally, I did not like all the chopping and changing of suppliers that went on, but I was only the office boy. For instance, the Ideal Home Exhibition was coming up again and Miss Miller was talking this time of employing an architect to design an AEI group stand and then put the construction work out to tender. I very much hoped that she would change her mind, but . . .

After a few months I became a full member of the publicity department staff and my salary was increased from four pounds a week to five pounds ten shillings.

The rise came as a relief. I was pursuing a pretty girl who lived in Norbury. She had expensive tastes and also a doting family. When my rivals gave her presents or took her out dancing to glamorous West End night clubs, her mother always took care to let me know. My parents approved of the pursuit. My father thought her stylish and amusing as well as pretty. My mother's approval was less straightforward. She believed that the most disgraceful thing that could happen to a young man of my age was that he should get 'mixed up' with a married woman. She was glad that the Norbury girl was safely unmarried. She was also glad that the girl had expensive tastes. One of the American records I sometimes played for the solo piano bit on it had as well a male vocal chorus of 'I Can't Give You Anything But Love, Baby'. My mother always used to make the same comment on it. 'There's a lot of them like that about,' she would say darkly and give me a meaning look. I could think of myself as one of them. So could a girl with expensive tastes.

One January day I arrived back at Croydon to find that my father had come home early from his office and then collapsed in great pain. His doctor, who arrived a few minutes later, diagnosed a perforated duodenal ulcer and peritonitis. An ambulance took him to a nursing home. Later that evening a surgeon came down from London to operate.

My father lived for three weeks after the operation. He had had many friends and they were a great help to me in doing the things that have to be done at such times: things like choosing a coffin and the fittings for it. My mother would not go to the funeral and insisted that no other women should. So, it was a men-only occasion. A large number attended, over fifty. Some must have regretted doing so. It was a cold, rainy day and I blubbered noisily at the graveside.

My mother said that I was now the head of the house, but, of course, did not mean it. She had held the post for years and would continue to do so. Until she married again, her three children filled in as a series of makeshift lieutenants.

Early in 1929 we became semi-detached again instead of double-fronted, and the Hudson-Essex was replaced by a secondhand Austin Seven. I also lost the Norbury girl.

One evening in the spring at a pub in Upper Thames Street a printer bought me too much beer. I drank it and, as usual, was sick. However, on that occasion I was also a bit drunk. Too late I remembered that I was due in Norbury, so telephoned to say that I was ill. It was true, in a way; but I had never before failed to keep a date with her. As a result, my illness was taken seriously. When I got home I went straight to bed. A few minutes later she arrived with a rescue team consisting of her mother and brother. Her concern for me cooled instantly and permanently. My mother, who was indignant, amused but not wholly displeased, said that I had no one to blame but myself. I could only agree.

I found friends too. One was the librarian of the Public Library at Addiscombe who would let me have six books at a time instead of only one or two. It was on his shelves that I found Jung's *Psychology of the Unconscious* and *Collected Papers*. Jung led me to Nietzsche and *The Birth of Tragedy*. In the same part of the library I found my way to Spengler.

That same spring I showed how right my mother had been about me by getting mixed up with a married woman. She was legally separated from her husband at the time, but all the same I took care to be discreet. In other respects, though, I was less careful. It was during the run-up to that year's General Election that I was summoned to a sudden emergency meeting in a tea shop. I went expecting to be given the dreaded news that her husband wanted to return to her. What she really had to tell me was that I had made her pregnant. If her husband found out he would be sure to use the pregnancy as grounds for divorcing her. She must have an abortion. But not the back-street kind. That would be too dangerous. It would be dangerous to delay too. Her doctor knew a nursing home where it could be done overnight. But it would be expensive and she had no money. At this nursing home you had to pay cash. How much? Well, that was part of the urgency. If it was done next week it would be sixteen guineas. Next month it would be twenty-five.

Of course, in England then all abortions were, in a sense, 'back street'; but I knew what she meant. I, too, had read the Sunday paper horror stories about drunken midwives wielding skewers and operations performed on kitchen tables. The words 'nursing home' and 'guineas' were reassuring. But sixteen guineas was a large sum. I had nothing worth anything like that to pawn or to sell. I would have to borrow the money. I promised that I would get it somehow for the following week.

When she had gone I telephoned Uncle Sidney at his office and asked if he would lend me fifteen pounds.

'What for, my lad?'

'To meet a pressing obligation, Uncle. It's terribly important.'

'Been backing horses?'

'No.'

'Does your mother know about this obligation?'

'No, Uncle.'

'Come and see me tomorrow. We'll talk it over.'

I have been trying to think why it was that I chose to go to Uncle Sidney rather than to the more affluent Uncle Frank. It may have been that I thought it would be easier to deal with Uncle Sidney's manly condemnation of my disgraceful behaviour than with Uncle Frank's secret amusement and too-searching questions. If so, I was mistaken. It was easy to make mistakes about Uncle Sidney. He looked and often sounded deeply conventional. He was not. In matters of the heart he was his own man. Auntie Ida, his wife, had come from a family of strict Orthodox Jews who had sternly refused to accept Sidney Andrews as a son-in-law. When the two of them had defied the prohibition and married anyway, her family had banished her for ever and denied Sidney's existence.

He lived, with his exotic Ida, near Shepherds Bush. The following evening I met him in a pub there. He had the money in an envelope. He put it on the table beside his drink.

'What's it for?' he asked again.

I told him.

'How do you know she's not pulling your leg?'

'She's not like that.'

He put it in words of one syllable for me. 'How do you know the child's yours?'

'It couldn't be anyone else's. She's separated. There's nobody else.'

'I see. She says that and you believe her. I only asked. Just wanted to be sure. You won't ever let your mother know, will you?'

'No.'

'Right.' He gave me the envelope. 'I'd like to say, "Keep it, it's yours", but I can't afford to. So, I'll expect you to pay me back fairly soon, say in three months' time. Right?'

'Yes. I can't tell you how grateful . . .'

'That's all right. These things happen. Sixteen guineas seems a lot. Is that the going price?'

'She says it is.'

'You could buy a small diamond ring for that.'

He was probably right; and the same ring today would probably cost several hundred pounds. In some civilized countries abortion is still illegal, and so, I dare say, still costs a lot; but inflation statistics and price comparisons are always tedious. I recalled my uncle's remark about the small diamond ring because I would still rather not think about the days that followed her visit to the nursing home. She had a bad time, and in the particular back street that we had to go through there was only pain, blood and fear.

It is easier to remember time wasted in walking the back streets of Epping on a summer's night.

As Election Day approached an invitation came down from the Chairman of the Board. It called for volunteers from the staff to go down to Epping after office hours to canvass the electorate there on behalf of the Chairman's friend, the Right Hon. Winston S. Churchill MP, who was standing in the Conservative interest. Charabancs would leave the office for Epping at 5.30 p.m. and sandwiches would be provided. With the official typed memorandum came a muttered unofficial warning. Pressure of work would not be accepted as an excuse for non-attendance. It was assumed that all members of the staff were staunchly Tory and against Socialism in any shape or form. I was reading the novels of George Gissing at the time and was not staunchly anything.

However, not a word of protest was heard from any of the staff. At Epping we were met by local party workers who divided us into squads. Each squad was given a group of streets to cover and cards bearing the names and addresses of registered voters. Our instructions were to knock on their doors, announce that we were there on behalf of their Conservative candidate, Mr Churchill, and ask who they were going to vote for. We were to write down their answers on the cards.

The question sounded heavy-handed to me, and my reception at the first house in my pack of cards confirmed that impression. A stout woman answered my knock and stood there peering at me as I recited the set speech. When I asked who she was going to vote for, however, there was a yelping sound from the background and a small angry man in his shirt-sleeves erupted into the passage. He swept the woman aside and shook his fist at me.

'The ballot is secret,' he cried. 'You have no right to come here asking how I am going to vote.'

'I was only trying to . . .'

'Get out or I'll call the police.'

I got out and wrote 'Refused to say' on the card. The next door people said that they were going to vote for Churchill, but farther up the street I had two more indignant refusals. At the corner our squad compared notes. One man had been threatened with violence. We went looking for the party worker and when we found him asked for clarification. Was what we were doing legal or was it not?

He was offended. 'It's not illegal to ask a simple question. They're not obliged to answer or to tell you the truth. I thought you people had come down to help.'

'We were asked to come here and canvass.'

He became patronizing. 'Obviously we don't expect you to be able to argue the Conservative case well enough to convert the heathen, but you *are* gathering valuable information. We have only so many cars available to pick people up and take them to vote on polling day. Naturally, we only want to pick up people who are going to vote for our man. All that's called for is a little tact on your part. If they don't want to show that their hearts are in the right place they can't expect a nice ride in a motor car, can they? Now, let's get on, gentlemen. We have a lot more ground still to cover.'

We went on, but agreed between ourselves to change the question we asked to, 'Do you think that you may be voting for Mr Churchill?' Those who had to think twice before they answered were put down as 'Would not say.' Only one voter that I spoke to had any political comment to make. 'If the Conservatives get in they won't make him Chancellor of the Exchequer again, will they?' she asked anxiously. I said that I did not think they would and put her down as 'undecided'.

Mr Churchill got in again without any trouble. I cannot believe that our working for his cause cost him a single vote.

A few months later Miss Miller told me that she had plans for my future that she wanted me to think about. I was much relieved. When she had called me in that Friday afternoon I had thought that it might be to tell me that my request for more money had made her decide finally that I must be sacked. Formation of the AEI group had involved the merging of three large manufacturing companies. In theory, the resulting rationalization should have cut the managerial work forces by two thirds. In practice, it cut them by only a half; but the in-fighting had been fierce and the strain of it still stretched the nerves of the survivors, including those of Miss Miller. Besides, there was a depression deepening all around us. As we moved into the thirties not even survivors could feel very secure.

The reorganized department headed by Miss Miller was heavily dependent on the advertising agency she had chosen to employ in easier times; but it was no longer giving satisfaction. It would be simple enough to move the account elsewhere; a single telephone call could start that process; but would that kind of change necessarily solve the problem? Part of the trouble was that the company had grown untidily in too many directions; it sprawled. Although its claim that it made everything electrical was absurdly exaggerated, it did make a great many different pieces of electrical equipment, too many. Such diversity created a corresponding range of marketing problems. For an advertising agency with heavy-spending clients of international standing in the breakfast cereal and patent medicine fields, we were a bit of a nuisance. That part of our advertising budget most profitable to the agency was that spent on national press advertising and poster work. Relatively unprofitable to the agency, but of prime importance to us, was all the technical, professional and trade press advertising. Naturally, the agency was equipped to perform best where the big money was. Copywriters and ideas men used to devising snappy campaigns for cornflakes, laxatives and soap flakes could also devise snappy campaigns for electric light bulbs and domestic appliances. However, faced with the problem of doing a series of full-page advertisements to explain, say, a new dry-charged battery plate to the motor trade or an improved system of strip lighting to readers of the *Architectural Review*, those fellows were stumped. They would have liked not to have to bother with such things, but knew that if they said so they were out. So, they went on submitting technical and trade paper copy that invariably had to be rewritten; formerly by Miss Miller, now, generally, by me.

Her proposal was simple. Since I was doing a substantial part of the agency's work, the agency should employ me. They should also give me a little more money. I was worth more. I had talent. And there was another thing, she added thoughtfully: in the high-flying London agency world I would meet fewer lunch-hour beer drinkers and printers' reps with expense accounts.

My career as an agency copywriter began with a playful little deceit.

On the Friday before it began I had had the authority to okay agency copy and layouts without reference to Miss Miller. Three days later, on the Monday, I had a desk in the agency copy department and no authority to okay anything. Nevertheless, on the Monday afternoon and under the smiling eyes of the agency account executive concerned, I okayed and initialled all the copy for Miss Miller that I had written in the morning. That meant that it did not have to be sent for her approval. When I boldly back-dated the okays by a week, I was given an even warmer smile. He paid me compliments. He said that I was entering into the spirit of the game. I was a pragmatist. I would be a handy man to have around. I was my father's son.

SIX

Students of the period have been known to describe the copy departments in the big London advertising agencies of the early thirties as hotbeds of Far-Left conspiracy and fellow-travelling Communism. It is an understandable error. The techniques of commercial persuasion may be seen from the outside as differing only slightly from those of political subversion; but at the time, and to those inside, the hotbed notion would have been received as a puzzling and probably unfunny joke. The copy department I joined was fairly typical I think. Some of us there may have been a bit odd, even eccentric, but politics were not a common topic of conversation.

The head of the copy department, a man with few friends, had what would now be described as an identity problem. When I got there he had just discovered the early Marx brothers' films and fancied himself as Groucho. His moustache, although not painted on like the real Groucho's, was trimmed to resemble it and he could move his eyebrows and roll his eyes like Groucho. He was word perfect on *Animal Crackers* and needed no encouragement to demonstrate his mastery of Groucho's multiple-gag routines. It was a relief when *Monkey Business* arrived to supply him with fresh material.

All of us sat in one big room then and conversation could be lively. For a time we had two notable stammerers. One was Robin Fedden who tended to use his slightly hesitant delivery as a way of calling for order when he had something of interest to say. Phillip Taylor's stammer, on the other hand, was an affliction that he fought tooth and nail. When it reduced him to silence he would seize the nearest piece of paper and scribble what he wanted to say. He had a joke about two scribbling stammerers having a heated argument. One seizes the other's paper and in his haste to write snaps the point of the pencil. Incensed, the other snatches the paper back and scrawls *DON'T SHOUT* on it.

98

Phil Taylor had a quick temper and strong views about homosexuality (he was against it for men, in favour for women) but I never heard him express a political opinion. I cannot believe either that Robin Fedden was ever a secret Marxist. He had been to Oxford and later followed a first novel with an interesting non-fiction work about suicide.

If our copy department was any sort of hotbed it was a literary one. Most copywriters wished that they could be writing something else. This is not to say that there was no pride at all in the work. Some copywriters could even be pretentious about it. At one agency there was a man who claimed that his best copy had poetic echoes in it of Keble's *Christian Year*, but he was an exception. With most of us literary ambition set its cap at Grub Street. Dorothy L. Sayers, writing novels of detection in the copy department of a rival agency, seemed to have the right idea. We had one published two-book novelist, Cecil Maiden, and several aspirants, one of whom, Gerald Butler, did well a few years later with a novel called *Kiss The Blood Off My Hands*. The short-story writers, aiming at the Amalgamated Press pulp market, usually missed by a mile. It has always been a mistake to suppose that good trashy stories are easy to write; they are not; they ask for natural talents of a peculiar kind.

I can remember clearly the first novel I saw in typescript. The author of it, who also worked for the agency, lived with an attractive wife in a Bayswater flat. They had asked me to go to a theatre with them and then stay for the weekend.

The typescript should have told me that all was not quite as it had seemed. Every paragraph ended with an ellipsis . . . instead of a full stop. I thought it a curious affectation and asked the author why he did it.

'It's my style,' he said.

On Sunday morning, before breakfast, he brought me a cup of tea and sat down as if for a chat. Soon, though, after some heavy breathing and a declaration of love, he tried to get into bed with me.

I fought him off, not in an unkind way I think, but in a squeaky sort of panic. His wife was in the kitchen making toast. I could hear her and smell the toast. I was afraid that she would hear my protests and come to investigate. What would happen if she were to come in and find me clutching a sheet to my chest like . . . well, like a *Peg's Paper* heroine defending her honour? What, I asked him, would she think?

'Nothing,' he said impatiently; 'she doesn't mind.'

But I minded. My refusal to co-operate was objectionably prissy, no doubt, but he was fairly objectionable too. Thereafter, his attitude towards me was one of glum reproach. All writers were bisexual he told me mournfully. If I wanted to be a writer I would have to be bi-sexual too. Everyone knew it.

I remained unconvinced. Jung had said nothing like that; neither had Kraft-Ebbing. Had Dostoievsky been bi-sexual? Had Gogol? Who could tell? On the other hand, how about Wyndham Lewis? After reading *The Apes of God* I had felt that no deviance could ever again seem improbable. Had Ibsen been bi-sexual? Shaw? Better ask Candida or Mrs Patrick Campbell. Or was it only novelists who had to be bi-sexual? Could it be optional for playwrights?

All the same, I did wonder if my reception of the stylist's advances might have been different if he had not made those treacly declarations of love and had been physically more attractive. I had never set much store by my ability to resist temptation. A day might come when . . . Fortunately, I was not the only object of his attentions; he had eyes, too, for those who worked in the art department.

One there with whom he had no success at all was John French. This was the John French who later became a photographer. In the agency he was a poster artist. Outside he was a vorticist painter with a palette that owed much to Léger. I envied him his colour sense. I envied even more the smiling ease with which he fended off the hot-handed passes and ignored the murmured endearments that so embarrassed me.

'At school we called it the secret of the old iron pot,' John told me one day over lunch. 'I know it's a terribly camp expression, but as it's illegal for boys to do anything about being queer there has to be a way of talking about it that everyone can understand. I don't know what they called it at his school, do you? Something dreary like You-Know-What, I shouldn't wonder, or the love that dares not speak its name.'

John introduced me to vorticism, the cabaret songs of Douglas Byng, the Ballet Rambert at the Mercury Theatre and the downstairs tables at the Café Royal. He also introduced me to Vere Denning, then a fashion editor. She had a precise, deliberate way of saying what she meant that was most beguiling. They were kind to my innocence, and under their influence, I think, I became less of a bumpkin.

*　　*　　*

100

I arrived home one day to find my mother in tears. This was most unusual; she was not much given to weeping. It took me some time to discover the reason for her distress.

'The disgrace of it,' she kept saying, and that was all she would say at first.

For a while I thought that some misdeed of mine must have come to light; but no, it was Uncle Frank who was in trouble. He had been arrested, charged and committed for trial on a multiple count indictment involving a variety of serious offences ranging from embezzlement and conspiracy-to-defraud to forgery and theft.

The company for which he worked was engaged on a national scale in the scrap metal trade, buying and selling many hundreds of thousands of tons a year. They bought by the railway truck-load. It had been Uncle Frank's job to do the buying and then, when he had enough truck-loads sitting ready in factory sidings, organize their sale. Trains would be assembled to take the scrap consignments to the foundries which wanted them or, more often, to seaports for shipment overseas. Uncle Frank had no computer to help him, of course; however, he was able to carry a surprising amount of the information he needed in his own memory. What he had done to improve on his salary was to manipulate the paperwork, and some of the people, involved in this complex network of commercial transactions. He arranged it so that in every long scrap train that rolled there were one or two truck-loads of steel briquettes or non-ferrous alloy scrap that would be sold separately for his account. He was caught out, it seems, through the boastful talk of one of the minor fiddlers to whom he paid cash. The man was a yard foreman somewhere up north.

It was estimated that over a period of six or seven years Uncle Frank had stolen more than a million pounds.

'I know he was a prisoner of war,' my mother said, 'but I feel that I never want to set eyes on him again. Poor soul.'

The poor soul to whom she was referring was Uncle Frank's wife. Poor was indeed the word. Some of the stolen money may have gone on silk shirts and swanky living, but most had gone to the bookmakers. My Uncle Frank was one of those gamblers who believe in doubling their stakes every time they lose.

He got seven years, a lot for a first, non-violent offence. He served the sentence in Maidstone Prison. This was convenient for his former employers whose accountants spent a lot of time interviewing him during the first two years. He and his memory

101

co-operated fully and the mess was cleared up eventually, more or less. He was a model prisoner.

'He'll need feeding up when he comes out,' my mother said.

My progress as a playwright had been slow. My tastes had changed. I no longer wanted to write the kind of play that William Archer admired; I had seen a repertory company performance of *The Green Goddess*, which he had written, and despised it. For a while I was a slice-of-life man. Though I still looked on *Playmaking* as a sound instruction manual and was all for thinking of the theatre as a place in which to reveal 'the inner beauty and the meaning of life', I could not bring myself to believe that Gordon Craig's 'total' theatre was going to reveal anything but handsome set designs. I thought that Wedekind and the German Expressionists had the right ideas. I set out to speak with their voices.

From what I can remember now of my first attempt at a play in the manner of Ernst Toller, it had nothing at all to commend it except a plot; and that was probably stolen from another source. It was about a street-corner evangelist. He is supported in this work by his wife who is, though he does not know it, a prostitute. What he preaches is the certainty of redemption through love. What he does, when he discovers the truth about his wife, is commit murder.

It was during a reading of the play that I discovered how truly dreadful it was. After the first act I wanted very much to leave. However, as I was reading the lead that was impossible. There were three of us reading and, I think, six or seven in the 'audience'. They nursed gin-and-tonics and at the end said polite things about the play. Perhaps we read well; perhaps the drinks were stronger than I knew; I can think of no other reasons for politeness on their part. I have also, for psychological reasons no doubt, forgotten where the reading took place and who attended. I regret this; I would have liked the audience to know that although their names are forgotten their kindness is not.

I have just remembered the title of the play and the memory makes my toes curl again. It was *White to Harvest*. Biblical, of course, and culled from the evangelical rantings I had written for my hero. One of the things I had learned at the library was how to use a concordance.

It was the year after D. H. Lawrence died and literary reviews like Middleton Murry's *New Adelphi* were full of reminiscences and critical essays by persons who had had tea with him. Some of the better reviews could be bought secondhand in the Charing Cross Road, but I always bought the *Adelphi* as soon as it appeared. I knew that very clever people despised Murry and that the admired Aldous Huxley had made fun of him as Burlap in *Point Counterpoint*, but I was grateful to him for a single descriptive phrase and an observation. What he was describing was depression. He called it 'the nadir of desolation' and seemed to know it well. He went on to say, in effect, that once one had reached the lower depths all one needed was strength enough to open one's eyes. After that, there would be no more to fear in the empty darkness. It was, I thought, unfair to laugh at anyone who could write such things or who had been married to Katherine Mansfield.

That was about the time that I began to discover that some things were done better abroad.

I had already found my way to France and Germany and learned the smells to be encountered on the way: that of the Newhaven–Dieppe cross-channel steamer, the Gare du Nord in Paris, the Gare de l'Est (quite different), Basle, the Baden-Bahnhoff, Freiberg-im-Breisgau, a mountain cable-car terminus; but I had yet to smell the fabled sea that Sandhurst Road had taught me to spell.

However, I was able to become more adventurous. John French had earlier given up his job in the agency and gone to Italy to paint. In September he was returning to England. He wrote suggesting that I go to Positano and stay with him while he still had his studio there. We could then travel back to London together.

I found that I could get to Naples easily and cheaply by sea. The outward bound Orient Line boats stopped at Naples to pick up passengers for the Far East. The third-class return fare for the five-day trip was only twelve pounds and it was possible to use the return half of the passage towards payment in Naples for a rail fare home. I went on the *Otranto*, a comfortable old ship with a predictable roll and a speed and wake that seemed friendly to dolphins. After Gibraltar we called at Palma and Toulon before docking at Naples.

In the early thirties Positano was still a little-known and fairly primitive fishing village with a small fleet of boats that went out at night for cuttle fish. There were only sixteen foreign residents and most of them lived up near the church in a *pensione* run by two

German sisters. John's studio was down by the beach, a hop, skip and a jump away from the caffé-bar Rispoli where the fishermen congregated. We used to have meals there and I mention the hop, skip and jump because they were the necessary steps to take when crossing the street from the studio for breakfast coffee; there were open drains to be negotiated and, in the early morning, a build-up of night soil. When John told me that Giulio Rispoli, the proprietor's son, was planning to redecorate the bar and call it 'Buca di Bacco' to attract tourists it seemed a good joke. The drains could be covered over perhaps, but how were tourists to come and go? The best way was by steamer. At six in the morning, not a tourist hour then, the ferry between Capri and Amalfi would usually, weather permitting, stop outside Positano and wait for a boat from the beach. To leave by road meant taking a horse-drawn *carrozza* from the square by the church up to the Sorrento–Amalfi bus route. I felt that Giulio himself also thought the idea of the Buca di Bacco a trifle far-fetched. In Positano then any sort of change seemed unlikely. Some Americans had tried to build a villa there; but all they and their architect had got in the end had been yet another house in the tenth-century Saracen style of the rest. Only the church (eighteenth-century baroque) was allowed to be a little different. The planning authorities in Sorrento used to take their duties seriously.

John's kindness and determination to educate me knew no bounds. So that I should see how well those with a little money lived in the old houses higher up he took me to lunch with 'Papa' Pariso, a plump chichi old rascal with busy hands and a flow of anecdotes about the local *scandales*. 'Has John told you about our priest being surprised naked in the church drinking fountain by the horse of one of the *carrozza* drivers? No? Well. . . .' The lunch was memorable chiefly for a beetroot salad with caraway seeds in the dressing. I knew that I would have to re-read *South Wind*.

We went to Capri, where the drains had long been covered over, and to Ravello where John supervised the installation of a stained-glass window he had designed for a monastery chapel. It was a round window on a narrow end wall and well suited to a vorticist design. The fathers were pleased with the result and showed their pleasure by giving us too much wine to drink. It was their own wine, they explained, made from their own grapes and they had cellars full of it. We were offered cells to sleep in after lunch, but our return later down the steep track to the Ravello bus stop was still a bit unsteady.

It was time to go. Before we left, though, we spent a night out with the fishing fleet.

It sailed always at sunset. None of the boats was very long; most were beamy, undecked caiques with a single mast and lateen sail. A few had auxiliary engines. All carried powerful acetylene lights which were hung over the side of the boat near the stern before fishing started. The sea off-shore there is very deep and the lights would attract cuttle fish up from the extreme depths to the intermediate ones where they could be offered large six-point hooks generously baited with fresh sardines. Passengers like us, friendly but non-paying outsiders, were expected to make themselves useful by handling extra lines when we reached the fishing area abreast of Capri.

The lines were cords of hemp hundreds of feet long, and the process of paying them out, then keeping the baited hook moving and then hauling in the catch proved tiring. The bringing aboard of the catch required some care. As a cuttle fish was pulled from the water for the first time it would squirt a jet of brownish black ink high into the air. The ink would usually hit the sail which was used to that treatment. The fisherman would then return the fish to the water for a moment before pulling it out again. The second jet would be of diluted ink. The third would be of clear sea water. The fish was then brought on board, unhooked and left to lie in the bottom of the boat. There it would make sighing noises, and go on doing so at intervals all through the night.

For our supper, the Rispoli kitchen had provided us with square cakes of cold spaghetti bolognaise and several bottles of red wine. After it, neither the hard lying in the bottom of the boat nor the heavy sighing of the catch could keep us awake for long. In the early hours of the morning, though, I sat up to ease a cramp and saw a strange sight. A bank of mist had rolled across the entire surface of the sea just up to the height of the boats' gunwales; we seemed to be afloat on a vast cloud. Two miles away across the cloud the stern lights of the Amalfi fleet glowed in the mist as ours did. Sound was muffled and all I could hear clearly was the sighing of cuttle fish. It was as if we had ghosts in the bilge. I had never quite been able to believe in the eidetic visions of William Blake and had disliked the Victorian illustrators who had tried to imitate him; but for a moment there I could have believed anything, even a troupe of angels and the strong right arm of a bearded god reaching down from a halo round the moon.

105

In Rome we had a four-hour wait between trains and, to pass the time, went to a much-advertised cultural exhibition showing Fascism's achievements since 1921. That had been the year of the Congress of Rome before the famous march from Milan. The exhibition was in a cavernous modern building somewhere behind the Vittorio Emanuele monument and, aside from pro-Duce graffiti, was the first Fascist propaganda that I had seen. John had doubts about our going in, but I was interested; besides, admission was free. John gave in but warned that we must not send anything up or show amusement. The Italians in Rome, he said, were quite different from those in Positano.

The central exhibit was a 'shrine' commemorating the fallen heroes and martyrs of the movement, a political lying-in-state. It consisted of a series of brightly lit tableaux depicting with life-size waxwork figures the decisive moments of heroism and martyrdom. Each tableau had a stage setting to itself and the stages were arranged like framed paintings around a dark rotunda. The wax figures all postured extravagantly and a lot of prop blood had been used. Though I found it absurd I did not find it amusing. The martyrs, I noted, were all former deputies of the Italian parliament and were shown as they were shot or stabbed in the back by Communist assassins.

John murmured something disparaging about 'static representation of dynamic objects', but I had a different thought. During Mussolini's rise to supreme power, the event that had brought most discredit on his regime had been the kidnapping and murder by Fascist *squadristi* of the socialist deputy Matteotti. It had happened in 1923. Yet here, years later, it looked as if Fascism was still trying to efface or confuse memories of the crime (and perhaps hoping to retrieve the mistake of having committed it) by parading some of the other parliamentary casualties of the period.

I had just started to ask John what he thought of the idea when there was a sudden, sharp hissing sound.

I have said that the exhibit was a lying-in-state. It was not only the way the thing was staged that gave that impression. At intervals all round the rotunda stood a guard of honour consisting of smartly-uniformed Blackshirts. They were armed with carbines. The carabinieri at the entrance only had holstered pistols. It was one of the Blackshirts who had hissed and he was also pointing his carbine at us. He now hissed an order which I did not understand and slapped the butt of his carbine for emphasis.

John translated for me. 'It is forbidden to show disrespect by speaking. If we don't leave at once he'll tell the green ones to arrest us.'

The green ones were the carabinieri. We left without further discussion or backward glances.

It was not the first time that I had had a gun pointed at me. My second camp with the LRB had been at Aldershot and we had taken part that year in a divisional tactical exercise. It had been designed to culminate in a small battle and, to everyone's surprise, things had gone according to plan. The day ended with our side defending a long ditch on the reverse slope of a hill and the enemy trying to smother us with a mortar attack followed by an assault from a flank. The final stages had been as realistic as blank cartridge fire and smoke grenades could make them. All the same, total suspension of disbelief had come as something of a shock. When the attacking line suddenly materialized out of dead ground on our right, everything for a minute or two seemed all too real. Taken by surprise, we began to fire blanks as if our lives were truly at stake. After all, the uniformed men attacking us did not belong to our regiment; they could have been issued with live ammunition by mistake; and their bayonets (which we in the rifle regiments still called 'swords') were not made of painted cardboard.

As they came, screeching and yelling at us, we ran out of blanks to fire and the sergeant told us to fix swords. Then we stood up in our ditch to receive them. I do not believe that at that moment there was any of us who did not have a small twinge of the kind of fear that used to be experienced on those old battlefields when both sides could see a human enemy.

In Rome I had no way of knowing whether or not the Blackshirt's carbine had live rounds in it; but the slap he gave the butt had been convincing. My twinge of civilian fear had been convincing, too, and interesting. I noted that it had taken about three seconds to turn fear into fury and a further half second to remember that I was a foreigner there and, for that reason probably, objectionable.

It was at about this time that I became an income tax payer. For puberty I had been more or less prepared. My affair with the Inland Revenue people began without any preparation at all.

The first word I had from them was a police court summons to appear before the Marlborough Street magistrate and explain why I had not paid the sum of six pounds fifteen shillings that I owed.

In those days employers did not act for the government as tax collectors, but were sometimes required to report their payrolls. However, the agency accountant, to whom I took the summons for advice, was puzzled.

'Didn't they send you a Schedule D form and ask you to make a return?'

'No.'

'Well, I should write and ask them what they're playing at.'

I read the summons again carefully. The wording of it seemed all too clear. If I did not go to court I would be a lawbreaker and only a step or two away from arrest. Then it would be prison like Uncle Frank, perhaps even Maidstone. I told no one else about the summons, only the accountant. Even if I had the impudence to write in the way he had suggested there would still be the summons to face. Now, I was a wanted man. Now, I was on the slippery slope to perdition and going down at a speed that would have surprised even a wet-eyed and gloating Dean Farrar. Well, sod Dean Farrar. He was dead and I did not have to worry about him any more.

I found the magistrates' court strongly reminiscent of early Edgar Wallace. When I got there the Black Maria had just arrived from the remand prison and police cell doors were being opened. Accused persons and the policemen in charge of their cases had begun to mingle in a friendly way. Cigarettes were being offered and accepted, bargains were being struck. 'Tell you what, Gordon. This time you plead guilty and I'll do my level best for you.' I went to a door-keeping policeman, showed him the summons and asked for directions. He gave me a suspicious stare before motioning with his head. 'Go in there,' he said, 'and stand at the back. When you hear your name called you speak up. If they want you in the dock they'll tell you.'

I did as I was told and stood among the friends of the drunk-and-disorderlies and insulting-words-and-behaviours of the night before. The magistrate dealt summarily with their cases and then had a brief discussion with the clerk of the court. When it was over the clerk called loudly for Mr Something-or-Other, Inland Revenue. A pale, neatly dressed man stepped forward at once; he went into the witness box without waiting to be asked to do so. The clerk administered the oath and then proceeded to read out at great speed a list of names. He did not speak very clearly and it was almost by chance that I heard by own name called. I spoke up squeakily.

'Here.'

108

The clerk stopped between syllables and raised his head. '*Who* is here?' he demanded.

I gave my name and the magistrate peered at me. 'Step forward,' he said, and when I had done so he looked at the Inland Revenue man. 'How much?' he asked.

The Inland Revenue consulted a list. 'Six pounds fifteen shillings, Your Worship.'

Someone in the court tittered. I did not know why. In those days six pounds fifteen was not an absurdly small sum to owe. The sound seemed to anger the clerk. He glared at me. 'Have you brought the money?'

'No, sir.' I said my piece about not knowing that I owed it.

The magistrate looked at the Inland Revenue. 'I am not going to make an order in this case,' he said deliberately. 'You can talk it over with the young man later, outside.' To me he said: 'Perhaps you'll be good enough to wait a few minutes.' To the clerk he said: 'Now, let's get on please.'

There were over a hundred and fifty names on the Inland Revenue list of summonses. I was the only person on the list who had responded by putting in an appearance. The policeman on the door was now quite friendly and showed me where to stand so that I could be found later.

'His Worship doesn't like the Inland Revenue,' he told me. 'They have to mind their Ps and Qs around here. You'll be all right.'

The Inland Revenue man was superficially affable, but the mouth was petulant and the eyes had a long-suffering, put-upon look. 'How much can you pay now?' he asked.

'I have one-and-six in my pocket, but I'll need that for lunch.'

The affability faded. 'I am trying to be helpful. The fact that you made no return and received no demand note does not mean that you don't owe the money. How much a week could you pay? A pound?'

It was agreed eventually that I would pay ten shillings a week, but he still wanted to be liked as well as paid. 'I'd be glad to give you more time,' he said, 'but this magistrate is most unfriendly to us. If we don't get after you as soon as the money is owing he won't make an order to pay, ever. I don't know what he's got against us. After all, it's the public purse we're collecting for. *We* don't get anything out of it.'

He quoted Dr Johnson on death and taxes and we had a wry little smile over that before he let me go. I warmed to the Marlborough

Street magistrate and his court. To feel at one with the law was an unfamiliar sensation. I was surprised to find it such a pleasant one.

It was at about that time that I was able to make myself useful to Madam Lillian Ginnett. She was then Professor and Examiner in Elocution and Dramatic Art at the Guildhall School. However, I never heard anyone address her as 'Professor'; she came from a French theatrical family and preferred to be addressed as 'Madam'. I was introduced to her by Alan Martin Harvey. He was related to the English acting family the head of which was then the actor-manager Sir John Martin Harvey. I thought that Alan found the theatrical name a slightly more reassuring distinction than his membership of the Institute of Practitioners in Advertising.

In the thirties the Institute was endeavouring to provide the more sensitive and better-educated agency executive with a set of letters to put after his name and a cloak of professional respectability of the kind worn by architects and accountants. It offered further business advantages. Agencies which had members of the Institute on their boards were allowed to call themselves on their letter paper *Incorporated Practitioners in Advertising*. Alan and his father ran such an agency with clients mainly in the food-processing industry. It was natural that Alan should need a way of escape and that he should find it in the amateur theatre. He was involved with the work of the British Drama League and, in particular, with the League's seasonal competitions for one-act plays.

So was Madam Ginnett; though for strictly professional reasons. Guildhall drama productions in the concert hall that was shared with the music departments of the School were of limited value to the students of acting. Productions in accessible commercial theatres, such as the old Scala, were expensive to put on for two or three performances even when audiences of parents and friends paid well for their tickets. Accordingly, Madam Ginnett bought extra experience for her acting students by entering School productions in the Drama League competitions. The finals, which the School usually reached, were held in a well-equipped London theatre with a competent back-stage staff. No one ever objected that students from schools of acting were not, strictly speaking, amateurs. It was left to the judges, always paid professional producers, to apply the critical standards they thought appropriate. It was also, perhaps, recognized that a school of acting, however professional its intentions, laboured under difficulties of casting and choice of subject usually overcome with ease by well-funded amateur societies.

Madam Ginnett's students were all young persons of about the same age and there were more women than men; a few had natural talent, most were no better than intelligent; she had no mature character actors; the one-act plays available were either hackneyed or hard for her to cast; vehicles for star students had nothing in them for the rest; the Guildhall School did not take kindly to paying fees for performing rights when the music departments were making do with dead composers or writing their own new music. So, Madam was open to offers of assistance from volunteers who wanted nothing for their services but the satisfaction of giving them.

Alan Martin Harvey was in his thirties then and baldness made him look older. He was also an experienced character actor who enjoyed working in Guildhall School productions. His name looked well on the programmes. He introduced me as a semi-pro performer who did not mind helping out with walk-on parts. If a one-act play I had written could be read by Madam and possibly considered for performance I would shift scenery or make tea as well.

I can remember what the play was about but not what it was called. If I were to search the British Drama League records for the period I could probably dredge the title up; but I really have no wish to do so. The title, I think, was quite good; the play itself was important to me for its disaster value. I learned something from its performance.

Those were the days of coal gas suicides. My central character, a young man who has reached the nadir of desolation, decides to put an end to himself. As he dies, he is confronted by the ghosts of his past; the men and women he has wronged are conjured up by a prosecuting, persecuting superego figure. The young man is tried and convicted. Sentence is pronounced. There will be no easy way out for him, no wallowings in self-pity, no sweet dream of death. The shilling in the gas meter runs out and the sentence begins. He has been sentenced to live. Bad luck. Curtain.

The script was deceptive. It did not read badly. Madam thought that something might be made of it. The part of the would-be suicide, she thought, might be right for one of her more talented young men. He came from a family which had recently moved from Budapest to Hampstead. He would have some showy, set-piece speeches and neither his slight residual accent nor his youthful portliness would seem out of place in such a harsh, un-English context.

Alan Martin Harvey played the prosecutor efficiently and the students who played the ghosts were good too. The early perform-ances went surprisingly well. Audiences found it unusual and evidently did not mind being pelted with words and then left to wonder what they were all about. However, the finals were another matter. The theatre was a fairly old one that used to be in the Tottenham Court Road, and although it was not particularly large it had awkward acoustics. All competitors were warned to speak up. Students taught to speak by Madam Ginnett did not need such advice, but for some unknown reason our leading man took the warning seriously. As a result, his performance, that had been contained, thoughtful and quietly effective, suddenly became shrill. Instead of an actor we saw and heard a tubby young elo-cutionist trying too hard to project elaborate speeches to the back of the circle. The play, never very steady on its pins, at once fell flat on its face.

The judge was John Fernald and he had some disagreeable things to say about the play which he had clearly detested. He was all for experiment in the theatre, he said, and for the occasional breaking of rules; but that did not mean that all the rules could be broken at once. He congratulated the cast on the gallantry they had displayed. Their courage and their producer's skill had been worthy of better things. Wounding stuff.

Madam shrugged it all off. The audience had liked the play, she said. As for Mr Fernald, he had made his way in the theatre as a professional producer of amateur companies. The nearest he had ever got to being experimental had been a production of *The Duch-ess of Malfi*. We would do better next time. Meanwhile, she had the abiding problem of finding new plays for her young women to do. Did I know that there were no one-act plays on the Samuel French list with all-women casts of five? There was a challenge. Why did I not try writing one?

I did try. The result was a one-act play in two scenes called *Feminine Singular*. The central character was a business woman and she was based on what I believed I knew about Miss Miller. I cannot remember much more about it except that it was 'well-made' and that it worked as an entertainment. Madam used it more than once and promised that she would one day reward me: I would be allowed, under her supervision, to stage a play myself. In the meantime, if I was going to use words like 'exquisite' I had better learn how to pronounce them correctly. With exquisite, the accent was on the first syllable, not the second.

I saw a production of Ibsen's *Ghosts* at the Arts Theatre and decided to forget about Wedekind and Toller. William Archer's appreciation of the 'crutch is floating' line in the master's *Little Eyolf* was still the right signpost to follow.

At the agency I was being tried out on a patent medicine account. The product was a chocolate laxative. In the copy department this was seen as a promotion for me. I tried to see it that way too.

That summer I had a fortnight's holiday and spent ten days of it in going to and from Marseilles by P & O ships. The four days I spent ashore in and around the city were both stimulating and, ultimately, productive.

In the old port of Marseilles then there was a quay from which fishermen with motorboats ran cheap excursions round the modern deep sea port, along the coast to Cassis and out to the Ile d'If and its château. With boyhood memories of Dumas to prod me, I chose the Château d'If trip.

The fancy lettering on the fishermen's signs had prepared me for guides and souvenir postcards, but the peculiar nonsensifications of the place surprised me. The Château d'If was a sixteenth-century state prison built to house in reasonable comfort persons of rank and consequence who had made political nuisances of themselves. It had real historical associations. Yet these had been brushed aside in favour of bogus relics of a body of fiction.

A series of pickled pine notice boards proclaimed the more obvious lies in poker-work Gothic script. Two adjoining 'dungeons' with views out to sea and a southerly exposure were labelled as those once occupied by Edmond Dantès and the Abbé Faria. The Man in the Iron Mask had had a two-dungeon suite complete with fireplace and a small observation turret. The dates of each prisoner's arrival and departure, dead or alive, were also given, and the attention of visitors was drawn to features of special interest. 'Note the tunnel,' one notice said, 'between the dungeon of the Abbé Faria and that of E. Dantès. This is the original tunnel excavated by the Abbé himself and the route by which Dantès escaped to become the Count of Monte Cristo.' When I suggested pleasantly to the guide that this was a joke that we were not expected to take too seriously, he was indignant and thumped the stone wall with his fist. 'Voyons, Monsieur,' he said sharply, 'ce n'est pas un roman, ça.'

This was a call for suspension of disbelief on an impressive scale. Who had authorized it? The dotty curator who had also authorized the excavation of the tunnel, or some romantic bureaucrat in Marseilles? Dumas *père* would have been pleased as well as amused, I thought. Feeling well disposed towards the rascally French, I proceeded to make a fool of myself.

I was staying at a bed-and-breakfast hotel on the Canebière and the concierge had drawn my attention to a convenient bar just round the corner. The bar was dark and cool, and so was the barman. At his suggestion I drank vermouth-cassis and let him teach me the game of pokerdice. I became interested, but it was only after he had totted up the score, when he smiled, that I understood the finer points. We had been playing for francs, not centimes as I had supposed. I knew that I had been cheated, but did not feel bold enough, or sure enough of my French, to tell him so. When I asked, a little coldly, how much I owed for my vermouth-cassis he said with a generous wave that the drinks were on him.

Back in the hotel room I assessed the disaster. It was Wednesday. The P & O boat for England would not dock until Friday morning and I could not board before midday. I would need enough French money to pay the hotel bill and to take a taxi to the docks. My steamer ticket was paid for, but my cabin steward would have to go without a tip. I would need English money for the fare home from Tilbury. The hotel daily rate included coffee and rolls for breakfast. If I spent nothing more on food I could just manage. If there were any surprise extras on the hotel bill I would be in a real fix.

Before the expedition to the Château d'If I had bought a Tauchnitz edition of Joyce's *Portrait of the Artist as a Young Man*. I spent most of Thursday reading that. There had been brioches for breakfast that day but by the afternoon I was feeling hungry. To take my mind off my stomach I planned an assassination.

I was in a corner room overlooking the intersection of the Canebière and the side street where the bar was. Outside my window there was a narrow balcony with a wrought-iron grille. Through the spaces in the grille I could see the roadway at the point

114

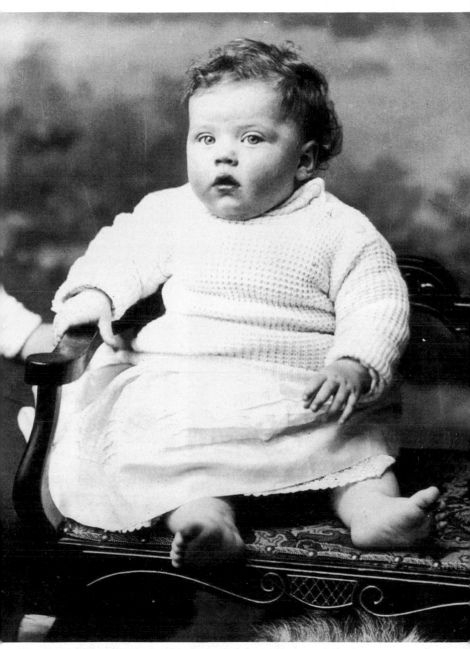

Myself, 1909. The solicitous hand in the lower left picture is my mother's.
To my mind, this portrait of the child gives clear warning of things to come later
in the man – a certain surliness of disposition and a tendency to put on weight.

left and below: My father and mother at about the time of their marriage in 1906. He was born in Lancashire, the eldest son of a printer's proof-reader and a mill-girl. He left school at the age of twelve to earn his living and so was mainly self-educated, though a friendly choir-master fostered his considerable musical talent and made him a proficient organist who could expect fees for playing. My mother he met when his family moved to London. Her father was a master cabinet-maker and her mother a lawyer's daughter. She was better educated than my father, though I don't think that either of them ever became aware of the fact. Their great bonds were music and the making of laughter. They were both stage-struck.

below opposite:
Another theatrical advertising photograph. When living marionettes went out of fashion my parents turned to the organizing of 'concert parties'. These were troupes of performers who, for a suitable fee, would provide evenings of vaudeville entertainment in a small hall or theatre for one night or a week or a whole season. The concert party, too, is now a bygone fashion. This picture (circa 1919) shows one of my father's troupes which called itself *The What nots*. My mother, the soubrette of the show, is sitting on the piano. The man roguishly tweaking the bow on her hair is the comedian, my father.

My parents on stage. They billed themselves as 'Reg and Amy Ambrose'. This photograph was contrived to advertise their 'living marionette' show to theatre booking agents. The art of the living marionette, once common in England, has now completely disappeared. The face was live, the marionette body was operated by the owner of the face through slits in a black back-cloth. Reg Ambrose was a technical innovator in the field, devising a back-cloth which appeared to remain stationary when the marionette moved sideways (it was stretched on spring rollers) and articulated marionette hands that enabled him to light a cigarette on stage and even play a miniature piano.

Family group, 1920. In those days, evidently, when a beach photographer told you to smile you did so. This particular cameraman must, however, have been a singularly persuasive fellow. My mother, a formidably strong-minded woman with a quick temper, did not take kindly to stage directions from strangers. It can be seen, perhaps, that her smile here, though fairly broad, does not quite reach her eyes. The boy seated at her feet is my brother Maurice. My sister wasn't then born.

University student, aged eighteen. What I was doing here with my posturing was trying to make the girl holding the camera laugh. I seemed to spend a great deal of time in those days trying to make girls laugh. That is possibly because it was my belief then, a belief that I have since learned was unfounded, that if you made girls laugh you could more easily persuade them to go to bed with you.

left: No more clowning. The first-novelist, aged twenty-seven, is hoping to be taken seriously. Such a sensitive face! But where did all that hair come from? And where has it gone?

Lance-Bombardier Ambler, Royal Artillery, 1940. In British artillery regiments a corporal is called a bombardier. The reason for my rank then was that I had become an instructor. Those who have ever had to suffer in the army will at once recognize in the hooded eyes and that hint of a sneer on the lips the innate sadism typical of all instructors. In the space of a few months the gentle author of *The Mask of Dimitrios* (and five other novels) has become a brutish martinet.

below: In wartime armies' promotion tends to be rapid. Although there are no available photographs of Colonel or Major Ambler, here is one of Captain Ambler on the Fifth Army front in Italy. If he looks much less pleased with himself than the Bombardier, that is because the picture was taken (by a US Army Signal Corps photographer) in December 1943 and at a place near San Pietro.

Map-reading, Italy, 1943. John Huston (*left*) did not like being photographed while he was trying to think. Lieutenant Ibba, the Signal Corps cameraman in the foreground on my left, was later killed in action.

left: My sister Joyce and brother Maurice. She is fourteen years younger than I am, married to an airline executive and has a career of her own as personnel officer in a multinational corporation. My brother had a highly successful career as a photo-journalist until, in middle life, he abandoned all to become a Lutheran pastor. That look of cheerful confidence in himself and his faith is not assumed.

Post-war film-making, 1953. With *Judgement on Deltchev* I had returned to writing novels, but screenwriting still had its attractions. The man on the right is Nicholas Monsarrat. My screenplay of his best-seller, *The Cruel Sea*, earned me an American Oscar nomination. The man on the left is Jack Hawkins, star of the film. A fine actor and a delightful man, he is telling us how he sees his part in the film now that it is made. Note the respectful attention with which both writers are listening.

where the barman would cross to the tram stop. With an imaginary rifle in my hands I lined up a space in the grille with a brass curlicue on the base of the standard lamp. I waited and watched, with the intersecting curves of the tramlines in my sights, for nearly an hour. The barman never came and I returned to James Joyce.

It was quite a shock, a few weeks later, to see on the newsreels that same piece of the Canebière with the interesecting tramlines. The spot I had chosen for my sniper shot at the barman had also been chosen by the Croatian assassin of King Alexander of Yugoslavia. The King had come by sea to Marseilles on a state visit to France and had been met at the quay by the French foreign minister, Barthou. They had been driving slowly in the state procession up the Canebière when the Croat had run forward boldly firing his pistol into the back of the open car. He had mortally wounded both the King and Barthou before he was cut down by an officer of the escorting cavalry wielding a sabre. It was a messy death. If he had taken my room, I thought, and used a rifle he might have had a chance of getting away.

I saw the newsreel several times and cut out news pictures of the scene. I felt oddly guilty, but also pleased. In the Mediterranean sunshine there were strange and violent men with whom I could identify, and with whom, in a way, I was now in touch.

That winter I was promoted in the copy department from the patent medicine to a baby food; and I wrote my first book. This was a manual for prospective mothers on the problems of pregnancy and was published by the baby food people who gave it away free to those who sent in a coupon. Of course, I did not really write the manual; I revised and rewrote an earlier edition and added material from recent gynaecological studies. I made all of it easier and less depressing to read; and I enjoyed myself doing so. The earlier edition had been embellished on every page with epigraphs on the subject of motherhood. They were gooey in tone and most of them seemed to have been dreamed up by greeting-card versifiers. Many of the authors quoted had unfamiliar and improbable names like Janice Barton Proudfoot and it seemed likely that most of them had been invented by my predecessor as editor. As the new edition had twice as many pages as the old I had to invent some authors of my own. The epigraphs were fairly easy. 'Children are vicarious immortality' was paraphrased Santayana. I ascribed it to Jeremiah Cleat (the Cornish Sage), but cannot remember now whether I used or discarded him.

Memory also fails when I try to recall the title of a one-acter I wrote at about the same time for Madam Ginnett. I can remember the idea because that was stolen from an Austrian novelist, Leo Perutz. A man escapes from police custody and spends a day and a night trying to free himself from the handcuffs he is wearing. Perutz wrote it as a thriller of the kind that German film makers of the period used to like, with plenty of inexpensive location footage punctuated by character 'cameo' scenes. I made a forty-minute play of it. The setting was a tea shop. Alan Martin Harvey played the man in the handcuffs and Guildhall students played the other parts.

Audiences seemed to enjoy it and Madam duly rewarded me; not, though, with a play to direct, but with something I needed much more just then. This was a roll of old carpet she had in her basement. Her husband said I could have it for nothing as long as I made the arrangements to take it away. I made them immediately. I needed the carpet to cover some bare boards in a Pimlico tenement.

I had met Betty Dyson and was on probation. She objected to the prudishness of British hotels. It was essential, she said, that I had a room of my own.

116

SEVEN

Betty was the daughter of Will Dyson, the political cartoonist of the London *Daily Herald*, and had been born when he was working for the Sydney *Bulletin*. Her mother had been a Lindsay, one of the talented Australian ones, and Betty was proud of that side of her family; her uncle Norman's novel *Red Heap* was still causing a stir there. She lived with her father in a house just off the Chelsea side of the Fulham Road. His studio was on the second floor. Hers was downstairs, though that winter she did not use it much. She had been engaged by Lilian Baylis as costume designer for a season at the Old Vic and had found that she preferred working at the theatre.

A gossip writer who knew Betty a little wrote, in a book of his reminiscences published after her death, that she was 'a girl of strange decisions and rather loose morals'. He followed those prim judgements with the assertion that she was the talent-scout who had put my feet on the 'ladder of success' as a writer. She was also 'ebullient and masterful'.

Ebullient? Well yes, I suppose she was; at least, that was how she must have seemed to someone who usually saw her when she was at her best and enjoying herself at a party. Masterful? That, I think, is clearly a euphemism.

Betty was not quarrelsome, but she had a quick temper and was a forceful user of bad language. Public places did not inhibit her. When she was being boisterous heads would turn and eyes would stare. How could that lovely blonde head, that clear-eyed intelligent face with the dazzling smile, conceal such a rough tongue? Easily, in fact. Betty was not trying to shock anyone; she did not care what strangers thought. If they did not like what they overheard they should not listen. A fluent French speaker, she had a vocabulary of *milieu* indecencies that could cause heads to turn in Paris too. In La Coupole once an indignant woman at the next table declared loudly that Betty had been *mal elevée*.

117

Perhaps she had. Her mother had died when she was a child and Bill, as she always called her father, had been in France as official war artist with the Australian Corps. She had been cared for by relations. When I got to know Betty and Bill they were more like a couple who had finally decided to get a divorce than a father and daughter. There was still some common ground. Her respect for him as an artist was unshaken; she still admired the wit and force of his best cartoons; she knew that she would never draw as well as he did. She had even forgiven his turning away from radical Socialism towards the quackery of Social Credit. The thing she could neither tolerate nor forgive was his disapproval of her social behaviour.

Betty had many Asian friends, mostly Hindus, and a lively interest in Hindu arts and culture. It was a genuine and informed interest, though undoubtedly deepened by a prolonged love affair with the Indian dancer Uday Shan Kar. She was not discreet about that or any other relationship. With Betty, to be discreet was to apologize. Bill, for all his radicalism, was a white Australian with the race prejudices of his generation. Betty took pride in her Asian friends, despised the English-speaking Commonwealth and considered herself a free soul. Her father saw her as an ill-natured, self-destructive baggage.

When Betty was working late at the theatre and the cartoon for the next day's paper had been collected by the *Herald* messenger, Bill would sometimes give me a drink while I waited for her. He knew about the room in Pimlico because Betty had borrowed some Gavarni prints of his to decorate the walls, but he would never have let me know that he knew; that would have embarrassed us both. Mostly we talked about such things as the bad news from abroad and the problems of helping German refugees. Once or twice he told me tales of the Australian infantry on the Somme. Although, as an official war artist, he had been technically a noncombatant Bill had been wounded twice. He had seen trench warfare as a participant and well understood the business of killing at close quarters. There were times when the Aussies had felt like taking prisoners and times when they had not. He could talk about those events easily to someone who seemed interested. He found it more difficult to talk about Betty. I remember only one occasion.

She was later than usual and he was going out to the Chelsea Arts Club. As he went he told me to help myself to another drink. Then he paused and gave me one of his thin-lipped grins. 'Don't ever think of marrying Betty,' he said; 'she'd make your life a misery.'

'Oh, she wouldn't think of marrying me.'

'That's good,' he said and left.

At the time Betty had no intention of marrying anyone; I had by then a clear idea of her thoughts on the subject. If she ever took a husband he would have to be not only rich, cultivated and highly athletic in bed but also doglike in his devotion to her and infinitely complaisant. If, for example, she chose to go off for a few weeks to stay with Greek friends in Nice or Juan les Pins, he should not expect to know which Greek friends or where they lived. If she brought him back from her travels abroad a gift of something unexpected – crab-lice, say, or clap – his discovery of it must be an occasion only for amazement at the tricks that nature was capable of playing on the innocent and the unwary. Mutual sympathy would be in order; raised eyebrows would not. All questions should be left unasked. He must learn to expect and shrug off such surprises.

I became very fond of Betty. She could behave appallingly, but if you were a friend you had to understand that often she did not quite realize this. She wanted, sometimes too fiercely, to enjoy herself. She wanted her friends to enjoy themselves, and to succeed, too, if success was possible. She liked to help by praising and by arranging for people to meet.

Most of her non-Asian friends were non-English homosexual artists and actors. I was the odd one of the bunch, an English, pinko-grey, more or less heterosexual writer. Did she put my feet on the rungs of a ladder of success? She would have laughed explosively at the idea. For her, ladders were the things used by snakes to succeed in business. Artists (and craftsmen like writers) could only develop by working. Everyone knew that. What do these sods mean by success? Money? Christ Almighty!

Rashly, I took Betty to a student performance of one-act plays. One of them was by me. She made it plain that she did not care for it. Later, however, she relented enough to ask why I did not write three-act plays.

'Like *Night Must Fall*, you mean?' Emlyn Williams' new play had made a deep impression on me.

'No,' she said; 'more like *Richard of Bordeaux* or *Spring 1600*. Then I can do the costumes instead of bloody Motley.'

She was working at the Old Vic then and envious of the West

End production budgets enjoyed by the design team of Motley. She went on to point out that the author of the Richard play also wrote detective stories. I could do that too if I put my mind to it.

Betty did not read many novels. When I gave her a bound page proof of *The Dark Frontier* she looked at it suspiciously. She knew, of course, that I had been writing a book, but this was the first she had seen of it. We were sitting in a Kings Road cinema waiting for the Sunday showing to start.

'Is it a detective story?' she asked.

'No, a thriller. Or a parody of one. I'm not quite sure which.'

She had brightened up at the word 'parody', but was still reluctant to commit herself to reading it. 'Well, I can't read in this light.'

'You can read the dedication. It's to you. I can change that if you don't like it.'

She read it. 'Oh well . . .'

'I could change it to Elizabeth Dyson if you like.'

'Christ no. Who's doing the jacket design?'

'That's up to the publishers.'

The house lights began to dim and she handed me back the proof copy. I don't think she ever managed to read the book.

She had been mistaken about my writing skills. They did not extend to costume plays about the death of kings; nor could I hope to match the Golden Age ingenuities of crime novelists like Anthony Berkeley and John Dickson Carr. What I wanted to be, failing success as a playwright, was a contributor to the *Adelphi*, or possibly the *New English Weekly* for which Will Dyson wrote occasional pieces. The only kind of popular novel about which I had strong feelings was the post-war thriller. I could no longer find any worth a second reading.

It was the villains who bothered me most. Power-crazed or coldly sane, master criminals or old-fashioned professional devils, I no longer believed a word of them. Nor did I believe in their passions for evil and plots against civilization. As for their world conspiracies, they appeared to me no more substantial than toy balloons, over-inflated and squeaky to the touch, with sad old characters rattling about inside like dried peas. The hero did not seem to matter much. He was often only a fugitive, a hare to the villain's hounds, prepared in the end to turn pluckily and face his pursuers. He could be a tweedy fellow with steel-grey eyes and gun pads on both shoulders or a moneyed dandy with a taste for adventure. He could also be a xenophobic ex-officer with a nasty anti-Semitic streak. None of that really mattered. All he really needed to function as hero was abysmal stupidity combined with superhuman resourcefulness and unbreakable knuckle bones.

As I saw it, the thriller had nowhere to go but up. I was not lacking in self-confidence. With *The Dark Frontier* I set out to start the upward trend. Fortunately, I had only a very modest success with the book.

The villainy I plotted was sound enough. The reading done years before when I was playing truant in the IEE Library had given me a little knowledge that in 1935 was still fairly esoteric. I knew something about the work that had been done on the structure of the atom and I understood some of the more obvious consequences of it. I knew, for instance, or had deduced, that an atomic bomb would eventually be made and that the first possessor of it would have awesome power over the rest of mankind. I had realized, too, that the threat it represented would, at the moment a practical bomb existed, be translated into overwhelming political power.

The first mistake I made was to underestimate the economic and industrial resources needed to develop the bomb. I believed that it could be made in a single laboratory by a team of Ruritanian scientists. Today, no doubt, it could be made by their students. In 1935, however, my solemn nightmare of fascist plotters in a Balkan state using atomic blackmail to dominate the world was flawed by my ignorance. If I had known a little more I might have written a science fiction novel of some consequence.

My reduction of the atomic bomb threat into melodrama had other trivializing effects. Using C.G. Jung as my psychiatric authority (without his permission, naturally) I played dual-personality games with the hero. This was plain cheating. The 'Carruthers' half of the personality was a parody hero put there largely for my own entertainment. I enjoyed making fun both of him and of the early E. Phillips Oppenheim kind of thriller writing that went with that type of courtly superman hero.* Among my other indiscretions was an American newspaper man. He was an observer hero, introduced halfway through the book and writing in the first person, who suddenly took it over. This was simple desperation on my part. It was this intrusive late-comer who made

* My impudence did not always go unpunished. Forty years or so later, in a formal critical piece about me, Clive James quoted a phrase from this awful parodied Oppenheim stuff as a significant example of my own early prose style.

it possible for me to resolve all the story problems I had created for myself earlier on by breaking, or ignoring, other sound storytelling rules. He made it possible for me to finish the book. I told Betty that it was a parody of a thriller. That was what I had meant it to be when I had started out. It changed as I went along; and, no doubt, as I began to learn how such stories could be well told.

My first publisher was John Attenborough, a director of Hodder and Stoughton. He showed me their regular readers' reports on the book as well as his own and he asked me a lot of questions.

Those were the days when good trade book publishers were more interested in the whole bodies of work to be expected of new writers than in their early efforts. They hoped not to lose money on a first novel but did not expect to make any. Authors were looked upon as speculative investments which might, or might not, become profitable later on. First books were no more than guide lines. John Attenborough wanted to know about my second and third books. What plans had I for them? He was glad to hear that I had a steady job.

By then the job was somewhat steadier. Martin Harvey senior had decided to retire and Alan had asked me to join the agency. I joined as production manager, but when we later amalgamated with an up-and-coming Birmingham agency, became a director. I could have afforded to move from the Pimlico tenement to a flat with a bathroom and its own toilet, but had a feeling that I should stay put. I did not want to believe that the only future I had was in advertising. My room in Moreton Place might be squalid, but the rent was only sixteen shillings a week and I had written a publishable book there. Besides, the lack of a bathroom did not mean that I went unwashed. During the first month there Betty had found (at Harrods she said) a strange object that looked like a heavy, cork-seated bathroom stool but was really a disguised, though unplumbed, bidet. I had soon become good at bathing myself in it, using only two kettles of hot water and a big enamel jug of cold by the kitchen sink.

The advance on *The Dark Frontier* was thirty pounds. The first printing was, I think, a thousand copies. The most important thriller reviewer then was Torquemada of the *Observer*. From him I received a guarded nod of approval – 'He has knowledge; and he has speed' – and from the *Scotsman* word that the book was subtly written and 'a genuine thriller'. There were other favourable reviews. I was pleased, of course, but not inordinately so. I had done the rounds with one or two of Hodders' London travellers and had seen how difficult it was to sell books during a depression. I was also hard at work on a second one.

I was helped to set about it by Eileen Bigland. She was a serious writer who worked as a reader of things like thrillers because she needed the money. She had been one of those who had read *The Dark Frontier* and it had been she who had pointed out most trenchantly its many faults. Over a drink or two she told me of the difficulties ahead. 'Some authors have second book trouble,' she said; 'some have third. I think you've been lucky. You've had first book trouble. With a bit of application you could do much better next time.'

'I was trying to do something different.'

'You did something different, but you did it in a mucky way. You set out with a clear intention. Good. You said what you were going to do. Then you changed your mind. But you didn't tell the reader that you were changing you mind. You left him to find out. You musn't do things like that. Don't let the reader get away. Take him with you. What models were you using?'

I gave her a list which began with Stevenson and wandered through Gogol and Compton Mackenzie to Pirandello and James Joyce.

She nodded, glumly; it was more or less as she had expected. 'Try Somerset Maugham,' she said.

'I've read his plays and *Cakes and Ale*. Do you mean *Of Human Bondage*?'

'I was thinking of *Ashenden*,' she said; 'and the other long short stories. He's not a great novelist, but he's a fine storyteller. And he never mucks about with the story he's telling. Another word of advice, my friend. Never read very good writers when you are trying yourself to write good trash. You'll only get depressed.'

I took all her advice. I also read *Extremes Meet* and *The Three Couriers* by Compton Mackenzie, another ex-MI6 man. The book I wrote that year was *Background to Danger* and was a more disciplined piece of work than the first. It also contained a few novelties: Soviet agents who were on the side of the angels and a disreputable central character who gets into a fix through losing too much money playing pokerdice. I also used a few thin slices of what I thought to be real life: the man who had bored me stiff on a Channel crossing with his belief in pasta as an infallible cure for gastric ulcers, and the English salesman who had sprayed me on a train

123

between Milan and Domodossola with crumbs from salami sand-wiches and his deadly hatred of all foreigners. The year was 1936, the year in which Italy invaded Abyssinia, Civil War broke out in Spain and Hitler ordered the German Army to reoccupy the Rhineland. It was a year of yet more refugees and of marriages arranged to confer passports. It was also the year in which the League of Nations was at last seen plainly to be impotent.

Those were the things that I was trying, in my own fictional terms, to write about. Most of my information came from refugees, but there were other sources.

Before television came, published authors, however unimport-ant, were thought of as communicators and could receive the strangest invitations. Young male authors who might have suits of evening tails and white waistcoats would be invited to make them-selves useful at deb dances. Scruffier authors, of both sexes, would be asked to literary get-togethers where coffee and biscuits were served. Since I had inherited my father's tails as well as his golfing tweeds I could accept invitations from any or all who cared to issue them.

The deb dances I went to because they excused indulgence. If I had changed at home the other denizens of Moreton Place would have made cutting remarks or accused me of doing someone out of a job as a waiter. So I would pack a suitcase, book a changing room at Austin Reed's and luxuriate in a real hot bath before dressing up. The dances were dreadful affairs and the dinners that preceded them not much better; but I learned how boorish and ill-mannered many well-brought-up young men could be. The girls, whom they despised and whose feet they trod on, had a rotten time.

The literary get-togethers were generally organized with the object of enlisting support for a cause. The causes were usually liberal and the support requested was in most cases only moral. It came to be understood by most of those who attended these func-tions that the organizers and lenders of premises were, if not actu-ally members of the Communist Party, fairly sympathetic to it. If the term fellow-travellers had been used in its present pejorative sense at the time I think that many of us could well have been described in that way.

All the same, I can recall only one get-together at which the cause of the Party itself was the one being promoted. It took place at a club in Great Newport Street and the proceedings opened with an address by Stephen Spender. He said, I think, that a great many writers seemed to be troubled by recent reports from Republican Spain. There seemed, I think he said, to be apparent contradictions of a dialectical nature between the views of a certain Trotskyite faction there and the established front-line convictions of the Communist Party fighters for democracy. It was for this reason that one or two of those who had the facts of the matter at their fingertips had come along that evening to answer questions and to set doubts at rest. He introduced Randall Swingler, who then took over, speaking in a language that I have never been able to understand, that of the academic philosopher. He had friends there who also spoke the language and a keen debate developed. I did not understand a word of it; and there were others in the same predicament. This was not the ordinary jargon of slap-and-tickle dialectical materialism but a more rarefied cant. From the glazed look he wore as he wound up the proceedings I thought that Spender, too, may have found the evening a bit of a strain. I cannot believe that it assuaged any doubts.

The only Communist Party speaker who ever carried conviction with me was one of those who set up every Sunday in Hyde Park. He could use phrases and sometimes whole sentences from the Communist Manifesto with a sort of hesitant wonder and passion that made you feel that he had just invented them. Listening to him could be a stirring experience.

He needed his dais, however. Without it he became vulnerable. One Sunday I stayed behind after the dais had been removed by his assistant and asked if he would care for a cup of tea. I think that he would have preferred a small donation to *Daily Worker* funds but after a momentary hesitation he accepted. A small, neatly dressed man with a rolled umbrella who had also been in the listening crowd then asked if he could join us. The speaker shrugged and led the way out of the park. He had had no dinner, he said. Personally, he was going to have something to eat with his tea.

In the Lyons shop on the Edgware Road the speaker ordered a poached egg on toast and then set out to clarify the thoughts of the man with the umbrella. The man looked like a middle-rank civil servant in his early forties; his umbrella was an expensive one with a malacca handle and a gold band. It was the umbrella, I was sure, that had marked him for the speaker as in special need of dialectical assistance and straight-from-the-shoulder Marxist common sense.

The umbrella man proved strangely unco-operative. He had, after all, asked to join us. Yet, instead of listening to what the speaker had to say he kept asking questions; awkward, simplistic questions. It was all very well to talk about the redistribution of wealth and public ownership of the means of production, but which parts of the public were to get what? And what did each according to his needs mean? Who was to do the deciding? Someone like you or someone like me? Stuff like that; amateur heckling.

The speaker's patience did not last long. He pointed his teaspoon accusingly at the umbrella man. 'And what, may I ask,' he said with heavy courtesy, 'do you do for a bloody living? Plain clothes divisional CID is it, or Special Branch?'

The umbrella man gave a diffident little smile. 'No,' he said; 'I'm a burglar.'

The speaker stiffened with outrage. 'I asked a civil question,' he snapped; 'I think I'm entitled to a civil answer.'

'I told you,' said the umbrella man. 'You asked me and I told you. I'm a burglar. Professionally I mean. I suppose you could say that I redistribute wealth.'

The speaker, who had had a mouthful of toast, spluttered and became speechless with a fit of coughing. I took advantage of the moment. The umbrella man was clearly a wag, but I thought he might be telling the truth. 'Ever been caught?' I asked.

'Only once,' he said; 'but it won't happen again. I'm too respectable now, and strictly on my own.' He stood up and put the price of his cup of tea by his saucer. 'Doesn't do to speak too plainly nowadays, does it?' With a smile and a nod to us both he left.

When he recovered his breath the speaker was bitter. 'Some of them'll do anything,' he said. 'In my position you have to be careful. You saw what he was up to, of course.'

'Pulling our legs you mean? Saying he was a burglar?'

The speaker became indignant again. 'He wasn't pulling *my* leg, comrade, whatever he was doing to yours. Taunting me, that's what he was doing. Proudhon said that all property is theft. This geezer has property. Ergo, he's a thief. Burglar, my foot! Special Branch, that's what he was. I can smell it a mile off. Don't tell me about that lot. Provocators, all of them.'

I did not believe that the man with the expensive umbrella read Proudhon and I still thought that he was a respectable burglar; but there was no longer any way of finding out. To end the argument I paid for the speaker's poached egg on toast as well as his tea.

When I was rewriting the last chapters of *Background to Danger* I heard from John Green, my agent at Curtis Brown, that Alfred A. Knopf, the famous American publisher, was in London and would like to meet me. He had read *The Dark Frontier* and been interested by it, but could not publish it because I had lost copyright in the United States. In those days Bern Convention copyrights were only briefly valid in the States. Could he read *Background to Danger* as it was, unfinished?

He could, he did and he liked it. I had an American publisher; and one of the best there was. He was also the first man I met who could wear pink shirts and make them seem conservative. He asked for no changes to be made in the book apart from his house-style American spelling. For some reason that I never understood Hodders objected to the word 'background' in the title. So, in all English-speaking countries except the United States, the book was published as *Uncommon Danger*. It did well under both titles. Reviewers in many places said that I had written a new, more realistic and better kind of thriller.

It was about the time that I was reading those reviews that I began to have sharp pains in a part of the body quite near to the appendix. Betty sent me to an Indian doctor friend of hers. He was both charming and efficient. Within a few days I was in a big surgical ward at Bart's and a consultant surgeon who charged a hundred guineas for removing a private patient's appendix had taken mine out for nothing. In 1937 the removal of an appendix involved a stay in hospital of about three weeks. After the operation had been done an almoner came to see me. She wanted to know if I could pay anything towards the cost of my stay there. Could I, for instance, pay as much as two pounds a week? I could pay more? Ah no, sorry. Two pounds a week was the upper limit. If I felt able to give a donation to the hospital later on when I left, that would be greatly appreciated. While we were all patients in the ward together it was better if we all paid more or less the same. The surgeon explained his generosity by claiming facetiously that with us charity patients he only made very small incisions. In my case it had been no more than an inch and a quarter. Only four or five stitches. Quick and cheap.

Betty nearly ruined his work by bringing me a stack of old *New Yorker* magazines. I had not realized how painful it was after abdominal surgery to want to laugh. When the stitches were eventually removed it was discovered that I had broken two of them.

Back at Moreton Place I found that my mother had bought me a knee-hole desk, but did not feel up to using it. Betty decided that Tangier would be a suitable place for my convalescence. We went there for seven pounds a head on a P&O boat.

It was not at that time an obvious choice for a place in which to convalesce. The mounting violence of the Spanish civil war was never far away. Tangier was then an international zone with a multinational administration of some complexity. Gibraltar, of course, was not far away across the Strait and as further reassurance there were French and British post offices selling their national stamps; but it was Spain that counted. The zone had a land frontier with Spanish Morocco, a Spanish national bank (solidly for General Franco), a Spanish post office (straunchly loyal to the republican government in Madrid) and a Spanish business population of mixed loyalties. In the harbour of Tangier, the warships of the British and the French and the Axis powers showed their flags and sometimes even landed armed parties to show that they meant business; but the business concerned was intervention on one side or the other of the war in Spain. In the city, and the souks, all sorts of rearguard actions were still being fought; and not only with the weapons of undercover work, kidnappings and discreet murders. The peace of the warm, soft nights was constantly shattered by the sounds of rival political bands fighting gun battles in the streets. The big event of the day could be the smoke-belching departure of the train to Meknes or the arrival of a warship new to the place; but the nights were not so restful.

There was a French destroyer named *Simoun* in the harbour and Betty had taken a fancy to one of the junior officers. While they went off together I stayed out of the sun in a ramshackle wooden beach café called L'Onde Bleue, drank mint tea and thought about the future. I knew enough about the book I would write next to put a title to it, *Epitaph for a Spy*. What I had to think about was leaving advertising and becoming a professional writer. I still made my mother a small allowance. That would have to continue; but I had no other responsibilities. I had no intention of getting married. I knew by then that I could live more cheaply and more comfortably in France than in England. A good Swedish publisher, Bonnier of Stockholm, had made an offer – my first for a translation right – for *Background to Danger*. Surely, all I needed now was a little determination.

When I got back to London I talked the problem over with Leonard Cutts, the Hodder editor who nursed their thriller writers, and he spoke to John Attenborough for me. Word came back that I would be ill-advised to take chances until I had written many more books, ten or twelve. I said that I intended, even though ill-advised, to take my chances as a writer now. I said the same thing to John Green at Curtis Brown. He said that he would see what could be done.

I have heard since, from John Attenborough, that my various statements of intent, some bloody-minded in tone as well as ill-advised, were reported to the Chairman of Hodders, Percy Hodder-Williams, a man I never met. According to Attenborough, his nephew, Mr Hodder-Williams, then said: 'By Jove, he must mean it. We'd better see if we can help.'

They helped with a contract for six books; and on each one that I delivered I would get an advance of one hundred pounds. If I wrote two books a year that might just be enough. I had lived on four pounds a week before. I could do so again.

It was not until I had finished *Epitaph for a Spy* and delivered it that I began to get cold feet. I had told Alan Harvey of my decision as soon as I had made it and he had been sympathetic. We delayed telling the other directors for only a few weeks. I wanted the few accounts for which I had executive responsibility to be firmly in Alan's hands when I finally left. The reason for the cold feet was, I think, a throw-back, depression-years fear of not having a job to go to in a conventional work setting.

Leonard Cutts, who did not have to be told about the fears and frailties of authors, found a way of dispelling the gloom. He had inaugurated the Hodder 'Teach Yourself' educational series and gave me the job of editing a disastrous manuscript he had just received from one of his red-brick university dons. The subject of the book was Clear Thinking. The manuscript, however, was an undisciplined muddle; not a physical or typographical muddle, but, strangely, a thinking one. It was difficult to read. One could, after a bit, see what the author was driving at; but only if one first rearranged and clarified his thoughts for him. For instance, his example of a false syllogism might be good, but he would present it in a way that left the reader wallowing in confusion. It was a good book; and rearranging and editing it was a flattering job. I enjoyed doing it. I had also started another book of my own, *Cause for Alarm*.

Uncle Frank was due to leave prison shortly and my mother had decided to house him for a while and fatten him up again. *Epitaph for a Spy* would be published in the spring. By then, I would have left the agency and be in France. All I would be taking with me was one suitcase and a bag containing essentials such as dictionaries and the pads and school exercise books I used for writing. It seemed sensible to offer Uncle Frank – a divorced man now – my furnished room and kitchen as a *pied-à-terre*. Even my mother, who had always detested Moreton Place, could find no fault with this plan. 'It can't be worse for him than Maidstone.'

I never discussed it with Betty. One evening I went to pick her up to go to a theatre and found her with her hair down, collapsed and in tears. Bill had been found dead in his studio an hour earlier. A massive heart attack was suspected but the post mortem would deal with that. Bill's great friend Henry Rushbury, the etcher who had a studio at the back of the house, was there to help, but Betty had retreated into uncontrollable weeping and there was nothing any of us could do but mourn. Only gradually, during the weeks that followed, did Betty find that she could stop talking about the unhappiness she had caused everyone, especially Bill. In due course it was found that he had made a will in her favour and that she had now enough money to live on without working.

When she cleared out his studio she gave me two of his Great War cartoons for the original *Herald* and an artist's proof of a lithograph he had done then called *Nacht Verdun*. She said that he had not liked it and there was only the one proof. I was glad to have it. She told me, too, to keep the Gavarni prints. She had decided to live in France and marry a Frenchman. I had not met him. His name was Yves and he was a Breton with an old baronial title.

The few weeks after I left the agency and worked at Moreton Place seemed very long. I could not get used to the weekdays. From Monday to Friday I heard daytime street sounds that were completely new and strange to me. I heard women talking to one another and the sounds of milkmen and window-cleaners and delivery boys on their rounds that made the street a different, unfamiliar, hostile place. I felt a stranger there, a lodger without a job. I used to have lunch round the corner at a delicatessen in Moreton Street. The man there, who had very good black puddings, knew me well; but even he looked oddly at me when I went there in the middle of the day. 'Lost your job?' he asked me once. It was said in the friendliest way; he was probably offering to give me tick; but when I tried to explain that I was a writer now and working on my own he only nodded vaguely. He did not really believe me.

One good thing happened. I had been to dinner with Alan and Félice Harvey who lived round the corner in St George's Square and when I got back to Moreton Place found a telegram. It was from Curtis Brown and informed me that the *Daily Express* was going to serialize *Epitaph for a Spy* and pay one hundred and thirty-five pounds for doing so.

This was wealth. It meant that I could sometimes travel second class instead of third. I was lucky, of course, and well served by my agent. I see now that it was not a very good time for thriller writers or for their publishers. It was the custom then to publish such books only in the spring and autumn. It was also becoming customary for the Axis powers to make their more threatening moves towards the eventual havoc of the Second World War at the same seasons of the year. In March 1938 when *Epitaph for a Spy* was being subscribed Hitler invaded and annexed Austria. In those circumstances a thriller with a refugee as its central character was bound to lose some of its appeal.

Uncle Frank was unimpressed by the Nazis. Nothing the Jerries did could ever again surprise him. Prison did not seem to have changed him much. My mother reported no nightmares. He had some prison slang which I memorized carefully for possible future use. One old lag's adage – 'There's no taste in nothing' struck me as interesting as well as totally meaningless. I used it, later, more than once. Uncle Frank used it constantly in connection with the giving and taking of bribes.

He inspected Moreton Place thoughtfully and seemed impressed by the portable bidet. I showed him the rent book and told him about the people downstairs who worked in a brewery and were apt to monopolize the communal toilet on Saturday nights.

'When are you off?' he asked.

'Thursday afternoon. I'll take the night crossing, Newhaven–Dieppe. That all right with you?'

'I'll be here.'

He arrived at about two in the afternoon, not exactly drunk but just a bit unsteady. Part of the unsteadiness was certainly due to the fact that he was carrying on his shoulders an enormous hat rack made of stag antlers.

'Got it for twenty-five bob at an auction,' he explained.

'But what for, Uncle? You've only got one hat.'

'Those are magnificent antlers. I'm not putting any hats on them, my lad. Besides, I thought the place needed cheering up.'

It did, I knew. I had removed the Gavarni prints and put them in a safe place. The hat rack, though, was really hideous. It was clearly time for me to go. I would never see the room again anyway.

When I left he was trying to decide where on the wall the hat rack should best be placed.

EIGHT

The pound then was worth eighty French francs and I knew a hotel near the Sorbonne where I could get a room for ten francs a night; but I was not ready to stay in Paris yet. I was sure I would work better farther south. I had been told that some of the lesser ski resorts were, out of season, the cheapest places of all to stay for long periods. One looked, apparently, for the small *pensions* run and lived in by the families who owned them. They could not afford to shut up shop, even in the worst weather.

I had decided to try the Alpes Maritimes. I stayed one night in Nice and then took the bus up through the hills towards Sospel. I got off at Peira-Cava just below the snow line. There were a few patches of white slush and hillsides of dripping fir trees floating in a landscape of fog. Even the bus seemed unwilling to stop there. I stayed for three months.

My bedroom was cold and became colder as the heating system deteriorated. I took to working in the *pension* dining room. Since I was, for most of the time, the only guest, this caused the family no inconvenience. When, after a mild explosion, the heating system gave up altogether, all occupants – the waiter, two chambermaids and the family as well as me – were given hot bricks to keep us warm. The bricks were heated on one of the kitchen stoves and then wrapped in thick layers of newspaper. I asked for, and received, two bricks. The dining room, in which I wrote the last part of *Cause for Alarm*, was bitterly cold. While writing I nursed one brick on my knees and used the other for my feet.

The family, with just the daughter at home and the son away in the army, allowed me to make myself useful. In the evenings, when they needed a fourth at whist, they taught me how to play using the French names for the cards. This also meant that, as they had an efficient fireplace in their sitting room, they did not have to keep me supplied with hot bricks. The heating boiler could not be repaired until the summer. In the evenings sometimes, when it was not too cold, neighbours would drop in for an infusion of vervaine and a chat. The only one of these visitors who always refused all refreshment was a middle-aged woman who invariably smelt strongly of hospitals. She was often escorted by a uniformed chauffeur. I thought of her at first as probably the matron of a local hospital or clinic. However, my reference to her in those terms was greeted by the family with gales of laughter. It was explained to me that the lady, a wealthy member of the famous arms-making Schneider family of Creusot, was hooked on ether. She drank the stuff.

This was something I found difficult to understand. My first encounter with ether had been at the age of twelve when I had been given it as an anaesthetic for a tonsillectomy. It had produced copious vomiting. I had had it again, this time mixed with chloroform I think, at Bart's. More, and very painful, vomiting. Yet, they said, this Madame Schneider drank it. Regularly, her chauffeur would be sent down to Nice and her favourite pharmacist for fresh supplies. He bought it five hundred grams at a time. Grams? Yes, five hundred grams. The *patron* told me confidentially and a touch wistfully that, for those who did not mind the smell and flavour of it, ether was the only intoxicating liquor on which a man could get falling-down drunk and yet wake up the following morning without a hangover.

I could not believe that in France, the land of reason and the metric system, a liquid was purchased by weight instead of volume, but when I put this to the *patron* he only shrugged. The chauffeur said that he bought the ether by weight. Perhaps he was an ignorant man who knew no better. What difference did it make? If I wanted to try the stuff myself I could probably buy it in *decis*. I would still end up smelling like Madame Schneider. I should hope to be as rich.

He was becoming irritable so I dropped the subject. I did not want to lose him as a source of information. We had had a late fall of snow and for a few days skiers had appeared. Among those who came to the *pension* and froze with us was a Turkish family. They lived in Nice where, according to my friend the *patron*, there was a considerable Turkish colony. He had Turkish clients who came every year. He knew a lot about them. I was able, gradually, to find out more.

A few were royalists, a strange lot whose elders had once been middle-rank courtiers or hangers-on in the retinue of the last Sultan Mehmed son of Abdul the Damned; some were officer-class families headed by aging Young Turks who had chosen the wrong factions to join or in some other way played their cards badly. Most were the families of politicans, lawyers and businessmen in import–export and shipping who had found it simpler to cut and run than to bow to the reforming zeal of the Kemalists. Some, mostly those who had once owned land under the Ottoman regime, liked to speak of an eventual return to the country of their birth. One or two had even tried going back. Their children generally preferred to swim from the beaches between Nice and Monte Carlo and to ski on the slopes above. An old aunt who came with this family was easy to make friends with and I found her advice on the back-street residential hotels of Nice particularly useful.

The visitors melted away again with the snow. Allan Collins of Curtis Brown, New York, wrote to say that Knopf did not like *Epitaph for a Spy* because it was quite different from *Background to Danger* and would be confusing to reviewers. If I insisted, he would press Knopf to take it, but maybe it would be better to wait. I had nearly finished *Cause for Alarm* and maybe Knopf would like that. He was a publisher worth holding on to if you could.*

There were consolations. From Curtis Brown, London, came the news that Ealing Studios had offered three hundred pounds for the film rights of *Epitaph for a Spy*. Hettie Hilton, who dealt with film matters, said that I should accept the offer. I did.

I also finished *Cause for Alarm* and took the exercise-books of the manuscript to London to be typed. While I was there Hettie Hilton said that Alexander Korda wanted me to write a film story for Conrad Veidt. I went to Denham and saw Alex. I always liked him and he was never anything but charming; but on that occasion he had a bad idea for a story I should write. An airliner full of interesting and suspicious passengers makes a forced landing in the Maginot Line. All I had to do was to invent some fantastic characters and make it all exciting.

I wrote the story he wanted, but with a heavy heart. I called it *The*

* That, at least, was true. It was twelve years later that I received a sharp letter from Blanche Knopf, Alfred's wife and co-director, complaining that there was a book of mine *Epitaph for a Spy* that they had never been offered or even allowed to read. She dismissed as absurd my protestations of innocence. 'We'd better publish it, I suppose, but ex-contract, flat ten per cent. And we've lost copyright. You'll have to write a foreword and make radical changes in the text.'

Commandant. Mercifully, nothing more was heard of it. Conrad Veidt, poor fellow, died. He was to have played the lead.

Cause for Alarm was well received both in London and New York. Alfred Knopf was particularly pleased. However, he wanted to omit the whole of chapter seventeen. He hoped I would share his feeling that it was not really essential and that the book would read more easily without it.

I could see what he meant for minutes on end; then I would have doubts. I asked Leonard Cutts what he thought.

'Chapter seventeen happens to be the best in the book,' he said sturdily; 'it will not be left out of the British edition under any circumstances. That's American publishing for you. You must learn to expect it. Cheapjack.'

I am not sure if that was the epithet he actually used, but it was something like that. Rather shrewder, I think, was his theory that Alfred's letter had been drafted by a copy editor in whom the Knopfs then had confidence. I did not feel able to argue passionately about chapter seventeen, either for or against it. I have never been good at such arguments when my own books have been concerned. I always do several drafts; but when I have finished the last one I have finished with the book. I care about it, yes, but there is nothing more than I feel able to do.

Cause for Alarm was published in the United States later on that year without the original chapter seventeen. Its omission did not seem to make any difference. Allan Collins wrote saying that MGM had read the book in proof and expressed an interest in the movie rights. We should keep our fingers crossed.

I went back to Nice to find out more about the Turkish colony there. In the train on the way I scribbled, and drew, a note about the book I wanted to do. First there was a sketch-map of Europe made squiggly by the movement of the train. Across it all ran a still more squiggly line running from Istanbul to Izmir, then to Athens, to Sofia, to Geneva, to Belgrade and finally to Paris. The central character would be a criminal called, perhaps, Demetrius or Dimitrios. The spelling of the name could be decided later. If I wanted to start the story in Turkey, and if I were a serious writer, obviously I should go to Turkey. But what would I do there? I was not serious. I knew no one there. I could not speak Turkish. I was not the kind of person who knew ambassadors or who could employ interpreters. I was a nobody. On the other hand, there were Turks in Nice who spoke French as badly as I did and with whom I could communicate.

The hotel I chose was run by Belgians, but it was one of the back-street Turkish haunts mentioned by the old aunt in Peira-Cava. I was richly rewarded. Exiles may not always tell the truth about their native lands, but they like to talk about them. They talk a lot, and it is not absolutely necessary that one listens to the words. Sometimes the music that comes through is enough. It can be as little as the faint pain in a man's eyes as he remembers something he is *not* telling you. One woman proudly showed me a photograph of an old wooden villa on the north shore of the Bosphorus that her parents had once owned. It was imposing. What interested me, though, was a steel bracket with white insulators to carry telephone wires high up on one corner of the house. There was an incongruity about that bracket bolted to the old wood that stuck in my mind. I remembered it later when I wanted to describe a mortuary in Istanbul. I still thought of that city as Byzantium. How better to express decay than old wooden walls with telephone-line brackets on them or old stone walls, still contemptuous of time, but roofed over with corrugated iron?

In Nice I was learning too much about Turkey, so I went to Paris to work. Betty and Yves were there and warmly recommended the Hotel Libéria which was opposite the art school in the rue de la Grande Chaumière. The weather was still warm so I scarcely noticed that the heating and hot water systems were both defective. It was fairly quiet and near La Coupole where the food was good; so I began to work. I called the book *A Coffin for Dimitrios* and in the United States that is still its title as a book.

There were one or two interruptions. Word came from Allan Collins that MGM had offered three thousand dollars for the *Cause for Alarm* movie rights. After deductions for commission and US income tax, that was nearly eight hundred pounds. MGM's London office would complete the deal and I would have to have the contracts notarized there. I had other reasons for going to England then. I had new friends like Victor Canning and Charles Rodda (an Australian who wrote thrillers under the name of Gavin Holt) and old friends like Vere Denning, now married to John French. Vere I took to the oyster and champagne bars I could now afford. I also had work to do; I had to find out about Dimitrios.

I found out most of what I needed to know in the offices of *The Times* in the old Printing House Square at the lower end of Queen Victoria Street. There, one used to be able to go to a long mahogany counter and ask to see back numbers of *The Times* in huge leather volumes four or five inches thick. One asked for the year (1922, say) and the month, and watchful, motherly men and women would supervise one's search for information. No photocopies then, of course, and photostats had to be ordered. Most searchers brought a notebook and wrote down their notes. If anyone had ever tried to tear a piece out of any of those old papers there would have been a terrible shemozzle.

I took the loot back to Paris; and it was about that time, I think, that I discovered that night channel-crossings by sea were a waste of time. I took a fancy to commuting by air. The planes I chose, however, were not those of Imperial Airways, slow, stately and expensive, but the Lockheed Electras of a 'pirate' airline called (how odd it sounds now) British European Airways. They flew from Northolt, very cheaply, and the planes they used later became known to the RAF as Hudsons. The only difference was that in the tail of the old Electra there was a small toilet. In the Hudson that space was used for a gun turret.

In Paris I changed hotels and the quarter I lived in. This was not only because I had taken against the Libéria's plumbing and its habit of running out of clean sheets – on some lower floors it was little better than a *maison de passe* – but because it was too near Betty and her quarrels with Yves. Advised by mutual Australian friends who understood the problem, I moved to St-Germain-des Prés. At first I tried a very noisy place on the rue Jacob. Later, I moved to the Hôtel de l'Université round the corner. There I had a bathroom. The Café de Flore and the Brasserie Lipp were also handy.

I forget how I got to know Brian Howard. I think I was with John Hilliard, Jean Connolly and a young American couple in the Flore when Brian came in with his German friend Toni. I had heard vaguely of Brian Howard as someone to be avoided. No one had told me why. He was said to be extraordinarily talented, but no one seemed clear about the subject of his talent. I was unprepared.

He was a year or two older than I was, though he looked younger and was a highly attractive man. Within a few minutes of his joining us I had put him down as a moneyed, bitchy, petulant and altogether unpleasant scold. I felt very sorry for the young German with him whose role seemed to be that of whipping boy. It took me a few more minutes to realize that the scolding of Toni was part of their normal relationship. The scold was a genuine wit and part of Toni's function was that of straight man, of Judy to Mr Punch. It was not much longer before I discovered that Brian, far from being moneyed, was a notorious remittance man. Of course, he did a little good literary journalism, but not in the amounts required to produce the kind of income he needed. He showed me some of his poems and lent me his personal copy of Cyril Connolly's *Enemies of Promise*.

It is not a book which could be called in any way flattering to Brian, but I could see why he thought it important. He was a peculiar kind of snob, a very precious one, and extravagantly relieved at not having been ignored in a book by a more talented writer who had been a contemporary at Eton. Brian did not mind being lampooned. Before a respectful audience he would lampoon himself. He had remarkably little self-respect.

The respect he had for me at the beginning of our brief acquaintance was based on his recognition of the fact that, although I wrote books that made money, they were neither illiterate nor unreadable. He could identify enthusiastically with the paranoid hero of *Epitaph for a Spy*. He also seemed to feel that I responded well to flattery. He thought, I believe, that he might eventually get into the habit of touching me, perhaps every other month, for fifty pounds or so. Fifty, I had heard by then, was the usual figure.

The first approach came after a weekend at Grez-sur-Loing. This was a village near Fontainebleau with a small hotel whose *patron* did not mind a weekly influx of English-speaking foreigners who drank too much and did not care where or with whom they slept.

When we got back that Monday evening several of us had snacks at the Flore. Then Brian gave me one of his thoughtful looks.

'My dear,' he said, 'can you think of any reason why we shouldn't take a taxi over to Bricktop's and have a brandy? No, not you,' he added sharply as Toni started to say something; 'you had much too much to drink last night. I shall expect to find you sleeping it off when I return.' He looked at me again. 'Yes?'

'Isn't Bricktop's closed on Monday?'

'My dear, you mustn't be so literal. There are dozens of Bricktop's and Harry's Bars available every night of the week. If Madame Bricktop is closed, one of her friends will be open.'

He was right, of course. There were several cosy bars with bogus Anglo-Saxon names open on the slopes of Montmartre and we visited most of them. Towards two o'clock in the morning Brian made his first approach.

'They tell me you've sold the film rights of one of your books to Hollywood.'

'Yes. You think I should have refused the temptation?'

'Now, my dear, you're being arch. It doesn't suit you. Was it millions?'

'No, only hundreds.'

'Oh well, perhaps you should have refused. Still, hundreds aren't bad. Would you mind very much if I asked you to lend me fifty pounds?'

'Lend? Yes, I'm afraid I would mind.'

'Oh dear, I've offended you. People can be so funny about money and behave so oddly. I can never think why.'

'I'm not offended, Brian. If you need it badly I'll give you fifty pounds, but I won't lend it to you. You wouldn't pay it back.'

I had offended him deeply. He drained his brandy and banged down the glass. 'You really are a very common little man, aren't you?' he said with one of his sweeter smiles.

'Of course,' I said and signalled for the bill.

He gave me his most menacing stare. 'I can tell you this, my dear. I am not leaving you this evening without a cheque for fifty pounds.'

'I'm glad to hear it.'

'It will be a loan.'

'The cheque won't say what it is. I'm going to London tomorrow. You can write me a letter there, a promise to repay, if you want to.'

He wrote to me in England to tell me again that he was never surprised when people behaved oddly about money. He could understand and he could forgive. I did not hear from him again for several years.

Cause for Alarm was on Hodder's autumn list. Public attention was focused on what the Nazis were doing in the Sudetenland and what they were soon likely to do in Czechoslovakia. Neville Chamberlain had flown to meet Hitler at Berchtesgarden. A week later he had flown for another meeting at Bad Godesberg. Europe was very near to war. The following week Mussolini took a hand and the news that Hitler had invited him to join a meeting with Daladier as well as his friend Chamberlain was announced. The place of the meeting would be Munich. Who wanted to be bothered with fiction? Only reviewers were reading the stuff.

It was a strange time. Few persons of sense, and only a small group of eccentric politicians, thought that a general war could be postponed indefinitely. The trenches being dug in the parks were not just for show; and nor were the boxed gas masks. Yet almost everyone, even the bitterest of the refugees, still pretended to hope. I remember two of them in particular. One was a Prague newspaper editor named Czissar, the other a German historian, Herbert Rozinski. Both men were highly respected in their own countries; both had been marked for destruction if they fell into Gestapo hands, or the hands of the ever-increasing numbers of those who received and obeyed Gestapo orders. Czissar was a loyal Czech and a brave, intelligent editor. Rozinski had written a notable history of the German army and was an internationally acknowledged authority on the subject. It had been found, however, (God knows by whom) that there had been a Jewish element in his family; one eighth, I believe, though it may have been less. It had been enough, though, to deprive him of his university post and to turn him into the sad figure I knew.

His was a predicament I could easily understand. My brother Maurice had married a German girl whose father was the headmaster of a school at Leverkusen near Cologne and so obliged to be a member of the National Socialist party. For the marriage to be legally valid in Germany my brother had to go to Cologne and satisfy the authorities there of the Aryan purity of the Ambler blood. Birth certificates alone were of no help. Genealogical tables were requested. Certificates of baptism and confirmation and forthright letters from Church of England clergymen with unequivocally English names were the sort of back-up material they liked to see. The fact that, at the time, my brother bore a strong resemblance to a young Robert Donat was a handicap. All alien film stars were suspect, even British ones who looked Aryan.

As the tensions of the Munich days mounted, I had a letter from Betty. She said that rumours were circulating in Paris that when the war broke out (not if, when) Paris would at once be declared an open city and not be bombed. Hotel rooms there were getting scarce. Bank accounts were going to be frozen at any minute. I should think seriously about this. A few hours later a telegram from her arrived. I cannot remember now exactly what it said, but the tone was one of panic. Yves was about to be mobilized. He would need French money. She needed English money and moral support immediately.

I did not believe her about the money; she had plenty of English money and Yves had a job selling furnishing fabrics; but I had no reason for staying in London. My mother was thinking about getting married again, to Arthur Waters, and my presence would hinder rather than assist that development. I was strongly in favour of it. Besides, I wanted to get on with *Dimitrios* and I worked better in Paris. I telephoned BEA for a seat on their evening Paris flight.

They were, as always then, polite, but that time also sounded surprised. When I got to Northolt I discovered why. I was the only Paris-bound passenger. Both flights from Paris had come in with a full load. Nobody in Paris thought that the Germans would have the cheek to bomb London. Everyone in Paris thought that when Munich failed the Germans would bomb Paris first. Did I really want to go?

I did. Being the only passenger on a commercial airliner, even a noisy old Electra with loose rivets, was an experience not to be missed. During the flight, I had sandwiches and whisky-and-soda with the cabin crew. As we approached Le Bourget reports came from up front of unusual happenings. A few towns had blacked out, experimentally no doubt; most, including Paris, seemed to be showing rather more light than usual.

I found Betty in one of her wilder moods and Yves trying, foolishly, to talk sense. It was, he argued, only to be expected that rumours should be unreliable. One day you are told that Paris is an open city and not to be bombed. Clearly, that must be disbelieved. Now, two days later, Paris is said to be a prime target, *the* prime target according to some. Who can say? There are those in the cafés of the Boule Miche today who have already named the hour of the attack. It is to be at noon tomorrow. London, no doubt, would be attacked later by a second wave.

Betty and Yves were living in the Montparnasse quarter so, to be near them, I went back to the Libéria. On the following day – the final day of the Munich conference – the three of us walked to the Boulevard St-Michel in order to test the rumourmongers' prophecies.

It really was an occasion. There was no doubt that the bombing rumour had caught a lot of fancies. The cafés were packed. Then, at about ten minutes to twelve, everyone gradually drifted away from the café tables and moved out into the street to look up at the sky. We all wanted to catch a first glimpse of the huge fleet of German bombers that had been sent to destroy us and the city of Paris. Many of us there expected to be destroyed. The much-publicized bombing of Spanish cities and the belief in the omnipotence of the bombing plane that had been fostered by many respected military writers of the thirties had produced a widespread conviction that any general declaration of war would be followed by instant attack from the air against which there could be no effective defence. Films had reinforced the conviction. This was not, though, just a popular fallacy. The expectation of dreadful initial casualties from air bombardment and all the secondary consequences of such a slaughter had been calculated by thoughtful municipal authorities all over Western Europe. They were not over-imaginative; they simply believed what the aviation experts had told them. Nearly all of them over-ordered such things as body bags, coffins, stand-by generators and water-purification plants. Some were plagued for years with the problems of finding discreet bulk storage space for the coffins. Others, of course, eventually found a need for such things and were still able to use them; but at the beginning all were prepared for an apocalyptic Armageddon in the style of H.G. Wells.

That was what those of us in the Boulevard St-Michel were prepared for that September morning as we looked up into the sky. What we got, at about a minute before zero hour, was the mild drone of a solitary civilian plane. It was probably cleared for Le Bourget. All the same, it caused some excitement. The word 'reconnaissance' buzzed about. Then, as the hour became stale, people began going back into the cafés. Two hours later *Paris-Soir* had an extra edition on the streets with the news of the signing of the Munich Agreement and the first step in the dismemberment of Czechoslovakia. Everyone was much relieved. With the Nazis to help us rationalize it, we were getting used to shrugging off treachery.

As the weather was still warm I stayed on at the Libéria and worked at *Dimitrios*. Then, sometime in November, a letter came from Allan Collins asking if there was any chance of my taking a trip to New York the following year. He had heard that the American Export Line ran a regular cargo service between England and New York. They were small ships which took a few passengers along with the cargo at fairly cheap rates. I might like to inquire about them. Of course, there was no possibility of the trip being paid for by Knopf, but it was time I took a look at the New York book business and met some of those in the Knopf office who mattered, besides Alfred.

A combination of circumstances made me warm to the suggestion. I was having trouble with *Dimitrios*. I knew that I was breaking new ground with it and that only excellence on my part would be good enough. I had been trying to write too quickly. I did not need the hundred-pound advance so soon. I had film money in the bank. I had also become aware again of the Libéria's inefficient radiators. They were massive iron objects with the sort of surface floral patterns in the casting that was used in Victorian lincrusta. They did not look as if they had ever seriously been meant to work. I wrote huddled against the one in my room, but was never comfortably warm. I thought, too, of the private bathroom at the Hotel de l'Université that I had so casually abandoned. Betty and Yves were quarrelling steadily; Betty wanted to go and live in Martinique or Guadeloupe; Yves did not. Most of the patrons of the Flore had gone south to places like Fez and Marrakesh. The idea of taking ship somewhere, anywhere, suddenly became irresistible. I wrote to Allan Collins saying that I would be in New York within a few weeks. He was, I must say, thoughtful enough to write back at once to let me know that January and February were not generally considered the best months in which to visit New York for the first time; but by then I had made up my mind. There was a cargo liner, the *American Merchant*, with accommodation for sixty passengers leaving Tilbury on or about 9 January for Boston and New York.

The agents said encouragingly that there were still a few passenger vacancies. The passage time to New York was nine or ten days, the fare £30. There were no single cabins, but American Export Line ships were noted for their friendly atmosphere and the social acceptability of the passengers who used them.

All these claims were fully justified. In those days, of course, ships had no stabilizers and even the great and famous liners of the period were likely to sail in the month of January with quite a few empty state rooms. The *American Merchant* (just over 7,500 tons) sailed in January 1939 with a passenger list of about thirty. The only passengers who did not get cabins to themselves were married couples who had asked to share.

We sailed on time and after a little tumble in the Channel headed out into the Atlantic. We hit our first storm three days out, and found then that the ship had a most peculiar roll. At the port extremity of it there was a distinct pause, then a sudden and violent heave to starboard.

The passengers' public accommodation included a small bar about six feet long with bolted-down stools and a stout handrail for

144

safety. When the ship did one of its spectacular starboard rolls a dry martini not held down firmly on the bar would hurtle through the air to hit the far bulkhead high above the bar itself. The barman kept a score of the ship's achievements as a hurler of drinks with lines drawn on the bulkhead and dates pencilled in. On that trip the record was raised by no less than four inches. There were other diversions. A series of sliding chair races organized by some wild youngsters in the passenger saloon was cancelled on the captain's orders when one of the competitors received minor injuries in a collision with the piano. That had already been lashed down to ring-bolts. Thereafter, the chairs were all lashed down too. It made little difference to the passengers' comfort. All but six of us were by then badly seasick. The open decks were forbidden and meals in the dining room were occasions to be finished with as quickly and with as little spillage as possible. The bar with its anchored stools and handrail was the favoured refuge, but after a while the effort of just holding on and trying to anticipate the ship's movements became physically exhausting. Staying in one's bunk wedged in with extra life jackets was exhausting. Staying uninjured was exhausting. The only relief came one day when the wind increased to well over storm force and produced a list that made it necessary to turn the ship into the wind and heave to. In one twenty-four-hour period we covered only forty-three miles.

Our second storm was a more exhilarating affair with snow. The whole superstructure of the ship became a mass of ice, and steam jets had to be used to keep some of the deck machinery and lifeboat derricks working. We arrived in Boston five days overdue, and as we came alongside an ambulance backed up to take off our casualties. The remarkable thing was that we had none. Most of the passengers had stayed wedged in their bunks. Some of these – hungry as well as weary, no doubt – decided to leave the ship there and take a train to New York. The six of us who had relied upon the bar to keep us on our feet decided to go ashore and celebrate our aching muscles and nagging bruises.

One of the six was William Hayter, the British artist who had founded the famous Atelier 17 in Paris, and who was then on his way to teach for a while at a university in California. He wanted to see what an Ivy League university looked like so we took a taxi out to Harvard. In Cambridge, nearby, we had our first taste of American sea-food, the stuff I had always called shell-fish. We found that we were certainly hungry. The university had looked all right, comfortable rather than distinguished.

The voyage south to New York was smooth but very cold. There had been heavy snow storms in many of the Eastern states and the temperature in Manhattan the afternoon we docked was nine below. Although the streets had been cleared of snow for traffic, the last fall, frozen solid and filthy with mud, was banked up on the sidewalks. In places the banks were five feet or more high. What I knew about Manhattan then I had learned from Charles Rodda, who had worked there as a newspaper music critic before he had turned to writing thrillers. 'Let the publishers pick your hotel,' he said; 'they may feel they ought to be picking up the tab. And that way you'll know how you rate with them. The top hotel for writers when I was there last was the Algonquin. The bottom was the Barbizon-Plaza. There you never saw room service. They used to slide your breakfast to you through a flap in the door as if you were an animal in a zoo and dangerous.'

I was booked into the Lexington which he hadn't mentioned. It was old and the safety chains on the elevators made weird noises; but Allan Collins said that it had been chosen because it was near the Knopf office two blocks over on Madison. When I asked if there were not hotels even nearer on Park Avenue, Allan pretended not to have heard me and asked about money. There were royalties due to me that he could probably get paid, but what kind of money had I brought with me? Cash? You don't want to carry a lot of that about. Traveller's cheques had not then been invented. What I had was an elaborate two-part document called a letter-of-credit. Allan was pleased with my good sense and told me the name of a bank just a block from the Lexington Hotel (another plus for the old ruin) where they knew all about letters-of-credit and made no difficulties about paying out on them.

The Knopfs, both Alfred and Blanche, gave me a warm welcome. They took me to dinner at Twenty-One which still had the bottle chutes and other escape gadgets of its earlier days as a speakeasy; and they invited me for a weekend at their house in Purchase outside New York City. When they dropped me off at the Lexington ('Whose idea was it to put him in this dump?' Blanche asked) Alfred gave me a book. It was an advance copy of a first novel, he said, by an American writer from the pulps. It wasn't badly written though. The reviewers were liking it. He hoped to do as well with it as he had done with *Background to Danger*. The book he gave me was Raymond Chandler's *The Big Sleep*.

After a day or two Blanche decided that I was fit to be seen as her escort at the cocktail parties she was obliged to attend. The witch-like impression she often created on these occasions has been described in detail many times both by her friends and her enemies. However, it took me twenty years or more to discover that the claw with which she grasped your left arm when she entered a room, head up and ready to be recognized and greeted, was neither possessive nor a sort of hex on the potency of the other publishers there. It was just that she could not see where she was going and, except in her office when reading, was too vain to wear glasses. She never took to contact lenses either. However, as well as watching for steps ahead to save his own neck, and so guiding her, the escort had another duty. This was to carry Blanche's Yorkshire terrier. It was a well-trained little dog and never misbehaved with me; but I have heard of other writers who detested it and spoke of changing publishers on its account. The truth was, for me, that although escorting Blanche could sometimes become a bit of a bore, you did meet a lot of interesting people. It was a pity that most of them were publishers. Writers are interesting to them only if both profitable and available. I had more fun with a girl from the Curtis Brown office.

We began with a slight misunderstanding. She assumed, as many agents still do, that all writers want to meet all other writers. So, to set the ball rolling, she took me to a party given by Sinclair Lewis. She called him 'Red', as everyone else did, and I actually shook hands with him; but the meeting ended there; he was too drunk to say anything more than, 'What'll you drink?' I met other writers at the party, a great many probably, but never caught their names. I think I used to be too casual about writers in person, even of writers such as Lewis, whose work I greatly admired. All I can remember of him is that he had some sort of skin disease on his face or a pock-marked complexion. Very soon I asked the girl from Curtis Brown if she thought it likely that we would be given food at the party. She thought it unlikely. I asked if there was anywhere we could go where we could eat and hear jazz music at the same time. She said there sure was. Did I mind a subway ride? We left immediately.

Sinclair Lewis's apartment was somewhere up in the eighties, I think, so the subway ride to 14th Street was quite a long one. But it was worth it. The Italian food we ate was not great, but the music was. There were several restaurants on 14th Street then and it was perfectly safe to wander from one to the other and sample the music for the price of a drink at the bar or a bar-area table.*

The jazz groups playing were mostly in threes or fours and there were some great men among the musicians. In the mid-town places that winter the groups all had Hammond organs and played the new hits like 'This Can't Be Love'. On 14th Street they didn't go for Hammond organs. For the rest of my stay in New York, 14th Street was where I liked to spend my evenings, generally with the girl from CB. There were some fine piano players on the street, but my favourite among the musicians was a black drummer named Zutty Singleton. After I had been to the place where his group played (was it Nick's?) three nights running he became curious. Told that I was a British mystery writer, he gave me an auto-graphed 10 × 8 of himself. On it he said nothing about mystery writers, only that I was 'a great guy and a lover of jazz'. I valued the photograph and kept it carefully.

By the time I boarded the *American Exporter* to take me back to Tilbury Docks I had a clear idea in my mind of how I wanted to end *Dimitrios*. I told Alfred that he would have the completed type-script in a few weeks.

The interest he expressed was no more than polite. My weekend at Purchase had not been a success. Alfred was a gramophone snob with a big collection of records and a passion for Brahms. On being asked, too carelessly I thought, which of the symphonies I would like before dinner, I answered as I thought Zutty Singleton would have wanted me to; I asked for the Fifth. 'But there is no Brahms Fifth,' Alfred said and smiled kindly at my ignorance. Then, it occurred to him that I might have been gently sending him up and the smile faded. No more was said about music before dinner. To put me in my place he served a red Algerian wine with dinner and pretended he was giving us all a treat.

It was Blanche who blew that one. Their manservant was French and she used to speak to him only in French. However, he had not been warned that I might understand the language and when she asked why we were being given that plonk (*pinard*) that someone

* Most of New York City was fairly safe then. Up in Harlem, in or near big dance halls like Roseland, whites who behaved themselves and brought their own partners ran no risks.

148

had sent them for Christmas, he said simply that he was obeying Alfred's changed orders. Alfred, now flushed, defended himself by saying that in a lot of Paris bistros now they were saying that some Algerian table wines were becoming better than French.

'I've not heard that,' I said.

Alfred was quite angry now. 'Perhaps you don't go to the right places.'

'Bistro' had not yet become a vogue word; not, at least, in France. Then, it was still the word for a modest café-restaurant used by locals.

'The only bistro I've been to lately', I said, 'is next door but one to the Dôme. A lot of cab drivers use it in the evenings. There's a good *prix fixe* for six francs. The Algerian wine they serve is included in the price of the meal. It's not bad but the cab drivers still call it *pinard*.'

Alfred sulked and Blanche announced that she was going to have an early night.

The voyage back in the *Exporter* was smooth enough for writing. When I delivered *Dimitrios* to Hodders there was much pleasurable excitement. In reviewing *Cause for Alarm*, Phillip Hewitt-Myring had said in the *News Chronicle* that one more book as good would mean that he had to call me 'the best living writer of thrillers'. That was the sort of selling quotation that Hodders wanted to decorate their Yellow Jacket editions of my books. They thought that *Dimitrios* would convince him.

However, they did not like the title. I never knew exactly why. My best guess, arrived at through hints and sighs heard in Leonard Cutts' office, was that someone upstairs, a senior director possibly, had strange theories about the ill effects of certain words when they were used in titles. He knew when a word was wrong. He could not explain; it was like a second sense. 'Background' had been wrong, so was 'Coffin'. Instead of *A Coffin for Dimitrios* why not *The Mask of Dimitrios*? Would it not look and sound better? I thought not, but have never found the unexplainable second senses of higher authorities worth challenging unless one is prepared for a fight to a finish and to shed blood. Another time, perhaps. It is only fair to mention that when Warner Bros came to make a film of the book two years later, they too preferred *The Mask of* title. Another second sense at work.

Brahms' Fifth and Algerian wine handsomely forgotten, Alfred wrote me a very warm letter about *Dimitrios* and said that he intended to see that it was seriously reviewed. He liked the title I had given it and thought the change foolish. Canadian booksellers who sold both American and British books would not be pleased.

Meanwhile, Hitler had torn up the Munich Agreement and invaded Czechoslovakia. I went back to Paris where it was easier to read, without losing one's temper, about British guarantees of Polish territorial integrity. I was reading a great many French periodicals as well as the British ones and I went often to the W.H.Smith's shop on the rue de Rivoli. It had a teashop on its upper floor and I went there too. I had developed to a regrettable extent over the years the habit of listening to other people's conversations. Smith's tearoom was a first-rate listening post. Clandestine love affairs made the best listening, but there were other matters. It was at Smith's that I heard about a hotel called the Mont Thabor. It was just round the corner in the street of that name. I liked the sound of it.

I liked the look of it, too, and had a talk with the Spanish manager. He had a top-floor suite that he said I could have on a residential basis. It was an odd shape as it had recently been built into a loft space under a steeply pitched roof; but it was fresh and clean and comfortable. I moved in at once with my one suitcase and bag of books.

I mention the suitcase and the books because I was conscious of them at the time; together they were a source of satisfaction and, in a way, a conceit. They were my only possessions. So, I had little to lose. They represented a freedom I valued. If an idea looked too easy or too obviously successful I could turn my back on it and walk away without a second thought. 'If it's straightforward it probably stinks.' That was the creed I wanted always to be able to afford.

Callow? Yes, distinctly. I must, I think, be considered a late developer, and, at that stage, a totally self-absorbed one. I can remember what the manager of the Hotel Mont Thabor looked like, but I cannot remember how I met my first wife. I think John Hilliard introduced me to her in a café near the Rond Point, but I really can't be sure. Callow, and light-minded as well.

Louise Crombie had been born in Portland, Oregon, and graduated at Mills, a women's college in California. She also went to an art school. When her father died, the family moved east to New Jersey. While trying to break into the New York fashion world as an artist Louise earned her living as a jazz piano player in a sheet music store. She had married, had three children, discovered that her husband was an incurable alcoholic and divorced him. To

150

avoid paying alimony he had promptly skipped to another state. She had to earn her living again. Her mother, a teacher of languages in the New Jersey State school system, undertook to take care of the children, two girls and a boy, while Louise pursued her career as an artist.

Through the art department of one of the American second-string fashion magazines she secured accreditation as a fashion correspondent in Paris. There, she became a *croquis* artist for illustrators on American *Vogue* and *Harpers Bazaar*.

In the world of Paris high fashion the *croquis* had a curious place. The top designers, such as Balmain and Dior, were in the business of selling designs and collections of designs to foreign (mainly American) department-store buyers. The showing and buying seasons were critical times. Design copyright could be effectively protected only by total concealment. The buyers understood this; they wanted exclusivity; but they also wanted the maximum amount of fashion magazine publicity. The designers had stood firm. Photographers, who made design-pirating all too easy, would have to wait at the end of the queue. The compromise was the *croquis* artist who could be trusted. How it was decided who were the ones to be trusted I don't know. It all worked like this: the *croquis*, an annotated sketch, was sent to New York where it told the artist–illustrator all he or she needed to know about the design and colour features of a garment; the illustrator, using his or her own imagination and experience, could then give an attractive rendering of the new design. The published result was of little use to the design pirates, but it was what the fashion magazine reader wanted, an artist's impression of a new fashion. The trusted fashion photographer was a later development.

I met Louise when she was covering the big summer collections, the annual revelation of Paris fashion thinking for the year to come. It was her busiest time.

She lived in a room rented from a fiercely British spinster named Winifred Harle who ran a secretarial and translation bureau with offices in the rue Marbeuf. Miss Harle's apartment was over her offices and rather too big for only her and a cook–housekeeper. Louise fitted in nicely. Miss Harle liked her personally and had soon noted that Louise's fashion work was largely seasonal. A qualified French–English legal interpreter, Miss Harle was often employed for rogatory commissions by the American Embassy. This legal work could be time-consuming and her commercial clients would start to complain. When hard pressed she would persuade Louise to go downstairs and help out with the French staff at a typewriter or duplicating machine. My intrusions on Louise's spare time caused her inconvenience. She had a bad-tempered Sealyham named Bingo which, with a mystified smile at the old darling's strange likes and dislikes, she would let off its leash to attack me. I was frightened of the thing. The only defence I could think of was to make the suggestion that Bingo could not really be well-bred – too heavy and long in the legs. Could I really be British? I was clearly no gentleman.

When the fashion shows ended for the time being and Louise moved into the Hotel Mont Thabor with me, everything became much simpler. Louise needed a vacation, so I took her down to the Hotel Réserve at Agay on the coast between Toulon and St Raphael. It was Agay that I had used as the St Gatien setting in *Epitaph for a Spy*.

Soon after we got back to Paris Louise went to 19 rue Marbeuf to pick up a suitcase she had left with the concierge there. At least, that was the reason she gave me. She had never taken my suggestion about jealousy very seriously. Instead, she had amused me with an account of her mother's dismissive comment on first reading Radclyffe Hall's *The Well of Loneliness* – 'Oh, we don't have that sort of thing in Portland, Oregon.' It was to prove, I think, that we had not had it either in the rue Marbeuf that she went to make her peace with Win Harle.

In Agay we had talked about getting married. Rashly, over tea at the rue Marbeuf, Louise mentioned the fact and was stunned by the fury with which she was denounced by the woman she had thought of as a friend. Angered, I telephoned Miss Harle to ask for an explanation and demand apologies. She was as nice as pie, invited me to call her Win and insisted that we came and forgave her over a glass of sherry later in the week.

The sherry was the 'nutty' kind and, although the dog was leashed, Win was not. She was inclined to tipple, usually while taking Bingo for his after-tea walk. Her habit was to stop at certain cafés in the Elysée–Montaigne–Marceau triangle and have quick nips. She favoured port. At our peace conference she added to her earlier port intake by drinking most of the sherry. Soon she became bellicose. What, she snarled suddenly, was a middle-aged American divorcée with three children doing marrying an unemployed British bachelor six or seven years younger than herself?

She did not even have alimony or a settlement to fall back on. It could only end in disaster. I protested that I was not unemployed. Not only unemployed, she snapped back, but soon to be earning a private's pay in the British army. They only gave commissions to gentlemen. Unless, that is, I did a bunk to America or one of the colonies when war came and let my aging wife support me with her artistic talents. At that point Win lost control of her dentures. We thanked her for the sherry and left.

We tried to laugh it off, but not altogether successfully. Although Win Harle had no right to express views for or against our marrying, we both had families who were entitled to, and no doubt would, speak freely on the subject. Suppose that the children took a dislike to me or hated the British schools they might have to be sent to? And could I really afford to support a family? Where would we live? France? Sue and Ann, the girls, would soon be out of high school and, even if at college, mainly self-supporting, but what about Mike? And what were the chances of a war that year? The first thing, obviously, was for us to go to America so that I could meet the children and see how they felt. Would we be allowed, though unmarried, to share a cabin on a ship? Not, Louise told me decidedly, on an American ship. It had better be a French or an Italian one.

Meanwhile, we slept at the Mont Thabor, ate at the Belle Aurore and Chez Pierre and met our friends in the Ritz bar. We were in a lesser bar somewhere up the hill above the Place Blanche on the night of 24 August. That was when the devastating news came that Stalin's Russia and Hitler's Germany had signed a non-aggression pact.

The news was brought by a boy selling early editions of the next morning's papers. He sold out instantly. It was remarkable. Everyone in that bar understood immediately what the news meant. All other non-aggression pact signings had been fairly meaningless bits of pious ceremony. This one was the signal that a general European war was about to start, and very soon too; perhaps in a few days.

Getting from France to England soon became difficult. There were no more seats to be had on BEA. Probably their Electras had already been commandeered for conversion into Hudsons. Louise had work to be finished before she could leave and more clearing up to do than I had. Betty and Yves were at sea, married and *en route* to Guadeloupe. Win had announced for the benefit of her

153

clients that she was staying put. She told us that any Germans showing their noses in the rue Marbeuf would have Bingo to reckon with.* Eventually, Louise and I made a standing-room-only trip to England on the Newhaven–Dieppe ferry.

The Mask of Dimitrios had just been published and had the distinction of being made *Daily Mail* Book-of-the-Month during the week that Britain, Germany and France declared war.

Louise and I were married early in October at the Croydon Registry Office.

The immediate task for me seemed to be to make myself useful to what was by then being called The War Effort. I had long been divorced from the LRB and so could not pretend to be a trained soldier. I did an ARP First Aid course and joined a local unit based in an evacuated primary school as a stretcher bearer. At that stage, however, the only casualty we had to deal with was an elderly drunk who tripped in the blackout and broke a leg. It occurred to me that Curtis Brown, so good at doing business for me, might be able to steer me towards something more interesting. They did their best. Spencer Curtis Brown, by then head of the agency, introduced me to a Commander at the Admiralty who had something to do with organizing a force of coastal patrol boats.

The Commander and I got on splendidly. He told me about the boats' good points – wooden hulls, no trouble with magnetic mines – and about the drawbacks to the job. 'You'll be an RNVR sub and that's all,' he said; 'there'll be no promotion. Still, you might get an idea or two for a book out of it, eh? Oh, there's just one other thing. Which club are you?'

'Club?'

'Or perhaps you only crew. Spencer said you were an experienced yachtsman. I only need a name for reference.'

That was the end of that interview. The RAF man, a Wing Commander with silver hair and 1914–18 ribbons, was not even polite.

'How old do you say you are? Thirty? Look, my friend. Retreads like me are some use still because we know a bit about aeroplanes. We can't waste our time training old jossers like you, not even as air gunners. At the moment we can't even deal with all the youngsters we've got. Why don't you wait for your age group to be called up? The army'll get to you one day, never fear.'

* They did, as I shall explain later.

154

'That leaves the Ministry of Information,' Spencer said when I reported back.

'Writing advertising copy? No thanks.'

Leonard Cutts asked me to write a short story for a charity book, *The Queen's Book of the Red Cross*, and the old shiny-paper *Sketch* commissioned a series of short detective stories. I called the series *The Intrusions of Dr Czissar*. Dr Czissar was my detective, though as I described him he looked more like Rozinski. It was a sort of hand wave to them. I did not know where either was by then, and questions about important refugees were no longer being answered. I also started writing *Journey into Fear*.

While I was writing, Louise was trying to get a sea passage to the United States. It seemed likely that the phony war would sooner or later turn into a real one and certain that her place at that moment was with her children. I persuaded her in the end to get a British passport. The American Congress had passed a neutrality act with a provision in it that made it illegal for American citizens to travel on ships belonging to any of the belligerent nations. Most of the passenger-carrying ships then crossing the Atlantic were flying belligerent flags. She might get to New York with an American passport on an Italian ship via Genoa or one one of the 'mercy', or refugee, ships like the *Gripsholm*, but she would have to wait months. And how long was Italy going to stay neutral? She was entitled to a British passport, so why not get one and try for a belligerent passage?

Although I did the usual obsessional rewriting on it, *Journey into Fear* went very quickly. The typing bureau in Oxford Street that I had always used before was found to be still in business. I delivered the book to Hodders in time for their 1940 Spring list. In the same week Louise was told that she could have a passage on a boat leaving in March. All she had to do now was to get an exit visa. For her there was no difficulty about that; lots of married women were joining their children in America just then; but when she asked why I could not go too, there had to be some plain speaking. Rude bastards in the RAF might sneer, but men of my age, and older, would eventually be needed by the services before the thing was finished. I did not intend to be unavailable when called.

Spencer was consulted again. From someone in the Ministry of Labour he found that my age group would not be called for its preliminary medical for another four or five months. On the other hand, only the Foreign Office or the Ministry of Information's

American section could give me an exit visa. Forget the Foreign Office. However, plenty of authors were doing lecture tours abroad for the MoI. One had to admit that none of them so far had been thriller writers; but I had one thing in my favour: I was becoming a substantial dollar earner and could prove it.

I have forgotten the civil servant who began the interview at the MoI, but not the man with a Scottish accent who wandered in from another office. I was not introduced to him. The civil servant asked the easy questions.

'How long would you want to go for?'

'Two months.'

'Returning May or June?'

'About then. I suppose there would be no difficulty about getting back.'

'You'd find that the British Consul-General's office in New York would arrange all that. You'd be paying all your own expenses, of course.'

'Oh yes.'

The man from the other office had been standing there reading my application form and letter. Suddenly, he took over the interview.

'Who's your publisher there?' he asked.

'Knopf.'

'Ah. Where would you want to go after New York? California? That's where the money for writers is, wouldn't you say?' He spoke very rapidly; the words tumbled out. The speed and the accent together made him hard to understand.

'I don't know much about California. The place I'm asking permission to go to for a few weeks is New Jersey.'

'Where in New Jersey?'

'Nutley.'

'It's a nice little place. Suburban. Near Passaic. You say you could give talks to local groups. What sort of groups?'

'The Garden Club there has been mentioned as a possibility. I'm afraid it doesn't sound very exciting.'

'Other things could be arranged. Do you know what a Lions Club is?'

'Something like the Rotarians?'

'There are differences. How would you answer a bloody-minded American Rotarian who wants to know when Britain is going to repay her debt to America incurred during the Great War?'

'I think I'd dodge the question if I could. At the moment we're paying cash for the supplies we need to fight with. If our cash runs out the United States will have to think of their own interests. Who do they want to win? Hitler and Stalin, who signed a non-aggression pact before carving up Poland, or America's traditional allies?'

He gave me a sidelong look. 'Whose leading article did you pinch that from?'

'I think it was the *News Chronicle.*'

He put my application back on the first interviewer's desk. 'I shouldn't think he'd do us any harm,' he said.

With a farewell nod to me he turned away to talk extra rapidly to another man who had just put his head round the door to the passage. I tried to catch what he was saying – something nasty about a Chicago newspaper – but it was too Scottish and fast for me.

'Have you got your passport with you?' asked the civil servant patiently.

The man who had interviewed me so briskly was the historian Denis Brogan, a Fellow of Peterhouse and Professor of Political Science at Cambridge. It was towards the end of the war, four years later, that we met again. Then, he was able to help me in a different way and we became friends. He never remembered the MoI interview and I never thought to remind him of it.

Security was fairly strict. Two or three days before the sailing we were told to go to Liverpool and be at Dock so-and-so, Shed such-and-such early in the morning of a particular day. When we got there it seemed that about two thousand other people had had the same orders. Many of them, we soon found, were customs and security personnel. They worked hard. They thoroughly searched every piece of baggage, they searched pockets, they counted money and they even read letters. Since many of those sailing spoke poor English and had letters in other languages, the process was slow. The ship was one of the smaller Cunarders but it took all day for us to board her. She was an efficient ship. Although fast enough not to travel in convoy she took no chances. The lifeboat drills were serious affairs and we carried life jackets with us at all times. During submarine alerts we zigzagged and had the lifeboats swung out and partly lowered. In spite of this, we docked on time in Hoboken.

Molly and Don Stoddard, Louise's sister and brother-in-law

with whom we stayed in Nutley, could not have been kinder. Louise's mother was trusting enough to let me drive her car. The children found me, I think, an interesting novelty. The office of the British Consul-General in New York was extremely helpful and I gave a number of talks to friendly groups. They seemed friendly, anyway. Knopf was doing well with *Dimitrios*. The *Saturday Review* had described it as a 'masterpiece', a description, Alfred said, that they awarded sparingly, only once in ten years or so.

However, the news from Europe was becoming terrible. On the weekend after Paris had been declared an open city and the French government had moved to Bordeaux, Louise and I were at the Knopf house in Purchase. The French servants and Blanche were in deep mourning and there were several outbursts of un-restrained weeping. I recall an awful moment when the man-servant, in the act of choking back a sob, dropped a cup of hot consommé on his feet. He let out a cry and fled. Blanche took to her bed. Alfred got out the brandy.

On Monday I went to the Consulate-General and suggested that I should get back to England at the earliest possible moment. They agreed. No problem. They were used to repatriating merchant seamen. I could go with the next party. They would add my name to the list and let me know when and where to report.

I sailed, with a very mixed cargo and only sixteen fellow passen-gers, two weeks later on the liner *Georgic*. Louise and Molly drove me to the dock, but neither of them was allowed near the ship. The American dock police were sympathetic, but I was the only one with a pass. It made sense, didn't it? If I was going on the ship I wouldn't be trying to sabotage it, would I? It was a dismal parting.

The only thing I had to cheer me when I got back to England was the news that my books had not lost their knack of appearing before the public at the most inauspicious moments. *Journey into Fear* was the *Evening Standard* Book-of-the-Month for July 1940, the month in which the Third French Republic ceased to exist and the Battle of Britain began.

NINE

The army interviewing officer did his best to be helpful, but I was a bit of a problem.

'Writer,' he said thoughtfully as he stared at the form I had filled in. 'You don't by any chance mean underwriter or some kind of legal writer, like writer to the signet?'

'No, sir. I write books, novels, detective stories mostly.' I had found that with persons who did not read much detective stories were more respectable than thrillers.

He scratched his head; he was suffering from dandruff as well as perplexity. 'But is there anything you can actually *do*?' he asked plaintively.

'Well, as I told you, I can fire and take care of an army rifle.'

'But you can't remember your Territorial Army number.'

'It's over ten years ago since I had to, but surely there would be army records . . .'

'Oh, we can't start applying to War Office records without a number. It would take months and they're terribly overworked. Let's try again, shall we? Can you by any chance drive a car?'

'Yes.'

'Ah. Mind if I have a look at your licence?'

A few weeks later I went into the army. My first posting was to a Royal Artillery Driver Training Regiment stationed in Blackpool. There were about two hundred of us in that intake. Most had been employed in Civvy Street as lorry or van drivers, though there were a few London taxi men too. Among the amateurs, with me, were a Savoy Hotel waiter who had dreams of becoming a Rolls Royce chauffeur and a crane driver who had got in with us through a clerical error. He had never driven any sort of road vehicle except, for short distances, his father's horse-drawn cart. The thing we had in common was that we all came from the London area and were somewhat relieved to be getting away from it. The relief, of course, was strongly spiced with guilty thoughts of loved ones left behind. All the same, it was safer in Blackpool; and the air was better, too. At the beginning of the night blitz, I had been conscious of a mild sense of achievement when, in the early hours of the morning, the sirens wailed the All Clear. We had survived, some of us, to live another day. As the nights grew longer and the blankets and stretchers in our blacked-out, gas-tight First Aid post became smellier, I had begun to look forward to the army.

I had another, special and rather extraordinary reason for feeling guilty.

A year earlier, I had been sent by a man I had known in the advertising world a copy of a newly published first novel. With it had come a cheery message to the effect that my success as a thriller writer had inspired him to follow in my footsteps. He asked me to recommend a literary agent. I had written back recommending Curtis Brown, but without first reading the published book he had sent. When I did eventually read it I received a shock. It was a word-for-word plagiarism of *Background to Danger* with the names of the characters and other proper names changed. There were also a few transpositions and cuts. Most of it was directly copied.

I liked the man and was upset, so took the problem to John Green at Curtis Brown. He read a few pages and said, 'Oh, Lord, I'd better check.' My advertising friend had taken my advice about Curtis Brown and sent them the typescript of his new novel. It was out with a reader. Two days later John reported that the new novel was a full-scale borrowing of *Cause for Alarm* under a new title. He could stop that going any further, but Hodders would have to be alerted about the published plagiarism. Hodders acted promptly and discreetly. Fortunately, the other publishers concerned were responsible people. They immediately withdrew all copies of the offending book.

The author of it, in the service dress of a lieutenant RA with gleaming buttons and Sam Browne belt, was among the first officers I encountered in the drivers' training regiment at Blackpool. He had been a Territorial officer and was now in charge of a group of instructors.

He was very, he was dreadfully, pleased to see me again; and he was kind. When he was duty officer, alone in the orderly room and bored, he would send a message for me to report to him. Then we would have a chat about old times, the ones in advertising.

The Royal Artillery shared Blackpool with the Royal Air Force. They had a basic training establishment north of the Tower; we were billeted, in several acres of backstreet digs and boarding houses, south of it. The gunners of B troop occupied one side of a street of terrace houses, seven or eight to each house. The landlady of the house I was in allowed us to get hot shaving water from the kitchen where she also gave us a cooked breakfast. All the land-ladies had army ration books for us, of course. Their husbands sometimes helped with the washing up, but not often. We got on well with our landlady who was a widow.

Although we did not know it at the time, the driver training units were of some importance. In 1939, the British were still for the most part a nation of public-transport users; and in all three services there was a serious shortage of competent drivers. For an army trying to mechanize itself and to field motorized divisions the shortage was acute.

The idea of the driver training unit when I joined was not to teach men to drive, but to give men who could already drive and maintain heavy goods and other commercial vehicles a course of basic military training. At the same time, they would be taught map-reading and army written-signal procedures. They would also be introduced to at least some of the trucks, vans and gun-trac-tors they would meet with in artillery units. Some men would also be trained as motor cyclists capable of military convoy control and liaison with mobile field force units.

It should have worked. Some of it did work. By the end of three months most of our intake could march smartly, salute an officer, perform simple parade ground manoeuvres – our parade ground was the South Pier – and clean its webbing equipment. A few of us could translate the numbers of a map reference and then orient the map so that we could drive straight to the right place. A few, not necessarily the same few, could drive a gun-tractor and knew how to use the winch on it. One or two were able, using the most exquisite double-declutching, to change gears fairly quietly on a Guy 15 cwt truck. Only a very few could get into an unfamiliar truck and drive it well immediately. They rarely became drivers. They were usually sent off on courses to become driver-mechanics. The drivers from our sort of training regiment who reached the batteries which needed good and versatile drivers were often said by transport officers to be untrained. As the supply of experienced civilian drivers dwindled the situation naturally became worse.

The worst of our lot were, I regret to say, the London taxi drivers. I regret to say it because most of them were good company and

161

easy to live with in billets. The trouble was that the peculiar skill required to drive a London cab of the period appeared not to be transferable to any other kind of motor vehicle. Deprived of their cabs, the taxi men seemed to lose their road sense. It was not simply that the steering locks on army vehicles did not permit U-turns on narrow streets; everything became difficult; they seemed unable to adapt. Bert, an experienced lorry driver with whom I was billeted, put it down to bloodymindedness.

'They don't *want* to do it right,' he said; 'they're playing silly buggers. They'd better watch it, or they'll get posted to the machine gunners.'

In a way I saw what he meant; a Guy 15 cwt was a horrible vehicle with arthritic steering and the world's worst crunch-and-crash gearbox; it invited one to play silly buggers if by doing so one could avoid having to drive it. On the other hand, I could have reminded Bert that, on first being invited by the bombardier in charge to drive a Bedford army truck, he had pursed his lips doubtfully and said that he didn't know anything about Bedfords; he was used to Commers. The bombardier had told him to stop playing silly buggers and get moving and Bert had done so; but, of course, he had done so efficiently, not like the taxi drivers who stalled their engines and made simple left turns from the wrong side of the road as if, Bert said, they were towing trailers a mile long behind them. Bert took pride in his work. Oddly, he thought of himself always as much older than he really was.

'I shouldn't be here,' he told us one day; 'a man my age with a wife and kids, it's ridiculous.' When a quick check showed him to be the youngest of the eight of us he was unimpressed. 'I've got responsibilities,' he said.

His fear of transfer to the 'machine-gunners' and the barrack-room adages he was always quoting – never volunteer for anything, looking an officer in the eye is dumb insolence, bullshit baffles brains – had clearly been learned at his father's knee. However, he could invent his own if he felt it necessary. When I was picked for motor cycle training Bert set out at once to discourage me.

'Know what you've done, mate? You've joined the suicide club. Didn't you know that it's the Don R's, the poor bloody motorbike boys, that the machine-gunners always pick on first?'

'You mean it's safer to be a machine-gunner?'

'Safer? If you don't mind being the most hated thing on the

battlefield, if you don't mind being straffed and mortared until you're silenced for good, it's as safe as houses. Don't make me laugh, mate. None of it's safe. It's all bloody dangerous. That's why you should never volunteer.'

'I didn't volunteer. I was picked.'

He knew that this was an evasion and dropped the subject with a snort of disgust. Everyone knew that riding motor cycles was more dangerous than driving and that you didn't get picked for it if you played your cards right. I could only have been stupid.

Sergeant Easton, the former film stunt man who was in charge of motor cycle training, was tall, skinny and bursting with energy. His battledress trousers flapped as he walked and in a high wind he looked like an animated scarecrow. He communicated enthusiasm and he had a way with him. When he needed new blood he would go along the ranks asking each man individually if he could ride a motorbike. When he asked me, I was bored with driving trucks along the road to Southport. I said that I could ride.

That was stretching the truth a lot. When we had left school, Sims' father had bought him a 250 cc machine as a present. I had been deeply envious and had begged to be allowed to try it. Very reluctantly, Sims had let me ride three times up and down the street outside their house. That was the whole extent of my experience solo. The machine that I had ridden to London on the first day of the General Strike had had a sidecar.

Those on Sergeant Easton's list were ordered to report to the motor cycle section garage that afternoon. He received us wearing a leather jerkin and a balaclava helmet as well as a woollen cap. When we all stood before him in the garage he addressed us briefly.

'You all say you can ride. Well, we'll see. All you have to do is follow me in single file. No riding two abreast. The weather's not very good so we won't be going fast or far. If you've got your gloves with you I'd advise you to wear them. Goggles will be issued to those who need them later on, not today. There are ten of you. Beside me here are ten bikes. They're all the same and easy to start. Don't start up in the garage. Wheel them out to the street. Then start up and wait for me. Watch for my hand signals.'

The weather that day was awful. There was an on-shore gale and it was blowing a mixture of rain, sleet and sea-spray. It was bitterly cold. The bikes were all 500 cc BSAs painted WD green like our trucks. Mine started on the second kick. I had just managed to discover which lever was the clutch when Sergeant Easton rode out of the garage and took station in front of us.

With a wave of his arm he signalled to us to follow him and immediately rode off.

Three of us were left standing. I was still trying to guess which was first gear and remember Sims' bike. That had been a BSA. Perhaps they would be the same. Somehow I found first and got going. By the time I caught up with the leaders, though, they were strung out along the sea front and on very slippery cobbles. I was still in first gear. Greatly daring, I managed to change up.

Sergeant Easton had said that he would go slowly, but he was going much too fast for my liking. The wind and rain made it difficult to see. At about the same time that I remembered that I had not investigated the brakes, the man in front of me did so and went into a terrifying skid. He recovered but dropped back, clearly shaken. I resolved that, if I could think of a way of doing so safely, I would drop back too. Sergeant Easton, I had decided, was raving mad.

We were outside Blackpool and on the road to Lytham St Annes that used to run straight along there for a mile or so with only an area of sand dunes on the left, when he suddenly slowed. I knew the dunes slightly. There was a single track over them that the gun tractor people used when they wanted to practise winching a ditched vehicle.

Sergeant Easton, however, was not interested in tracks. He had slowed to a walking pace. I was about a hundred yards behind him when he raised his left arm and pointed to the dunes. Then, with another cry of 'Follow me', he turned sharp left off the road and dropped out of sight.

I saw the man behind him hesitate, put his feet to the ground and then, paddling gingerly, turn to follow. At the edge of the soft shoulder of the road he looked down at the dune below and stopped. The man behind him did not stop. He disappeared too. Then it was my turn.

There was an almost vertical drop off the road into the dunes of about fourteen feet. It was frightening and I knew that if I thought about it I would ignore Sergeant Easton down below yelling 'Come on, it's easy', and stay where I was upon the road. So I went on.

All that happened when I got to the bottom was that I immediately swooped up the dune beyond and got stuck in the same soft sand as the man before me.

'Don't try to ride it out,' yelled Easton: 'you have to lift it out. I'll show you in a minute. Come on! Don't dither.'

The last bits were addressed to the next man upon the road peering down in his turn.

Of the ten who had started, two retired before they reached the sand dunes. They returned to the garage wheeling their bikes. The three who had hesitated too long on the road were told, quite kindly, to ride in single file back to the garage. The five of us on the dunes were then given our first training session by Easton. He led, we followed. When we got stuck in the sand, he showed us how to lift the back wheel out of it without rupturing ourselves. He would tolerate no excuses or refusals. If you got stuck, you got yourself unstuck and tried again. If you tried to avoid the steep bits with grassy overhangs at the top, you also tried again.

'If the bike's really going to turn over and roll back on you,' he said, 'you'll have plenty of time to roll sideways out of the way. We're on sand so you can't hurt yourself too badly here. If you have confidence and do it right you won't hurt the bike either. Why are we doing it? I'll tell you. Tanks and guns don't stick to the roads. If they do they're sitting ducks for low flying attacks from the air. So, where the tanks and guns go we have to learn to go too, if we're to keep in touch. Where we can, we must go as the crow flies.'

What he was training us for has now become a rather unattractive sport called 'motor-cross'. However, we had no carefully surveyed and taped circuits to ride around or machines specially designed for that purpose only. The 500 cc BSA with its slow-revving four-stroke engine and ponderous frame could not have been more unsuitable for cross-country work. When we got off the sand dunes and took to the wilds up on places like Garston Moor, the difficulties were multiplied. Going by motor cycle as the crow flies proved to be more arduous than it had sounded, even with the best maps: and errors of judgement – such as a decision to ride boldly through heather – could lead to extremes of exhaustion not soon or easily forgotten.

As the time for my posting away from Blackpool came nearer, Sergeant Easton asked me if I would like to stay on with him as an instructor. It would not be for long, he said, because he happened to know that my name had gone forward for an officer selection board; but a month or two as an instructor was better than a temporary posting to some God-forsaken ack-ack battery as a driver or motor cyclist. I would also be promoted to acting, unpaid lance-bombardier, which would help me when I went up for the interview.

I said that I would like to stay and was duly authorized in battery orders to put up one stripe. It was the cause of the only real telling-off I had while in the army. This arose from the fact that, until then, our billet had had no NCO in charge of it. When I was promoted it acquired one. I was unwise enough to regard this as an unimportant technicality.

Sergeant Mills, our troop sergeant, was a regular army reservist who had been a coal heaver in civilian life. He was a stern man but a fair and decent one, rather like Uncle Sidney. I had liked and got on well with him. However, the week before the general posting away, when the whole of our intake would be dispersed to make room for a new lot of recruits, was a busy one for him. Every man posted to another unit must arrive at it with every piece of army issue property accounted for and all his records correct and complete. Inevitably, there would be odds and ends of unfinished business. The battery office was understaffed and overworked. Sergeant Mills liked to help out.

It was to ask whether one of the gunners in our billet had yet received by post the doctor's certificate necessary to support his claim for a dependant's allowance that the Sergeant walked into our billet one afternoon. It was just after high tea. In the hall he encountered Bert.

'Where's the Bombardier?' the Sergeant asked.

By way of reply Bert shouted up the stairs in the general direction of my room: 'Hey, Eric, the Sergeant wants you.'

I clattered down the stairs to find the Sergeant standing, pink with fury, on the pavement outside.

'Sergeant?'

He motioned me away from the billet with a jerk of his head. When we were out of earshot, he turned.

'Stand to attention when you address me, Bombardier.'

I stood to attention.

'Now then.' He pointed to the stripe on my arm. 'What's that?'

'Stripe, Sergeant.'

'Do you want to keep it?'

I found that I did. 'Yes, Sergeant.'

'Then see that it's treated with proper respect. That gunner I spoke to, you've got on well with him, eh? He's one of your pals.'

'Yes, Sergeant.'

'Not any longer he isn't. He's a gunner and you're the NCO in charge. You remember that. It's not an NCO's business to be a nice chap or a pal. I've got sharp ears and I listen. When I hear gunners talking among themselves and they say "that bastard" about an NCO, I know I've got a good one. Next time I walk into that billet and a gunner calls you down, I don't want to hear any "Hoy Erics" or any other familiarity. I want to hear him address you smartly and in a respectful manner as bombardier. Got it?'

'Yes, Sergeant.'

'Right, we'll go back. It's about this gunner of yours who's claiming a dependant's allowance for his bedridden old Dad. He'll have to do better than a letter from his married sister. It'll have to be a chit from the Welfare or a doctor's certificate.'

My mother forwarded a cable from Curtis Brown, New York, saying that Warner Bros wanted to buy the movie rights of *Background to Danger* and *A Coffin for Dimitrios*. They offered three thousand dollars for each book. Swanson, their Hollywood sub-agent, advised me to accept.

I sent a cable doing so. I was sure that Allan Collins would have the sense to see that the bulk of the money went to Louise. Even so, there would be some for me. I was possibly the richest Lance Bombardier in the regiment. With my friend Bombardier Harrington, who was the map-reading and signals instructor, I celebrated by dining at the Tower restaurant, which still had a very good cellar, and ordering a bottle of Clos de Vougeot. We got hostile looks from some officers at another table but confidently ignored them. In civilian life Harrington had held an administrative post at the Staff College, Camberley. He would accept disapproval only from very senior officers.

Sergeant Easton's request for an extra instructor had been made in anticipation of a need. The next intake contained very few men who could ride motor cycles and even fewer willing, as I had been, to pretend to ride while they were learning to do so. Easton decided that, to save time, all who offered themselves as potential riders should be given an hour or two to get used to the bikes, and to be unobtrusively assessed, before they were introduced to the dunes. He called it 'the beginners' class' and turned it over to me.

With my own experience in mind, I would first identify all the controls on the machine. Then, when the tide was out, I would take the class down on to the sands by the pier to do sedate figure-eights in line ahead. When I raised my arm we would all remember where the clutch was and change up.

It should have been pleasant, easy work, and a bit boring. I never really had a chance to find out. I was doing figure-eights with a new class one day when, suddenly, one of the class broke out of formation, shot away up the sands, did a skid turn and then broadsided neatly to return to his place in the line. I rode over to him.

'What the hell do you think you're playing at?' I asked. 'Why didn't you say you could ride?'

'Nobody asked me, Bomb,' he replied blandly.

At the break I asked him what kind of bike he normally rode.

'Specials.'

'For racing, you mean?'

'No, Bomb, that's a mug's game. The glittery sort. You wear a shirt with sequins. Fairs and that. I did two years on the Wall o' Death.'

Sergeant Easton insisted that the Wall of Death was simple trick riding and that any fool could do it. He never took to the man who had confessed to sequined shirts and glittery bikes. He called him a show-off and complained – a much more serious charge – that his map-reading was unreliable. Before long, the beginners' class was cancelled and we went back to trial by ordeal on the dunes. One day in February I was summoned to go before an officer selection board at a Preston barracks.

This was before the more serious and searching officer selection process, with aptitude testing and psychiatric interviews, had been introduced. All I had to contend with was a row of officers, plainly regulars, sitting at a blanket-covered trestle table as if ready for a courtmartial. The senior officer, and the only one who actually spoke, was a very courteous brigadier.

They all looked at my gleaming boots, the crease in my battledress trousers and at my sleeves with one stripe on them. So far so good. The report on me from my commanding officer was encouraging, the brigadier said, and passed it along to the others. He asked about my maths at school. How had my trig been? How was it now? Rusty? Well, no doubt I could soon put that right. Only one thing remained to trouble him.

'I see that in Civvy Street you write novels, Bombardier.'

'Yes, sir.'

'What sort of novels?'

'Detective stories, sir.'

He smiled. 'Ah. Make a good living at it?'

'Pretty good, sir.'

'What do you call pretty good?'

They were all looking at me intently now. How much I earned was the crunch question. Was a writer fit to be seated in an officers' mess or was he not? The lowest rank at the table was captain. I framed my answer with that in mind. 'About fifteen hundred a year, sir.'

There was an appreciative murmur. Nothing long-haired or scruffy about fifteen hundred a year. I was asked no more questions. Three weeks later I was posted to the Royal Artillery OCTU (Officer Cadet Training Unit) at Llandrindod Wells.

It took five months then to make an AA gunnery officer out of a cadet and five months were not really sufficient. The guns and fire control equipment that concerned us were the 3.7-inch 'heavy' with the Vickers predictor and the 40 mm Bofors which could be aimed either by the Kerrison predictor through a system of oil motors or manually. Both these predictors were highly ingenious analogue computers; both were exceedingly cumbersome. The Bofors gun was more effective in the field against low-flying attacks when it was controlled by gunlayers and a cleverly designed manual sight known as a Stiffkey stick. No matter: we still had to know all about the Kerrison predictor. There was also much to learn about the nature of propellants and high explosives, about a mysterious secret thing then called RDF (radar) and about the need for such things as fuse factors. There was also a series of ballets that had to be endlessly rehearsed. They were known collectively as gun drill and the place of their performance was known as the gun park. On the gun park cadets were not allowed to walk; unless they were being paraded by the Guards officer who supervised drill, they could only move at the double. Drill was supervised because cadets were usually giving the orders. We took it in turns to be the troop sergeants and battery sergeant-majors of the day. The instructors were all officers or warrant officers, except those who took PT; they were sergeants, some with very nasty dispositions. The atmosphere was competitive and inter-troop rivalries were encouraged. To add to the pressure there were monthly examinations, written and oral. Cadets could be called upon to give impromptu lectures. Up to the third month of the course any failure could mean that the cadet was automatically RTU'd, or Returned To his Unit. In practice, this meant being returned to a depot as a gunner. Since most cadets had arrived as NCOs and taken stripes off to become cadets, this was punishment as well as disgrace. No one from our troop had to suffer, but we were constantly aware of the threat. We learned zealously to write military appreciations in the standard military way, we went on fatuous TEWTs (Tactical Exercises Without Troops) and mounted spit-and-polish guards with spotless rifles but no ammunition. We became, almost permanently, weary and short-tempered. The course, we were told, was designed to test as well as teach us. It probably succeeded.

There was a pleasant side. Victor Canning was in the same troop as I was. On Saturday nights, duty permitting, we would go to the local repertory theatre and on Sunday nights to the cinema. In both places, of course, we could sit down. I cannot recall our ever going into a pub for a drink where one had to stand at the bar. On weekday nights, if not on duty or cramming or cleaning equipment, one went to bed early.

In the third month I had a letter from Louise that troubled me. Curtis Brown had sent her none of the Warner Bros money. When she had asked Allan Collins about it he had said that Curtis Brown, New York, was affiliated to its parent company in London. Although he was American, he had to go along with UK exchange control regulations which said that all dollars held for the account of UK citizens must be remitted to the UK. I wrote to Allan asking him to think again and to my bank manager seeking advice. To the bank manager I also pointed out that, because she was outside the sterling area, my wife was not even receiving the army marriage allowance to which she was entitled. He wrote back sympathetically but could suggest no way round any of my difficulties.

Then, Allan Collins cabled to say that RKO wanted to buy the movie rights of *Journey into Fear* for Orson Welles. He would make it with Mercury Theatre players. I had earlier given Ben Hecht, who had wanted to make a play of the book, the dramatic rights, but RKO would buy him off by letting him do a screenplay. Orson Welles was the man who counted. RKO would pay me twenty thousand dollars. Swanson advised acceptance.

I cabled back accepting, but then did something foolish. In the cable I asked Allan to lend me ten thousand dollars, give them to Louise and with RKO's twenty thousand buy British Government bonds to hold as collateral for the loan. Surely that would have the same ultimate effect as remitting the twenty thousand by cheque to the UK.

The censor picked up my cable. Within twenty-four hours, I was in deep trouble. From the censor the cable had gone to the Bank of England Exchange Control people. What I had proposed to Curtis Brown, New York, it seemed, was a criminal offence, and a very serious one. Had I not been in the army and a potential officer, the Bank thundered, there would have been a prosecution. As it was, I would report to their nearest representative to receive an official reprimand and sign a document stating that I understood the enormity of what I had tried to do.

The representative nominated was a local Barclays bank manager; and, although he solemnly read out the official wigging and I had to acknowledge the reading with a signature, he, too, was sympathetic. So was my OCTU Battery Commander who had to give me permission to miss a lecture in order to be reprimanded at the ordained time. 'Lot of bloody nonsense,' he said. 'What you need is someone in the Merchant Navy who'll post a little parcel to your wife in the States. The Liverpool convoys are going there all the time.'

I could have pointed out that what he was proposing – bulk currency smuggling – was infinitely more serious than the offence for which I was being reprimanded and would probably carry a gaol sentence for the one caught. All I said was that it would be difficult to get to know a suitable Merchant Navy person well enough in Llandrindod Wells. He agreed, but looked disappointed. I have noticed over the years that exchange controls have the same effect on some people as exorbitant taxes; they inspire an instant determination to avoid or evade.

At the end of the fourth month our battery was told that it would be fairly safe for us to order our officer uniforms; and we duly submitted ourselves and our bank balances to the London tailors and bootmakers who awaited us with polite smiles in temporary premises along the High Street. The last month seemed the longest. There were no disastrous failures but one or two of the PT instructors became strangely vindictive. In one case we may have given the man cause. He was a joker with a tiresome line of patter at which we had been laughing dutifully for months. Then, there came a day when our troop stopped laughing. There was no consultation between us. He was never discussed; but, suddenly and spontaneously, we were all of the same mind. We still obeyed his orders, but with our silence we gave his act the bird. He became white with anger and had us doing knees-up-running-on-the-spot for almost twenty minutes without a break. We were all very fit indeed or we could not have kept it up. His only hope was to tire one of us into insubordination or, better still, insolence. Failing to do so, he tried teasing us with obscure threats. What was the matter with us today? Were we perhaps already thinking of ourselves as officers and temporary gentlemen? Well, we might be in for some unpleasant surprises. Jumping on the spot – begin! Higher. HIGHER! We obeyed and kept on obeying. In the end he had to let us go to change for a lecture. We had PT every day except Sunday, but never again with him in charge. The other PT instructors seemed to have heard of our slightly browned-off state of mind and behaved sensibly.

After the passing-out parade, the issue of officers' identity cards and the change of uniform, we were given two weeks leave. I spent mine going to the theatre and seeing old friends.

I was dining with Spencer and Jean Curtis Brown at the Café Royal when I was introduced to Sidney Box, the film producer. He asked me what I was doing and told me about an army film production unit that was being organized by Thorold Dickinson to make training films of quality. Most of the existing training films were so badly written and directed that they defeated their own purpose by boring, and so antagonizing, their audiences.

I knew what he meant; I had been obliged to sit through the kind of films he was talking about. The problem, he said, began with the script. Filmed instruction manuals were never going to be any good. Would I have any objection to giving him my army number so that he could pass it on to Thorold?

I gave him the number, though I did not think that it would be very much use to him. He was a civilian; so, I assumed, was Thorold Dickinson. The army had just taken a lot of trouble training me to become an artillery officer, and that, surely, was how they meant to employ me. Indeed, I already had my posting. It was to a Light AA Regiment then stationed in the West Country. The battery headquarters to which I eventually reported was at Wareham in Dorset.

A Light AA battery then consisted of three troops, each with four Bofors guns, and an HQ troop. There were two subalterns to a troop and, at headquarters, a major, who was the battery commander, a battery captain, who was second-in-command, and a subaltern who was transport officer, messing officer and the keeper of battery accounts. These included the imprest account which held government money for paying the troops and was a grave responsibility. At OCTU we had been given two short talks on the keeping of army accounts and the strange systems of double-entry book-keeping that the army insisted upon. The officer who had given these talks had concluded by advising us to rely, when in doubt, on our artillery clerks to see us through.

It was my experience with transport that landed me with the HQ job. When I joined, all our guns were deployed on static sites to protect the Royal Naval Cordite Factory at Wareham. Though built mostly below ground, the factory was a tempting target for hit-and-run attacks by the Luftwaffe from their airfields just across the Channel. The Regiment to which we belonged was an established Territorial unit with several middle-aged senior officers and strong West Country associations, and from the start of the war it had been a part of AA Command.

Now, for our particular battery, all this suddenly changed. We were taken out of AA Command and placed, for special duty, under direct War Office control. The duty in question was to protect the Prime Minister against enemy low-flying attacks when he was outside London, either at Chequers, near Wendover, or at Chartwell, his own country house near Westerham. We were to take over the guns and basic transport of a battery which had been stationed at Chequers and to make ourselves fully mobile like a field-force unit. With dozens of brand-new vehicles, from gun tractors to water tankers, and not enough trustworthy drivers, I was kept busy.

Battery headquarters were in a commandeered house on the other side of Coombe Hill just by Chequers. On top of nearby Beacon Hill there was an RAF radar hut to give us early warning of approaching enemy aircraft. There was also a company of infantry to mount guards and to patrol the Chequers grounds. We had private lines to the radar hut and to the infantry as well as to Chequers itself. After some initial confusion – the Prime Minister's personal assistant and his personal Scotland Yard bodyguard were both named Thompson – we settled in fairly quickly. There was only a little bother over our standing orders.

Someone at the War Office had taken a lot of trouble over them. We had a suspicion that the same man had decided where our guns should be sited. It is safe to say, I think, that if we had been subjected to a low-flying attack none of the eight guns we deployed there would have been of the slightest use.* One, indeed, was sited on a lawn outside the house and had a total field of fire between two tall trees of less than five degrees. The gun had to be placed there, we soon realized, so that Mr Churchill, out for a Sunday morning stroll with a distinguished weekend guest, could show it off and air his knowledge of such things as muzzle velocities; but the other sites were very little better. As, however, there was a standing order saying that we were on no account to open fire unless we were certain of hitting an attacking aircraft and bringing it down, the siting of our guns did not really matter. If he has to be absolutely certain of both hitting and destroying a target as elusive as a low-flying fighter-bomber, no gunner in his right mind is ever going to open fire.

There was also a standing order which said that when an enemy aircraft came within twenty miles of Chequers those responsible for the Prime Minister's personal security must at once be informed. This was so that he could proceed immediately to the safety of the Chequers air raid shelter.

Both Commander Thompson and the Scotland Yard man advised us to ignore the order. Chequers was in the southeast quarter of the country and enemy aircraft could often come within twenty miles of it on their way to other targets. It was explained that the Prime Minister himself, though familiar with the order, always ignored it. Our battery commander, youngish, handsome but only fairly bold, decided to go by the book. Next time the RAF radar reported an enemy plane twenty miles away, Chequers was at once alerted. Mr Churchill, who had been in bed and asleep, had to be wakened and told so that he could go down to the shelter as standing orders said he should. Instead, he got out of bed, went up on to the roof and then, when we did not open fire, complained of having been disturbed for a false alarm. We did not make that mistake again.

There were other hazards. While explaining the workings of the gun on the lawn to his guests one Sunday morning, the Prime

* We used two troops at a time at Chequers. Our third troop was usually deployed at RAF Benson, a few miles away.

Minister noticed that the Number Three of the firing team had a boot with a cracked toe-cap. Asked why he did not get a new pair of boots, the wretched gunner said that Q (the quartermaster) did not have his size. What size was that? Eight-medium.

Eight-medium was the most common boot size in the army; quartermasters were always running out of it; but the gunner, flustered no doubt by the Prime Minister's unexpected condemnation of the boot, had probably sounded as if a cracked toe-cap was keeping him awake at night. According to the sergeant in charge of the gun, there was a senior general among the Prime Minister's guests that day who could well have been the Chief of the Imperial General Staff. Whether or not the general really was the CIGS we never discovered. What is certain is that the Prime Minister turned to him and said, 'Look into it, would you?' and that two days later we were inundated by the area RAOC supply depot with dozens of pairs of eight-medium boots, more than we needed or had room for. The supply people were in a sullen mood and, when we returned the boots we did not need, complained of our underhand behaviour.

We were already on bad terms with that depot. I had refused to accept from them a brand new water tanker that already had a leaking crankcase and a loud big-end knock. Then, I had had to threaten them with an instant complaint to our War Office authority in order to get a replacement. We took no pleasure in such victories. We could only hope that when our tour of special duty ended we would not be stationed in the same supply depot area. Their revenge would have been terrible.

The Prime Minister enjoyed Hollywood films and had a favourite star, Deanna Durbin. There was a roomy projection theatre upstairs at Chequers and off-duty officers from the guard company and our battery would sometimes be invited up for the weekly film shows. On Mr Churchill's birthday in November 1941, I was one of those who went. As it was his birthday, his favourite film, *A Hundred Men and a Girl*, with Deanna Durbin and Adolphe Menjou, was being shown yet again.

Getting into Chequers after dark was difficult mainly because of the blackout arrangements. There were elaborate light-locks at all the entrances and the use of flashlights was forbidden. One had to wait for someone who knew how the locks worked. That night we had to wait for Commander Thompson to come down and let us in.

175

The film had already started, he said, but as we'd seen it before we wouldn't mind that. He had large whiskies ready for guests and we took ours up with us.

The battery commander was on leave. There were only three in our party: the battery captain, one of the troop commanders and me. When we got upstairs we found the theatre full except for the front row. That was where the Prime Minister was sitting; we could see that from the landing outside. Over his syren suit he was wearing a vast padded and quilted dressing down made of a beige material. Under the projection beam and in the flickering reflections from the screen he looked like a rumpled bed. Commander Thompson hissed at us to go ahead and sit down, so, crouching to stay below the beam, we scuttled in. When I got to the seats the only one left was next to the dressing gown.

Mr Churchill had a cigar in one hand and a brandy glass in the other. For a time, as the second projector took over from the first, I thought that the film had his undivided attention. Then, I became aware of an intermittent sound coming from the dressing gown. It wasn't snoring, he wasn't asleep. Then, by listening more carefully and leaning towards him slightly, I understood what I was hearing; he was rehearsing a speech. I could not distinguish words; what he was rehearsing was the way he would deliver the words; what I could hear were the rhythms and cadences of delivery being hummed in a nasal tonic sol-fa of his own. Dum-dum-di-dah, it went, and then dum-dum-di-doh followed by a challenging doh-doh-di-di? On and on it went. He was supplying the music to go with his words. The film, however, was only half-forgotten. When Adolphe Menjou had his big moment and gave the wicked orchestra conductor a knock-out punch on the jaw Mr Churchill responded with a deep, satisfied, 'Hah!' He knew the film well, of course, and before the end titles came up he was already on his feet. 'A great talent, Deanna Durbin,' he said and strode out.

We were about to leave when Commander Thompson said that, as it was the PM's birthday, we were expected to stay and have another drink. He led the way downstairs to a cavernous drawing room. The official monthly allowance of spirits for an officers' mess of ten was, at that time, one bottle only. At Chequers that evening there was a bottle of whisky on every small table by every chair. along with water and two glasses. Moreover, the moment a bottle was used to pour a drink, a footman would immediately replace it with a full one. The battery captain, a fatherly man whom we called

Gaffer, muttered that this was done so that any guest who wanted to drink a whole bottle at once could do so without tiring himself by pouring doubles. Gaffer had a small political axe to grind. In peace time he was a Tory Party agent in the West Country and belonged to that particular wing of his party that 'had never trusted Winston an inch'.

There were only a few civilians present. Among the ladies, the most remarkable, apart from Mrs Churchill, was an untidy-looking elderly woman who planted herself with her back to the fireplace at the end of the room and scratched her backside. The infantry officers stood nervously with us, ready to leave, as we were, the moment the smallest cue to do so was given. Off the drawing room, towards the rear of the house, was the communications and signals room. We could hear the sounds of that. The Prime Minister presently joined us from there. He had shed his quilted dressing gown and recharged the brandy glass. Mrs Churchill swooped down upon him with a bowl of soup, but he waved it away and decided to notice our group.

'Well, gentlemen,' he said affably, 'your war is going very well.'

Our war? We were unused to that notion but it was a bracing one. However, it is impossible to stand to attention with a glass of whisky in one's hand. Instead, we all tried to look respectfully attentive by inclining our heads in his direction.

'The Eighth Army are still advancing in the Western Desert,' he continued; 'they are being supplied by the Navy from beaches north of Sollum.'

In fact, on that November day, the Eighth Army was trying desperately not to lose a battle for the Sidi Rezegh ridge, and failing; the corridor to Tobruk would shortly be cut. Bad news did not always reach the Prime Minister as quickly as it could have done. On his birthday, though, we believed the good news and made appropriate sounds of pleasure.

'Your duties permitting,' he went on expansively, 'you must come and see the film we are having next week. It is a new Deanna Durbin film, *Bachelor Mother*.'

Bachelor Mother was not new; I had seen it the year before; and it did not have Deanna Durbin in it. I did not want him to be disappointed so, foolishly, I spoke up.

'I'm afraid *Bachelor Mother* is not a Deanna Durbin film, sir. It's Ginger Rogers.'

He gave me his bulldog-about-to-bite glare. 'Deanna Durbin,' he said sharply; 'I have been told so.'

It must have been the whisky. Instead of shutting up, I persisted. 'Ginger Rogers and David Niven, sir.'

'Well,' he said grimly after an ugly pause, 'we shall see.' But I was not to get away so easily. He was still glaring at me. 'How many rounds per gun of anti-tank shot do you carry?' he demanded.

'Forty-eight, sir.'

He grunted and turned away.

'Lucky you weren't wrong,' Commander Thompson said quietly; 'the Prime Minister's knowledge of guns and gunnery is amazing. He'd have known if you'd been wrong.'

'Yes, but *Bachelor Mother* is still a Ginger Rogers picture.'

'He would prefer to think of it as another Deanna Durbin.'

Mr Churchill was now a few yards away playing happily with a small dog that was leaping up at him. Mrs Churchill tried again to get him to take the bowl of soup and again failed. He signalled for another brandy and then, returning to our group, pointed a finger suddenly at the inner wall of the room.

'Which would you choose, gentlemen,' he asked, 'as my favourite picture in this room?'

It was an impossible question. Chequers was given to the nation for the use of its prime ministers as a country house. It has been poorly remodelled and added to, and has accumulated over the years a substantial collection of paintings, many of them pretty bad. A number are, or were, late-Victorian story-pictures of the kind I used to see reproduced in the *Children's Encyclopaedia*. The wall at which Mr Churchill was pointing was long and must have been over eighteen feet high. It was covered, almost from floor to ceiling, with very large paintings hung close together. They were scarcely distinguishable as separate works of art.

Gaffer answered for all of us. 'Couldn't begin to guess, sir.'

The Prime Minister swung the hand holding the brandy until it pointed to the top left corner of the wall.

'That's my favourite picture here,' he said.

It was an enormous canvas and could well have been reproduced in the *Children's Encyclopaedia*. It was the sort of thing that Arthur Mee had liked. The painter must have been an academician of the Leighton school; it may have been Leighton himself. The story of the picture was the fable of the lion and the mouse. The lion is caught and pinned down by the hunter's cruel net; a mouse nibbles away busily at a corner of the net to free the noble king of beasts who is watching him.

We all studied the picture intently. It was Gaffer who broke the silence.

'And which are you, sir?' he asked politely.

It was such an impertinent question that for a moment the Prime Minister was too startled to reply. Then, he managed to find a smile and flourish his cigar. 'Oh no,' he said, 'oh no. They're not going to catch me in a net.'

Mrs Churchill was moving in again with the soup and this time he accepted it. He had had quite enough of us for that evening. Soon we left.

Gaffer was in a merry mood as we drove back to battery HQ. 'You're a fine one,' he said to me: 'we'll never get asked again, of course. A pipsqueak of a gunner, not long out of OCTU, and you're contradicting the Prime Minister of England in his own house.'

'You asked him if he was a mouse. That's much worse.'

He chuckled. 'Ah, but I'm a member of the Conservative Party. You're not. Pity the major was on leave. He'll be cross about that.'

While the battery was still in Wendover, Louise arrived from America. She had applied for a passage back to England before Pearl Harbor, but the end of American neutrality had made the journey easier. I was given leave to meet her in London and while I was there we rented a furnished flat in South Kensington. Later, she looked for, and soon found, a small house to rent unfurnished. There were plenty available then. Ours was in Cavaye Place behind the Forum Cinema in the Fulham Road. Louise bought most of the furniture we needed from a junk shop near Stamford Bridge. The owner of the shop was overstocked with old furniture; what he liked was the modern furniture bought from people who had been bombed out in the first blitz. When he found that what she was after was early Victorian country mahogany, he was so pleased that he let her have it at knock-down prices. She enjoyed herself. The children were all right. Sue was going to get married; Ann had a good job; Exchange Control had agreed that I could pay the fees of the American boarding school to which Mike was going. At Gaffer's suggestion, Louise was invited down to dine with us in the officers' mess. He said that her being American gave the occasion an added distinction. It did. There was only one slightly off moment. Gaffer, a Roosevelt enthusiast, asked her who she voted for in the United States. Louise said, with a smile, that she had only voted once in her life; that had been when she had voted for Governor Alf Landon who had lost everything down to his underpants to Roosevelt in 1936. It made Gaffer uneasy to hear political disasters spoken of so lightly.

Louise had news of Win Harle. Towards the end of 1940, according to the *New York Times*, she had been distributing an anti-German news sheet in Paris cafés. Someone had informed on her. She had been arrested by the Gestapo, tried by a military court and condemned to death before a firing squad. The American Embassy people, who of course knew her well, had appealed for clemency. After she had spent three months in a death cell at the Cherche Midi prison, her sentence had been commuted to one of life imprisonment. That had sounded to us like committal to a concentration camp. We did not expect to see Win again.

Towards the end of our tour of special duty, Gaffer told me sadly that Regiment had received a request from the War Office for my transfer to a strange unit called the AKS. I was wanted for employment as a writer. Regiment had replied saying that I could not be spared. No doubt the War Office would have another try, or simply turn the request into an order. It was a damned nuisance and could not have come at a worse time. Why? Well, the battery would not be returning to AA Command, but going to Blandford, fully mobile, for field-force training with an armoured division. They could only take with them officers they could be sure of keeping. There were officers senior to me at Regiment who had been longing for a chance like this. I would have to be posted away.

So, I had my last hideous battle with the imprest account, and went to Corsham and a lively regiment of Belfast men who had escaped from France in 1940 via Le Havre. The battery I joined was about to go to a Bofors firing camp on the Cornish coast. Because of the absence of other officers on courses, I went as a troop commander. From Cornwall we went to Grays in Essex where for a few weeks I ran a kind of training school for drivers from driver training regiments. When we were at last fully mobile, we too went to Blandford. It was there that the War Office caught up with me.

The course at Blandford was designed both to assess the troops and to test the officers by seeing how they behaved under stress. The stress was applied by depriving us of sleep and changing our programme of training exercises constantly to cause confusion. I had had practically no sleep for three days and was in a fair state of confusion when an order came – an order this time, not a request –

180

for me to report to ADAK, War Office, Curzon Street House. It added considerably to the confusion, but I was grateful for the night's sleep I was able to get.

ADAK turned out to be a lieutenant-colonel with a very friendly manner and tunic buttons that hadn't been polished for weeks. The acronym ADAK stood for Assistant Director of Army Kinematography. The army preferred Kinema with a K because the 'c' of cinema had been pre-empted by other acronyms to mean more important things, such as Command, Corps and Catering.

ADAK's orders for me were that I was needed to help make a training film for the Combined Operations people. I should, therefore, go at once to Glasgow and from there to Troon. At Troon I should report to Major Thorold Dickinson. He would be able to tell me what I had to do.

TEN

Thorold was our military leader and, in a sense, the producer of the film we were supposed to make. As a civilian director, he had made such films as *Gaslight* and *The Next of Kin* which was about military security in wartime. Carol Reed, who was there to direct this one, had the authority derived from having made a number of fairly successful Gainsborough films such as *The Stars Look Down* and *Bank Holiday*. He had joined the army three weeks before as a captain in the Royal Army Ordnance Corps.

The fourth member of the team was Peter Ustinov, then twenty-one and just out of basic training as a private in the Royal Sussex Regiment. I had seen him on the stage the year before in a revue at Wyndham's Theatre where he had appeared in sketches written by and for himself. He had been very good. Though he was not a soldierly figure, only very senior officers appeared to notice it; he was already a *diseur* and impersonator of rare and magical talent. In his spare time he was writing his first play, *House of Regrets*.

We were billeted in a hotel on the seafront at Troon. With us were various technical advisers and liaison officers. These included a Royal Navy beachmaster who had been on the St-Nazaire raid and an American army major from a Wisconsin National Guard unit. Before Pearl Harbor the major had been a dairy chemist and could talk fascinatingly about the enzymes involved in the manufacture of cheese. On tank landing craft and the problems of loading and unloading them he was less sound. He was there as a 'presence' because all planning for the Second Front had by then become sedulously Anglo–American. He was there as the token American and saw his position as absurd.

Even without such absurdities to weigh it down, the training film about beachmasters that we had been ordered to make would have been long, boring and of no use at all to those it was supposed to teach. With access to modern animation techniques it might have been possible to explain visually the logistics of a combined operation; but, with almost nothing of visual interest to support and make digestible voice-over lists and explanations, there was no way out. We could not even describe our difficulty without being rapped over the knuckles. 'It doesn't have to be entertaining, you know. The film'll be part of the course. The buggers'll *have* to see it, *and* pay attention.' We tried to explain that, even with a captive audience, boring them stiff was not a good way of impressing them with what you had to say. However, the experts could not imagine an audience that would ever find their loading tables boring; it was we, the film-makers, who were the problem; we were light-minded.

We produced a massive script, and even got as far as having a conference with officers from No 6 Commando about location shooting along the coast. Then, suddenly, it was all off.

At first we were told that the film could not be shot because there were no landing craft available. Not even *one*? Not even one. Later, we were told that this was because of losses on the Dieppe raid. Later still, word began to filter through of mistakes having been made at Dieppe; there were tales of cock-ups and of tactical doctrine having to be rethought. Our script, already a secret document, was to be hushed up and buried. The only one of us, I think, who wept for it a little was Thorold. We were all sent back to London.

Our premature return from Troon created a problem both for Curzon Street and for AKS Wembley and there was talk of our being dispersed and sent back to our units. In Carol's case this would have been awkward. His unit was AKS and as a captain he would have been obliged to perform the military duties of his rank. At one point, indeed, some joker actually put him down for twenty-four-hour duty as Orderly Officer. With great dignity, Carol went to the studio and watched a guard mounting, said that it seemed to have been well rehearsed and asked what else the boys had lined up for his entertainment. That was the end of the matter. None of the uniformed technicians there really wanted to make an enemy of Carol Reed. The joke was not repeated.

In the end, the problem of what to do with our film-making team was solved, appropriately perhaps, by a team of psychiatrists.

DAK had two functions: he was responsible for the distribution and projection of both entertainment and training films in

British army barracks and camps wherever situated; and he was responsible for making training films. He was not, though, and could not be responsible for initiating their making. Someone in the Directorate of Military Training or of Army Education, say, or the Adjutant-General's office would have to request a training film on a specific subject and appoint a technical adviser. Having assessed the difficulties of the subject an Assistant to DAK would commission a script either from AKS or from a civilian documentary maker, and supervise the making of the film. Civilian production companies were dealt with on a cost-plus basis. Costs at Wembley were usually lower. AKS was located at the old Fox British studio where Thorold Dickinson had added extra cutting rooms and improved film storage vaults. With professional writers like Jack House, lighting cameramen like Freddie Young and film editors of Reggie Mills' calibre, all available for lieutenants' pay, AKS could make films of high quality quite inexpensively.

What the Directorate of Army Psychiatry was asking for was a small but exceptional film of the highest quality. It was needed, they said, for an unusual military purpose. DAP himself, Brigadier J.R. Rees, was still busy then with the case of Rudolf Hess, but he had given the project his blessing. We dealt with two of his assistant directors, Ronald Hargreaves and Tommy Wilson, both psychiatrists in civilian life and both lieutenant-colonels in the Royal Army Medical Corps. Their job was to concern themselves with the state and maintenance of army morale.

By the middle of 1942, call-up intakes were quite different from those of the first two years of the war. There were over-thirties and under-twenties in the same intakes, and many came from Civvy Streets that had had two years of war, seen a little of what high explosive could do and thought it enough. Some had considered themselves 'safe' in reserved occupations and felt cheated by a change in the rules. Others had family worries, often created by the war itself, that could not be left behind. The prevailing mood among the new intakes was becoming one of fatalistic bloody-mindedness.

The psychiatrists wanted a film made specially for showing to these new intakes. Ostensibly, it would be about the nature of the relationship between an NCO and a group of men under his immediate command. What it would really be saying was: 'Yes, we know how you feel. We understand. Everyone feels the same at first. But if we don't feel too sorry for ourselves we can just about make the job worth doing.' It was to be about self-respect and the consolations of an *esprit de corps*. If we needed a textbook on the subject, the psychiatrists recommended the one they had adopted for their own guidance: this was *Disenchantment*, C.E. Montague's book about morale in the 1914–18 war. Montague had been particularly good on the Rupert Brooke of 'Now, God be thank'd', and on army chaplains. He also had a useful chapter on 'The Duty of Lying'.

Peter Ustinov and I were well qualified to write the script that was needed. He was just out of his teens, I was in my thirties. We had both been called up and experienced basic training as members of a raw intake, a new lot. We understood bloody-mindedness, both our own and that of those in authority over us. We were capable of finding it funny. We were both strongly in favour of our side winning the war.

We called the film *The New Lot* and it ran for just under forty minutes. It was made at Wembley, Carol directing, with a cast that included Stanley Holloway, Raymond Huntley, James Hanley and William Hartnell. Our helpful psychiatrists were very pleased with it and proposed that it be shown to all new recruits on entering the army. That was when the film ran into difficulties.

The older chairborne generals, those who decided what should and should not be included in training curricula, nearly all disliked *The New Lot* intensely. 'You can't call those men soldiers,' spluttered one of them furiously; 'they do nothing but grumble. Real soldiers never grumble.' I actually heard that preposterous statement made in a War Office film projection room. Unfortunately, the psychiatrists were outranked as well as outnumbered. Their mildly expressed belief that British soldiers were inveterate grumblers and all the better for it was dismissed with the standard jibes about 'trick-cyclists'. *The New Lot* was condemned as subversive stuff verging on the bolshy. It was not shown to new recruits. It was scarcely shown at all outside the War Office and the Ministry of Information. When, a few years ago, the British Film Institute tried to obtain a print for their archive they were told that none existed, and that no copy of the script was available either.

However, the psychiatrists were not the only ones who liked it. There were high-ranking officers both in the Adjutant-General's office and in the Public Relations Directorate of the War Office who thought that the general public should see it. There were those in the MoI who agreed with them. If it had been made by the Army

Film Unit at Pinewood it could have been distributed as a second feature to the documentary-style *Desert Victory*. Unfortunately, official film-making was strictly divided into separate departments. The AKS at Wembley was there to make training films. The Army Film Unit provided newsreel footage and made army documentaries for public exhibition. Noel Coward's *In Which We Serve* had been made with naval assistance by Two Cities Films as a commercial film. The army wanted, and thought it needed, a morale-booster of comparable quality. Did this mean that they had to go commercial?

As a way round the difficulty, what the psychiatrists proposed was a follow-up to *The New Lot*. We should make a feature-length film dealing with the relationships between officers and other ranks. At first, their idea had seemed to be working. We had found a badly-needed ally and co-conspirator in David Niven, then a major in the Rifle Brigade and one of those who had seen *The New Lot*. He was a former regular army officer with friends in high places and negotiating skills acquired in Hollywood. Of decisive importance was the fact that he was an established box-office star to whom not even the stuffiest training general could object on the grounds that he wasn't really a soldier, or from a good regiment.

Our scheming, however, had not gone unnoticed. Peter was sent to face an officer-selection board, which he failed to take seriously, and then consigned to Wembley. I was instructed to do an outline treatment on the lines of the film requested by the Directorate of Army Psychiatry, but on no account to discuss the matter with Captain Reed. It would be better, perhaps, if I did not see him. This advice was given in the kindliest fashion by the colonel who had sent me to Troon. He was, I believe, an accountant in civilian life. Though he did not actually say that Carol could have a bad influence on a young writer, that was the message that seemed to come from his dull brass buttons and keen blue eyes.

Carol was living at the time in a suite at the Park Lane Hotel. It was quite easy for me in Curzon Street House to reach the back entrance of the hotel unobtrusively by going through Shepherd Market. There were a lot of tarts on the streets there then, but I had sense enough always to make my refusals polite. Eventually, mutual recognition was on a fairly stable nod-and-hullo basis. It was the safest one. Before the GIs arrived in quantity to take the strain, the girls had had a hard time. I had seen what happened when a man objected rudely to being accosted. The girls had ganged up and pursued him, swinging their handbags, with cries of 'arsehole' and 'cocksucker'. He had panicked and run.

In Carol's sitting room at the hotel I would read him what I had written since our last meeting and often stay to go on writing there. Occasionally, David Niven would arrive with news from what was becoming known as 'the brigadier belt', the highest level of army influence that we could count on as benevolent. Sometimes Carol left me working while he went out to lunch. On one such day he lunched with Diana Wynyard and brought her back afterwards. In the lunch hour they had been married. He had not mentioned this before, he explained, because he had not wanted to interrupt the work. Whereupon Diana said firmly that this didn't mean that we couldn't call room service for a bottle of champagne.

By the time I had finished the treatment, it had become apparent to all of us that the film could not be made on the small Wembley stages and that if it were to be made at all it would have to be a commercial production. Even so, army co-operation would be essential; the approval of Jack Beddington at the MoI would take us only part of the way; we would need the blessings of some of the War Office mandarins as well. With that need in mind, I had tried to make the treatment as readable as possible for someone not used to reading treatments. I gave it a meaningless but vaguely optimistic title – The Way Ahead – and in one or two places switched from the bleak treatment form to dialogue. The most important of these switches was a long speech written to be delivered by the regular army sergeant of the film. He was dressing down his platoon by comparing it unfavourably with its Peninsular War equivalent. It was a strong, rousing, hurray-for-us speech; so strong, indeed, that it was eventually delivered by the star of the picture, David Niven, instead of the actor who played the sergeant, only a featured player. However, we were told that it helped the treatment with most of those who were to decide whether the film should or should not be made.*

Approval came quite suddenly. Peter was sprung from Wembley and we began to write the script. John Sutro, who was the producer for Two Cities Films, gave us the use of their boardroom in Hanover Square as an office and we worked fairly

* Though not with the Directorate of Military Training. When, much later, I became a senior officer allowed to draw secret files from Registry, I had a look at The Way Ahead's history. It had had shaky moments. 'Tripe!' one general had scrawled across the treatment. 'Why can't we have a full-blooded story by a full-blooded soldier?'

quickly. Peter's first play, *House of Regrets*, was in rehearsal at the Arts Theatre, but he resisted the temptation to spend too much time with it. The studio shooting for *The Way Ahead* was to be done at Denham and before long we had an office there, the one left vacant by the death of Leslie Howard. Peter had an important part to play as an actor in our picture and he began to work on that. It would be time for me, soon, to return to the real army.

Meanwhile, I was learning more about film-making, most of it from Carol. He had never read Pudovkin and the only technicians he really liked were set designers. In the great days of the Mitchell camera and black-and-white film, good lighting cameramen could be prima donnas and were often outrageous wasters of time. Lighting a scene in which the camera moved in a long tracking shot could take hours. Carol moved the camera as little as possible. He preferred to keep the camera stationary and move the actors towards it in S-shaped walks that brought them into close shot for the significant moment of the scene. I sometimes rewrote dialogue to match the speeches to the walks. He doted on actors and most actors doted on him. He had a sharp tongue for front-office pretensions. 'Knows the whole business backwards, but none of it forwards,' was his verdict on one bustling incompetent. The only bosses I ever heard him admit to fearing were autocrats of his early days in the profession: the stage producer Basil Dean and Ted Black, the studio head of Gainsborough. He respected major-studio Hollywood deeply – 'Heart, that's what pictures are about' – and the American director he most admired was William Wyler. With a Billy Wilder or a Fred Zinnemann he was less at ease. He never told me how he felt about David Lean. I once saw them on the lot at Pinewood talking together. David was being boyish and respectful, a new prefect with the headmaster. Carol was looking wary and kept glancing over his shoulder as if afraid that Ted Black might be watching. David Lean had been known to go way over budget without turning a hair. Going over budget was something Carol rarely did. Aside from bad weather, the only misfortune that he could never find a way to shoot around was a Method actor.*

As well as *The Way Ahead*, there was a film called *Hotel Reserve* being shot at Denham Studios. It was being made by an RKO

---

* I did not work with Carol Reed again for nearly twenty years and then it was on his first, and last, Hollywood assignment. We were older men and friends again by then. It was unfortunate for us both that the picture was an MGM big-budget loser starring Marlon Brando in his 'No Man is an Island' period. Neither Carol nor I stayed the course.

producer new to the work and without a natural talent for it. The script, unfortunately, was an adaptation of *Epitaph for a Spy*, the film rights of which I had sold to Ealing Studios. Ealing had sold them to RKO. The leading man was James Mason, yet to become a star with such films as *The Seventh Veil* and Carol Reed's *Odd Man Out*.

Though I later became a friend and neighbour of James Mason, he could never speak of *Hotel Reserve* without a shudder. In his autobiography and in a book about all his films he tried, almost successfully, not to speak about it at all. I shared his aversion to it. The film had a rubbishy script, bad sets and an unsuitable director.

The writer of the script was John Davenport, that engaging John Davenport who later graced the book review pages of the *Observer*. As he was careful to explain to me when I met him at Denham, he was doing this screenplay hack work strictly for the money. He had worked as a writer in Hollywood so knew the form. William Faulkner, the novelist, who had done a lot of script-doctoring there, had given him the secret: do five pages a day, never more, and they believe you're working. Better that I did not read any of the script; it would only upset me. James Mason was a Cambridge man and quite civilized. Perhaps he would be able to make something of it, though it didn't really matter, did it? He was sure I agreed.

I was ready to do so. Although a cheapjack screenwriter ready to be paid for work he despised, John was an entertaining companion. He had been a schoolmaster and had, I believe, a vocation for teaching. He steered me towards books I would not have otherwise read – I think of Maitland's *Constitutional History of England*, of Djuna Barnes' *Nightwood* and of B. Traven's *Government* – and when Max Beerbohm's 1943 Rede Lecture on Lytton Strachey was published John Davenport read aloud to me on the train from Denham to Marylebone that resounding passage about the century of the common man. We borrowed Max's phrase 'the great pale platitude of the meantime' to describe the studios at Denham.

It was at the time when I was disagreeing, and bickering, with Carol about who should have the long speech I had written for the sergeant. I had done my best to fight the change. The psychiatrists deplored it but could not interfere with what was now a commercial film. I was making a nuisance of myself to no purpose. I went to Colonel Gluckstein, DAK's deputy director, and asked if I could go to Italy.

This was not an idle or frivolous request. Through some Office of War Information (OWI) Americans I had met the film director John Huston. He had asked me to go with him to make a film for the Psychological Warfare Division about civilian Italy under its new conquerors. I think that it was from one of the OWI people that I first heard the bromide, new then, about 'going for the hearts and minds' of a population. This was when Italy was on the point of surrendering and the Salerno landings were being prepared. The idea, dreamed up in Washington by Colonel Frank Capra, was that John Huston and a US Signal Corps film unit should go with the allied armies to Rome and make the picture on the way. There was, however, a snag. It had been agreed at some high-level meeting that all Psychological Warfare films for propaganda in occupied territories should be joint Anglo–American ventures. John Huston therefore needed a token Britisher. Would I go along as writer on the picture? OWI and the PW people were at one in feeling that I was entirely suitable. How did I feel about it?

I felt surprised.

For some time Louise and I had been hearing from the United States about my growing reputation there. Newspaper columnists sometimes mentioned my name. Warner Brothers had made a film of *Background to Danger* starring George Raft. MGM had announced that they were going to star Robert Taylor in *Cause for Alarm*. Dorothy B. Hughes, a rising American detective story writer, had been kind enough to dedicate a book to me 'because he has no book this year'. I had seen in a newspaper cutting the first use of my name as a generic term – 'as tortuous as an Eric Ambler plot'. It all added up to a feeling that I was no longer unknown.

I had tended to treat the feeling as an illusion fostered by the loving enthusiasm of Louise's family and friends who kept their eyes open for such items and reported them in their letters to cheer us up. Surely, reputations were made by writers who kept their names before the public. It was three years since a book of mine had been published. What I had totally failed to understand was how faithfully I had been served by my publisher. Throughout the war and after it, Alfred Knopf kept all four of the first books of mine that he had published constantly in print. Moreover, they were always in hard cover editions: book club reprints, an omnibus of all four titles with an introduction by Alfred Hitchcock, several library editions. He could not have done it in Britain, of course, because war-time and post-war paper rationing would have made it impossible. Why did he do it in America? Not, I think, because he liked me or the British war effort, or because he expected me to come roaring in after the war with a blockbusting bestseller, but because he was a true publisher; he invested in authors; the books and their success had pleased him, so he had made sure that the success continued. It came, then, as a surprise for me to be treated, in England, by intelligent and well-read visiting Americans, as if I were a writer of consequence. The OWI knew all about me; the MoI knew a little. The army, though, said that I would do as I was told when *they* had decided what that should be.

Fortunately, our DAK then was an Indian army regular who had served on the Quartermaster-General's staff and had few prejudices. Brigadier Carstairs regarded those of us who served under him on the film production side with an amused and kindly tolerance that I do not forget. I saw him with David Niven, who, when he had finished *The Way Ahead*, was going to start a new AK section making educational films.

'You want to go and play soldiers?' the Director asked me incredulously.

'I don't think there's much soldiering with the Psychological Warfare people, sir.'

'Well, Colonel Niven'll be wanting you back here before long. What rank is this American, Huston?'

'A captain, sir.'

'Then I think that, since you'll be representing the British interest, you'd better be a captain too. We'll hold you on our strength here.'

I was grateful to him for the thought; later, I became grateful for his foresight.

John Huston and I flew in an American Air Force transport plane from Prestwick to Marrakesh. On the tarmac there we were met by Jules Buck, a Signals Corps lieutenant whose job John had described as that of 'fixer'. He was there to do John's bidding and had been sent by Frank Capra at John's request. Jules was a Hollywood still cameraman who had worked for John before.

A son of the actor Walter Huston, John was then at the beginning of his career as a director. He had been a bit-player and a screenwriter. For his work, with three other writers, on the screenplay of *Sergeant York* he had been rewarded by Warner Brothers with a second-feature to direct. This was a remake (the sixth) of Dashiell

Hammett's *The Maltese Falcon,* and to cast it John had been given a list of contract players in whom the studio had at that point lost interest. It included Peter Lorre, Sidney Greenstreet and Humphrey Bogart. The film, as it remade Bogart's name as a star, also established Huston's as a director. John's next picture was for the US Army and was a documentary about their air force in the Aleutians. At Marrakesh that day, he produced, and I saw for the first time, the special air-crew dark glasses that had been given him by the US Air Force brass with whom he had worked. On his long, shoe-like face they looked like an actor's prop glasses.

In a way, that is what they were. In the Aleutians, the air force had given him, with the glasses, a somewhat exaggerated view of their own might and of the impotence of other arms. They had told him there of all their latest attack capabilities and curdled his blood with tales of skip and carpet bombing; assaults that no mortal, flesh-and-blood foot soldier, no matter how well dug in, could possibly survive. They had even convinced him that they always hit what they aimed at. In Italy he wore his air-crew dark glasses quite a lot, even in the rain. When he heard gunfire he tended to look up at the sky for planes.

Getting to Italy proved not to be as easy as it had sounded. C.D.Jackson, a former *Time-Life* man who was the civilian in charge of the Psychological Warfare office in Algiers, did his best to be constructive. He did not say – he was probably too appalled to say – that the idea of a film about the little people of Italy that dear old Frank Capra had dreamed up in Washington was in Algiers pretty silly and would be in Naples preposterous. All he could do was to suggest that we trusted our own judgements. He used what influence he had with the Eisenhower HQ at the Hotel St-Georges to get us out of our billet at El Biar and on to a plane. Our new orders said that we were to report to a Colonel Gillette, commanding the Signal Corps photographic section at Fifth Army HQ, Caserta, Italy.

In Caserta, we found the colonel and his section officers in a modern house that had belonged to the German Consul and next door to Fifth Army headquarters in the great Palace. What we did not know at the time was that, in common with many other buildings previously occupied by the German army, it had been left by them mined. Some of the mines, those fitted with delayed-action fuses of the acid type, took months to go off. The one in the consulate was ultimately discovered by someone probing the recesses of the house in search of a blocked drain. It was successfully defused.

Colonel Gillette was not so easily dealt with. He was a regular soldier who, on the outbreak of war, had been on the brink of retirement. This posting to Fifth Army, and the promotion to chicken colonel that went with it, had been the making of him. He knew how this man's army worked and he wasn't about to make any mistakes. His job was to indent for photographic supplies, distribute them to the trained personnel under his command – still cameramen, drivers, movie cameramen, interpreters, you-name-it – and get the results back for processing, censorship and distribution by public relations. Thanks to an eight-week guided tour of Hollywood studios to prepare him for this mission, he knew all about movie-making. You just set your camera up, pointed it at what you wanted to see and pressed the button or pulled the trigger, whatever. He knew nothing about psychological warfare and didn't want to know. He knew nothing about Captain Huston except that he made good movies. Well, that was good to know. As soon as camera equipment became available Captain Huston could go out to the forward areas and shoot newsreel footage, and Captain Ambler – glad to have you with us, Captain – could tag along if he wanted. Right now, as it happened, he was short of transportation as well as cameras and film stock. So, if we wanted to go anywhere beyond the junior officers' mess in the Palace, we'd have to hitch rides or walk. However, there was a Fifth Army transportation pool back of the Palace. Maybe we'd like to try borrowing one of General Clark's personal jeeps. We smiled politely at the jest. John set out to make Colonel Gillette believe that a good movie made while we were under his jurisdiction would bring him credit. It seemed an impossible task; Colonel Gillette was no fool. In the end, I think, John bored him into giving way.

Among the epidemics afflicting the allied armies in Italy hepatitis was one of the first to strike.* In the small room we used as a dormitory two extra camp beds were moved in for officers who had gone sick and for whom there were no beds in the hospital. The Colonel slept with us and even he was crowded. For all except the hepatitis patients, the local peach brandy, which had the smell of french polish but tasted worse, was much in demand as an aid to

---

* Others were typhus (swiftly dealt with) and a virulent strain of gonorrhoea.

sleep. It could also keep one awake. I woke in the early hours of one morning to hear John trying to explain the subtleties of film direction to the Colonel.

'Now you tell me this, Colonel,' he was saying in his most unctuous classroom voice; 'when you decide how you are going to shoot a scene, when do you decide to cut and when do you decide to pan? What's the difference, Colonel, huh?'

'Well, that would depend.'

'You bet your life it would. I'll tell you the difference, Colonel. It's this. When you want to establish a special relationship between two characters, or between characters and an object, a window, say, or a gun, you *pan*, got it. Otherwise, you cut. That's rule of thumb. Okay? Now, under what circumstances should you need to establish that special relationship? Most likely at the opening of a sequence. Right?'

'At the opening of a sequence you just set your camera up and you point it. Okay?'

'Not exactly, Colonel, not exactly.'

It went on night after night. To one of his biographers John has complained that I snored at night. I may well have done so.

By some miraculous piece of fixing Jules Buck did eventually succeed in getting a jeep assigned to us. This meant that we could at least look for the story material we needed. What we found, though, was not quite what we were looking for.

Our first friend in the field was the Counter Intelligence Corps detachment commander in Venafro. He had seen *The Maltese Falcon* and read *A Coffin for Dimitrios* so we were in. Venafro was adjacent to a corps HQ and separated from the hard fighting that was going on by a mountainous ridge. The fighting was for the town of San Pietro and the expanse of the Liri valley floor before Cassino.

Venafro was not badly damaged physically and still had a substantial civilian population. They had had to put up with an occupying German army. Now they were putting up with an Allied one. It should have been just the place to show how much better we were, or were going to be. Of course, those were early days in the campaign and not everyone cared about the quest for hearts and minds. New stories about the instant black-market friendships that had sprung up between the shady types working for Allied Military Government Occupied Territories and reinstated Fascist bosses (*AMGOT mit uns* was one current jibe) were told every day. Many of them were true.

194

'We're getting a lot of flack,' the CIC man told us; 'but here we have to have the guy who knows how the sewage system works. He was an important Fascist? Too bad. It's worse in the big towns. The black market's sitting pretty. The MPs stop a civilian in a car and ask to see his gas permit. He shows them his German one. Oops! Wrong pocket. He shows them his Amgot one. What do they do? If they arrest the bastard, Amgot will spring him the same day, within hours. What I need here is an anti-Fascist who knows drains.'

We were sitting in his office which was in a building on the main square. While he had been speaking a shouting match had been going on between a man and a woman outside in the street. Suddenly it erupted into the office. The Italian policeman on the door tried and failed to stop a woman, who was screaming at the top of her voice and brandishing one of her shoes in the air, from fighting her way in.

When order had been restored, an interpreter told the policeman to ask the American soldier at whom she had been shouting to step inside. Meanwhile, the CIC man had motioned the woman to a chair. She sat down warily and kept hold of her shoe. It was one of a pair of wedgies with solid soles, like styled clogs, that were standard wear then in that part of Italy.

'She claims', the interpreter explained, 'that outside her family house and in daylight, not fifteen minutes ago, she was propositioned by a GI. When she tried to come here to complain he tried to stop her. She hit him with her shoe. She is a respectable woman. She wants him severely punished.' He added quietly: 'I know the lady.'

The policeman came back, ushering in the offending GI. There was no doubt that he was the one. He had been hit hard with the shoe and there was blood still trickling from the gash on his forehead.

'Jesus, Captain,' he said plaintively.

That was the end of the informality. His particulars were taken and his papers checked. He was a Private First Class in the artillery and he was on a twenty-four-hour pass. A buddy had given him this address to go to if he wanted to get laid. He had gone there, asked how much and this woman had started yelling. When he had tried to explain, she had hit him and yelled for the police. All he had done then was try to stop her. Jesus!

He was told to clean himself up and wait at the MP post for

further orders. Then, the CIC man looked at the interpreter. 'Okay, what's the story?'

The interpreter wriggled with embarrassment and then told the policeman to take the woman into another room. Even when she had gone, the story had to be dragged from him.

The woman was one of two sisters who worked in a restaurant and shared a family house. The husbands of both were away in the Italian army, POWs somewhere in the Middle East. Times had been hard for the sisters and everyone had understood this. When the German troops had been there, young clean boys, it had become the custom, gradually you understand, for them occasionally to visit the sisters at night in their house. But only, you understand, at night. These were respectable women. They *still* were respectable women.

'During the day.'

'At all times, sir. But at night, occasionally, who could say?'

'So, this Pfc had the right house but picked the wrong time to go there? That's the only thing he did wrong, eh?'

'Well, sir . . .' The interpreter had a final struggle with his civic pride and his wish to avoid plain speaking; then, with a sigh, he nodded. 'To go in daylight, that was the only thing wrong, sir.'

The soldier was told to rejoin his unit forthwith and make sure to tell his buddy that that house was in future off limits. The plaintiff received a deep apology and an assurance that the offender would be severely punished. She was coarse-featured with a bad complexion and a figure too well-nourished by gleanings from the restaurant where she worked, but with both shoes on again she had dignity. We all stood up and the CIC man bowed slightly as she took her leave.

Guy de Maupassant might have found the story interesting, but it was obviously not the sort of thing to appeal to Psychological Warfare. The CIC man suggested that we might like to go on one of his search missions.

'Searching for what?'

'Anti-Fascists mainly.' He smiled. 'If we could find us a good, sane anti-Fascist, even if he's a Communist, we'd probably make him mayor and give a press conference to celebrate.'

'What else would you be searching for?'

'In the hill towns and villages, stolen PX goods. Cigarettes are getting lost by the carload.'

We duly went on a hill town search mission. While the CIC

squad levered up the floor boards of wretched houses to reveal caches of Spam, we interviewed the priest. The CIC man had warned us what to expect. 'If you ask who in the place is a known anti-Fascist, you'll always get the same safe answer – the priest.' That was the answer we had received.

The reception room in the priest's house had a marble floor and bright scarlet and gold curtains. It was bitterly cold. We sat with our interpreter on small gilt chairs arranged along one wall and drank a syrupy brown wine from sticky glasses. The priest harangued us in Italian from the floor, which he used as a stage, sweeping to and fro as he denounced with slicing gestures the iniquities of the Mussolini regime.

We listened, not exactly spellbound but with reasonably close attention, until there was a distraction. The priest's dog, a small, practically hairless animal, trotted in unseen by his master, squatted in the middle of the marble floor and there boldly defecated. Still unseen by the priest, it then trotted out again. It was remarkable that such a small dog could pass such a big, firm mess so quickly and effortlessly.

There was a moment, I suppose, when one of us could have told the interpreter, an American lieutenant, to break in and warn the priest; but none of us did. We just sat there. The priest was in the middle of his peroration, gesturing largely and appealing, over our heads it seemed, to an audience beyond and greater than us. He strode up and down the room three more times without mishap. It was the hem of his soutane, swirling as he turned to slice the air again, that finally caught the mess and sent it flying. It broke up and, almost immediately, the priest trod on one of the fragments.

We sipped our sweet wine and tried not to look. It was his sense of smell that told the priest that something was wrong. I noted then that he looked sharply at the four of us in uniform before he looked at the floor and began scolding the dog. He had a housekeeper who came running to clean the mess up. We refused a second glass of wine.

Outside in the fresh air the interpreter summed up for us. 'Completely nuts. Well, it's natural. To be anti-government in a place like this and admit it, you'd have to be crazy. Only the priest could get away with it. He's crazy but he's still the priest and he still says mass and hears your confession. He's not a Commie. The Commies are all up north he said.'

'Why was he anti-Fascist?'

'That wasn't too clear. He was against Mussolini because he used to be a socialist, but he was against the Italian monarchy too. All mixed up. Crazy.'

All the CIC searchers had found had been Spam and K-rations, no cigarettes. There were smiles all round when we left without taking the food with us.

Not all the hill towns we visited were left with anything to smile about.

In his campaign to persuade Colonel Gillette that we posed no threat to his Signal Corps career and that, on the contrary, any good film that we made would redound to his credit, John had made some progress. However, the time came when he had to make concessions. Word came down from the Palace that a regiment of French colonial troops from North Africa, the Goums, were joining Fifth Army. General Mark Clark, our army commander, had made it clear that he regarded this event as an important public-relations opportunity. We already had American, British and Polish troops in Fifth Army. Now we were getting some crack French troops, real killers but with civilized French officers. This was a big news story.

No World War II commander of men had worked more assiduously in the field of public relations than General Clark. If he said that something was a news story, it was. Colonel Gillette was suddenly prepared to do a deal. If John would cover the Goums story, he could have the cameras, camera crew and film stock to make his documentary.

John accepted. We spent a day or two with the Goums and then made ready to do our duty to Psychological Warfare. We had by then agreed that our best plan would be to move into a small town immediately after the enemy had left, and then make a film of what happened next to its inhabitants. So as to be closer to the action, we found a room for ourselves in a farmhouse near Venafro and made ourselves and the project known to G2 (Intelligence) at Corps HQ.

We still thought it possible to make that sort of documentary in a forward area without 'reconstruction', 're-enactment' or other essential falsification. We had not yet understood that for us, with our brief from Washington, nothing but falsification would be of any use, or even possible.

ELEVEN

The town of San Pietro stood with its back to the hills at the entrance to the Liri valley, and it commanded a main road north to Cassino. From San Pietro it was possible for a few German troops, well dug in and with plenty of fire power, to hold off indefinitely frontal assaults from superior allied forces.

There were two obvious ways into San Pietro from the south. One was down the mountain road from the ridge above Venafro and German engineers had blown all the culverts on that. The other way took one down through olive groves to the valley floor below the town. That was the route favoured by the frontal attackers. The valley floor there had become a killing ground for enemy mortar teams who had developed their own version of carpet bombing. It was not until someone on our side thought of making San Pietro untenable for the enemy by outflanking it, that the stalemate was broken. The outflanking movement had been achieved, with some difficulty, by occupying the summit of the mountain ridge above the town.

We received the news, or a rose-coloured version of it, early one morning. San Pietro was ours at last, we were told; we could walk right in and take all the pictures we wanted.

Colonel Gillette kept faith with us. We were given a Wall camera (which recorded sound with the picture), a camera crew and an interpreter. Jules Buck managed to secure an Eymo and extra film. The Eymo was a hand-held 35 mm movie camera much used then for newsreel work and very reliable. I was pressed into carrying the film and we set out.

The engineers were said to be still bridging the blown culverts on the road, so we took the olive grove route. It soon became apparent that Corps' story of the breakthrough had skipped a few important details. The enemy might have pulled out of San Pietro, but our people had not yet moved in. The town was thought to be heavily booby-trapped, but the engineers had not yet been able to check it out. Moreover, in an attempt to bypass the town and advance into the valley, heavy casualties had been taken. The enemy mortars and eighty-eights were showing no signs of pulling out.

That day we saw General Mark Clark for the first time. He was looking as an army commander should look – alert, determined, fighting fit – and he was being photographed doing so. As soon as his photographers had got the shots they needed, he climbed back into his jeep and was driven swiftly away.

We left our jeeps near a squadron of tanks laagered just short of the olive groves. One of the tank men warned us that there were still stump-mines around and advised us to walk in the tracks they had made. We took the advice. The stump-mine was an unpleasant invention. It was strictly anti-personnel, very difficult to detect, and would blow a foot off when trodden on. A little farther along the tracks a party of stretcher-bearers was adding to a row of bodies in uniform. The bodies were being checked for identification. They had all been dead for some hours and in that cold weather had already become awkward to handle. One had an arm raised and a finger with signet ring on it pointing rigidly at the sky.

The sergeant in charge of the camera crew stayed to have a word with the stretcher-bearers. When he caught up with us he was well supplied with bad news. There were a lot more casualties, both wounded and dead, to be brought in and many would have to be left out for yet another night. The Krauts were even firing on the medics. In his opinion, we should all turn around and get the hell out.

John disagreed. The only thing bothering him just then was an artillery-spotting Storch that kept flying slowly from one side of the valley to the other, banking lazily as it came to the hillsides. Why didn't someone shoot it down? Turn back? What for? The way to San Pietro was open, so that was where we were going. Did I agree? I did, but added that we ought to go in single file and spaced out, not all in a bunch. This suggestion was accepted.

When we reached the first of the olive groves we found a company of Rangers under the trees and waiting to leapfrog through after some troops ahead of them had started the attack. It was true, they said, about some medics having been fired on. Jerry didn't like folk treading on his heels when he was pulling out.

They were from Texas, young, smiling and enjoying the sun that had just come through. When they saw our cameras they wanted to have their pictures taken for the newsreels back home. Jules obliged them by shooting a number of brief close-ups with the Eymo. John used them later in the film he made about the fighting for San Pietro; it was the only part of the film that moved me when I saw it; I knew that all those smiling young men had long been dead.

We moved on to the valley floor. To the right, between us and San Pietro up on the hillside and screening us from it, was a belt of trees with a path running alongside. Both the trees and the path curved to the right. To the left was a field of stubble. Crouching in a deep draining ditch that bordered the field just there was a platoon of infantry. Some of them looked over their shoulders at us as we approached along the path. Their surprise was understandable. Why were we standing up and walking about when they had been told to keep their heads down? The lieutenant in charge of them half stood up as John approached him. What he clearly wanted to say was, 'Who the hell are you?' He compromised with a cautious, 'Hi, Captain.'

'Hi,' John said. 'What are you doing here, Lieutenant?'

'Waiting for orders to move forward.'

'Into San Pietro?'

'No. I don't think anyone's been right into San Pietro.'

'Well,' said John, 'that's where we're heading for. We just follow the path, right?'

'I guess so, Captain.' He noticed my uniform then, thought of asking what the British were doing there and then decided that he was already confused enough. 'Good luck,' he said.

John acknowledged the note of concern with a reassuring nod. He did not think that he needed good luck. He still had not understood what he had been told at Corps. The fact that San Pietro was, militarily speaking, ours had not meant necessarily that we were ready to go to the trouble of checking it for booby-traps and taking possession of it. It had been valuable to the enemy because of the approaches to the valley it had commanded. It would be valuable to us only when it had a serviceable road running through it again.

I followed John along the path. We had gone about two hundred yards and were approaching a right turn where the belt of trees curved away, when I saw him hesitate. After a moment he went on; soon I too came to the reason for his hesitation.

At the turn of the path there was a GI kneeling beside a tree with his rifle to his shoulder in the firing position. For an instant he looked alive, but only for an instant. A mortar bomb fragment had sheared away the whole of one side of his head. He had died instantly and it was the death spasm that had locked his hands on the rifle. He had already been leaning against the trunk of the tree to steady his aim, so there he had stayed. This was that part of the killing ground where the medics had been fired on and the casualties had had to be left where they were. I did not attempt to count them. A whole company had been caught on that patch of stubble and the bodies of the dead were dotted about everywhere within overlapping patterns of shallow craters that looked like splashes of brown paint. The bomb fragments had ripped through everything, haversacks and equipment as well as men. Scattered about among the dead were their possessions, their tubes of toothpaste and their shaving kits, their toilet paper and their girlie magazines, their clean socks and their letters from home. There were places on the stubble where wounded had been and places on the path that it seemed better to avoid.

Ahead of us now we could see, perched on a hillside ledge above a steep escarpment, the rubble of San Pietro. It was about a quarter of a mile away, but looked nearer. Between us and the base of the escarpment the path we had been following disappeared behind a line of small fieldstone buildings that the interpreter said were granaries. They were on the other side of a fast-flowing brook that had stepping stones in it for users of the path. The interpreter said firmly that it didn't look to him as if there were any Italians left alive in San Pietro for him to talk to for us.

'Well, we won't find out by standing here,' John said and began picking his way across the brook. I followed and saw Jules follow me.

The water of the brook was clear and made a fine chuckling sound, but the path beyond was sickening. This was where the wounded had crawled for shelter from the night cold, and this was where they had died. Most of the granaries were barely high enough for man to stand upright or deep enough for him to lie flat. They were like stone kennels. Yet in some there were five or six bodies. They must have been there for at least two days and nights. Those who had not died of their wounds and the freezing cold had, in trying to find warmth, probably suffocated.

Beyond the granaries the path, which had been on a rising incline, began to descend. John halted. 'It looks to me', he said, 'as if this path joins the road below the town.' And then he noticed that he had lost part of his audience. 'Where's the interpreter and the crew?'

'They didn't follow,' Jules said.

'Why not?'

Jules shrugged. He wasn't going to fool with that one. 'We've still got the Eymo,' he said and held it up.

'Okay.' John looked at me. 'I think we have a choice. We can go on down to the road and enter the town by walking up, or we can crawl up over this open ground here. Which one do *you* like?'

The open ground he was talking about was the escarpment. There was a ditch beside the path and then a stone retaining wall. Once over the wall and on the escarpment we would have no cover at all. I did not like the idea of going down to the road either. I did not like the idea of staying where we were. I was trying to think of a sufficiently half-hearted way of saying that we should maybe try for the road when the enemy lost patience with us.

The first mortar bomb landed on the other side of the retaining wall. This saved our skins just long enough for us to hit the ditch. As the rest of the salvo rained down I heard John yelling at Jules to get it all on film, and out of the corner of one eye I could see Jules trying to do so. He was brave enough but he was attempting the impossible. Rule one for makers of war films: shots of bursting high explosive are only convincing when they have been properly set up by a good studio Special Effects department. The only usable film that Jules shot during that minute showed the earth spinning round the sky as he tried to anticipate where the next ear-shattering blast would come from and at the same time keep his head out of the hail of earth and splintered stone that came with it. John used this spinning in his film as cutaway footage instead of conventional optical dissolves.

Our reunion with the camera crew and the interpreter an hour later was not very friendly. We probably looked more ruffled than we really were. John's trench coat was muddy and so were the equipment cases. In diving for the ditch I had pulled a leg muscle and had a bit of a limp. The deserters looked sheepish and were inclined to be defiant. At the stream after we had crossed, it seemed, they had held a council of war. The sergeant cameraman had said that he didn't like the look of things; whereupon, the lieutenant interpreter had told the sergeant that he didn't have to go on if he didn't want to. This new approach to the old concepts of military discipline on the battlefield met with instant approval and they had all trooped back to the jeeps to wait for us.

It should be remembered, I think, that film unit cameramen of all

203

nationalities in that war tended to have a casualty rate that was above the average. The reason must be plain: an infantryman or a tank crew went in and out of action; a cameraman went all the time where the action was; moreover, he always went to handle a piece of equipment with a compound lens quick to reflect light and to draw fire. The sergeant had been under the orders of officers who were strange to him and in whose judgement he had no reason to trust; one could not wholly blame him for being scared into taking the lieutenant up on his unusual offer of free democratic choice; but one could certainly condemn the lieutenant for making it. I don't know what John said or did later about the incident and was careful not to ask. I did not see the interpreter again, nor that particular sergeant cameraman. It was agreed that when we set out again Jules would operate the Wall camera (which worked well as long as one did not ask it seriously to record sound) and that for the moment we would do without an interpreter.

Remarkably, John still had faith in Corps intelligence. The following morning he came, pleased as Punch, to tell me that the road into San Pietro was now repaired and wide open. I was in the medical aid post having my knee strapped up to take the strain off the pulled muscle. With the stick they gave me I could hobble well enough. The doctor shrugged. If we were going by jeep, okay.

The mountain road down into San Pietro was unusual in one respect: although it zig-zagged down like a boot lace in the usual way, it was almost entirely without cover. Gunners looking through sights in the valley could pick and choose their targets and have plenty of time to decide where on the road they would hit them. Corps thought it unlikely that the enemy would waste expensive 88 mm shells on trivial targets like jeeps. Look, the enemy was falling back on Cassino. San Pietro was wide open. What more do you want?

Up off the road on the hillside a group in British uniform waved to us as we started down. We waved back. It was David Mac-Donald and an Army Film Unit crew. John was pleased and seemed to think that we were beating the British to San Pietro. I did not think so. We had talked to David MacDonald the previous week in Caserta. He had been with the British Divisions of Fifth Army at Monte Camino and was not optimistic about the war in Italy. We had let ourselves in for a series of sieges so that the Fifth Army could eventually capture Rome and score a political victory. Its military value would be nil.

204

This was at a time when *Desert Victory*, his film about the African campaign, was still the only outstanding war documentary to have been made in the Allied cause. The Germans had succeeded earlier both with their film about the blitzkrieg against Poland, which they had used at special showings to intimidate neutral governments before attacking them, and with *Victory in the West*, a highly skilful celebration of the fall of France and the defeat of a British expeditionary force. Obviously, it is easier to celebrate a victory than a defeat; attempts to celebrate Dunkirk as a spiritual and statistical victory never quite came off on film without strong soft-focus fictional backing and character actors in small boats; but *Desert Victory* had special qualities. It worked well as a film because it successfully combined true documentary footage shot in the desert, chiefly medium and long shots, with carefully-lit matching close-shots and close-ups contrived by Roy Boulting in Pinewood Studios. Those famous close-ups of Eighth Army men's faces could not have been shot in the Western Desert 'live' unless David MacDonald and the Eighth Army had also had, 'live', an enemy who was prepared to ignore things like lighting equipment and make-up men waiting to dab on artificial sweat. The enemy would also have had to become used to the sharp crack of clapper boards at dawn's early light. Captious critics of war documentaries, too, should have rules: for every gallant fighting man peering over the lip of a slit trench as the barrage flickers, we ought to remember a camera operator with his buttocks in the air and his back to the enemy. Unless, of course, the critic prefers straight newsreel coverage.

San Pietro was reluctant to yield footage of any kind. The blown culverts on the lower part of the road down to it had been bridged temporarily by the army engineers with pairs of steel I-beams. These were placed so that the inner serifs of the Is would just channel the tyres of a jeep driven dead straight along them. The tyres of a small truck with a wider track would line up with the outer serifs. All vehicles had to slow down to a walking pace at these obstacles to be sure of getting across without jamming the tyres and having to back off and start again. Those were the moments the German gunners waited for. When we arrived, engineers were still clearing up after an early casualty, one of their trucks.

By road one came upon San Pietro suddenly. The road was on a ledge cut round a craggy mountainside of deep ravines and small natural caves. The culverts had bridged the ravines, the caves had been handy for the road builders as shelters in bad weather and as dumps for surfacing material. As one entered the town one turned a corner into a kidney-shaped piazza. The mounds of rubble that faced one on the far side of it were the remains of the town. There were one or two stumps of wall still standing, but nothing, not even the church, that could be identified as a particular building. The town had been bombed, shelled and bombed again until all that happened now when it was hit was a change of shape.

We talked to a team of engineers who had been checking for booby-traps. They had not yet found any. There was really nothing left to booby-trap. There were still a couple of Italian families there, maybe more if we looked. They were in cellars under the rubble. No doors. They came and went through holes. The places most likely to have been booby-trapped were where the German heavy machine guns had been dug in. They were leaving those until last. 'If you see a German officer's pistol lying around don't try picking it up.'

We saw no officers' pistols but did note that the machine gunners had not troubled to dig latrines. They, too, had lived under and in the rubble. I wondered where they had got their drinking water. Had they gone down to the brook by the granaries? Perhaps the Italian families in the rubble had access to a well or an old cistern. What about rations? To judge by the faeces the enemy had left lying about he had been well nourished. Had these German troops been the kind to share their rations with stay-behind Italians or the other kind we had heard about? Maybe we should have brought the interpreter after all, even if he wasn't strong on military law.

Jules had parked the jeep on the piazza near one of the roadside caves. I said that I thought a less naked spot would be better. John said that first he wanted an establishing shot and showed Jules exactly where to put the camera, right in the middle of the piazza.

'We'll start long on the valley, holding it for a voice-over introduction, maybe titles too. Then, we'll do a slow ninety-degree pan on to what remains of the town. We hold that for maybe seven seconds. Then, we cut and move in.'

It was, I thought, an acceptable opening. How acceptable would be determined by what we moved in *to* and by what the voice-over said in those introductory moments. 'This is Italy as the barbarians from the north found it before the Christian era' – we are panning on to San Pietro – 'and this is how they left it in the twentieth century.' That, I thought, had the kind of unction that John liked to put into his own voice.

Jules had set the camera up and John humped the batteries over. The shot was lined up as John had directed and he had a look at it through the viewer. Jules did a final check, then switched on and said, 'Turning.'

As he did so, three planes came over low and going fast. They were, I think, almost certainly ours. However, a second later there was a different sound, the multiple whine of a salvo of incoming howitzer shells. We ran.

All the shells did physically when they burst was to move a ton or two of rubble and start a few ears singing; but they also sounded an alarm. The high-velocity eighty-eights did not whine their way in like that. We were in for something heavier.

The engineers had already taken cover in the cave, so we joined them there. The camera had been left running; when all the noise had started Jules had not even begun to pan.

The cave was about thirty feet deep and ten wide. A tall man could stand upright. It was dry. It faced out across the valley, not towards the German guns. As a place to sit out an artillery bombardment designed only to discourage the movement of supplies, it could not have been bettered. Unfortunately, John had taken against the place.

It became apparent only gradually that he had associated the arrival of the first shells with the sound of the planes and concluded that we were being attacked from the air. He was also put out to hear that the piles of large flat objects in the cave, which everyone was using to sit on, were German anti-tank mines. He moved away from them.

'They're not fused,' I said.

'How do you know?' John had put on his air crew glasses.

I looked for help towards the engineer lieutenant. He had been prepared to make a great many allowances for a bunch of eccentric movie people, but now he was really perplexed.

'Those things don't come fused, Captain,' he said. 'They're safe. It would be a pretty good gunner who could put in a shell in here.'

'A good air force pilot could skip a bomb in here with no trouble at all,' John told him. 'Jules, I think they've gone for the moment. Let's take a look around outside.' He glanced at me.

'I'll wait here,' I said.

The gunners were shortening the range slightly. After a minute or two they began to drop shells on to the road. The eighty-eights were banging away again at vehicles.

'They don't like us having this road,' said the lieutenant; 'if they weren't there we could be in Rome in a couple of hours.'

A short way up the road another truck had been hit and turned over. One of its occupants who had ended up somewhere on the hillside below the road started to call faintly for help. It seemed to me that the calls went on for quite a long time. Nobody in our group did anything about him.

After a bit Jules came scrambling back. 'John wants you with us,' he said.

'What for?'

'We found a cellar. John likes it better than there. Be nice. You know how John is. I can't go back without you. He'll just send me out again. Look, there are civilians in this place, Italians.'

I said I would go, but at my own pace. He could wait for me by the hole to the cellar to show me where it was.

The lieutenant grinned as I got myself to my feet. 'Don't give those people K-rations,' he said; 'we already did that. What they really need, I guess, is cigarettes and candy.'

The cellar John and Jules had found was beyond the far side of the piazza, over two hundred yards away. I went slowly. The strapping on my right knee held it slightly bent so that only the toe of that foot could take any weight. The stick had to do most of the work. I cursed John and his air crew glasses.

The camera was still on its tripod and I wondered if Jules had switched it off. If he hadn't, both the film and the batteries would have long ago run out. I thought for a moment of stopping to look, when the sound of the incoming shells changed and several seemed to be landing on the piazza at once. I did not flop down instantly as I should have done. I knelt first on my good knee and then sprawled forward awkwardly with my nose in the dust against my left arm. My ear drums had popped and I was being showered with stone splinters. I doubt if I could really have heard anything much, but I thought that I could hear the sound of another shell coming in. I thought it might be for me, of course. That was the moment my unconscious mind chose to play a nasty trick on me. I heard myself saying: 'Into thy hands I commend my spirit.' I said it aloud.

As soon as I found that I was not going to be torn to pieces and die there, or even be scratched, I was deeply ashamed. It seemed a disgraceful thing for someone who valued Winwood Reade to have said, even in a moment of stress. It had been mawkish, craven. I did not know, until I checked later, that the sentence came from the Psalms and was also in the Book of Common Prayer. I knew it, from a history book read at school, as something said in Tudor times by someone about to be beheaded at the Tower. I resolved, as I dusted myself off, never to say anything about it to anyone.

This was not only because I was ashamed of having been so suddenly scared witless, but because of Louise's cousin Hank. He was, as well as being an ordinary clergyman, secretary of the World Council of Churches and sometimes came to England on Council business. I had had quite a heated argument with him (heated on my side, indulgent on his) over his quoting an army chaplain as saying that there were 'no atheists in the foxholes'. *An* army chaplain? They *all* said it, or something like it. They said nothing else. They were delighted with a war that gave their complex superstitions a simple-sounding, cheap-and-easy endorsement.

The cellar John and Jules had found looked like the crypt of a church, and may indeed have been one. It was on two levels, the lower one having spaces in the walls that could well have been designed as burial niches.

John was curled up in one of them and urged me to come on down and join him. I declined. Apart from the fact that I was not prepared to fool with a flight of broken stone steps that led to the lower level, I did not fancy being entombed down there under a fall of rubble. It was a conventional B-feature set: shaky-looking beams overhead and the ghost of a studio prop man above them dribbling down handfuls of dust every time a shell burst.

The civilian occupants were a skinny old man, two exhausted middle-aged women and three quiet and very dirty children. The old man was concerned about my leg. 'Ferito?' he asked. I shook my head. No, not wounded. I did a mime of a prat-fall to explain. He at once went and got a rickety chair for me to sit on. I hesitated. I knew that it was his chair, but that was not the reason for my hesitation. It had a wickerwick seat that was crawling, moving almost, with lice. It was possible that they were not human body lice, but I did not want to risk it. I thought of the tedium of getting rid of them. I refused the chair, but to show my appreciation of his gesture offered a cigarette. Soon I noticed that he wasn't scratching himself and began to wonder how I could make him renew his offer of the chair. In my left leg I was getting cramp. Then, the heavy shelling stopped, John was persuaded to come up from his niche and we agreed to run for it. John and Jules would grab the camera; I would get to the jeep as fast as I could. I gave the old man my cigarettes and we set out.

The trouble came when we were in the jeep and on the road. Several jeeps were getting the hell out of San Pietro at that moment and the one ahead of us was hit by an eighty-eight. The men in it were flung into the air and for an instant Jules, who was driving, took his eyes off the road. We had been just about to cross a culvert. Instead of doing so, we took the I-beams at an angle and stuck fast.

John leaned over to Jules and said softly, more or less in these words: 'Now then, you filthy little shit, keep absolutely calm. Just back off, you bastard son-of-a-bitch, and keep calm.' A stream of abuse followed. It touched on Jules' religion, his parents and his personal habits.

Jules kept his head and drove us safely up the mountain again. David MacDonald and his crew were still on the hillside and gave us another cordial wave.

In Venafro that evening I asked whose side we were on in the war – the Allies or the editors of *Der Stürmer*? For some of the more unforgivable things he had said to Jules, John asked forgiveness. He received it, of course. Jules was the only one of us who had kept his head throughout the day.

Corps was saying now that Fifth Army's next move would take us right to Cassino. We decided to go back to the olive grove route and see what was happening; but all we saw was General Mark Clark with a map in one hand, pointing in the direction of Cassino with the other. When the pictures had been taken he handed the map back to an aide and was driven away in the opposite direction.

It seemed to me that we had nothing at all to say to that old man and his daughters in San Pietro that required saying on film. He was doubtless hoping that the next bunch of Allied officers who accepted his hospitality would have candy bars for the children and a whole carton of cigarettes instead of the remains of one pack of Camels. Meanwhile, he could do with more K-rations. However, John was reluctant to pull out empty-handed. He needed to know what Colonel Capra in Washington thought. The problem was to ask him without going through army channels and risking the displeasure of Colonel Gillette. John found a way. We went to an American airfield near Naples where John had friends in air transport command who would carry a letter to Washington. It had taken John a whole day to compose.

In Naples, after sending the letter, we spent a boozy night with Humphrey Bogart. He was there, with the first Mrs Bogart, to entertain the troops. Mrs Bogart seemed to shout a lot. Perhaps she had reason. John, Jules and I spent the latter part of the night dozing in the Bogarts' hotel sitting room. The plumbing in that suite was far from silent.

The following morning I suggested that we went to Positano and ate at the Caffé Rispoli. The Buca di Bacco was still there, but there were no fishing boats and the open drains had been replaced by pipes. Giulio had been caught in the north at the time of the Italian surrender but was thought to be all right. A Rispoli aunt told me that John French had been to see them the previous week. He was an Intelligence officer in the Eighth Army.

I do not know how Frank Capra replied to John Huston's letter; I think it likely that he sent a verbal message to the effect that John should do what he could with the facilities available. What John and Jules did was make a short film called *The Battle of San Pietro*. Most of it was re-enacted 'combat' footage of a fairly impression-istic kind. One sequence, however, came over very strongly. It showed a burial party at work after one of the frontal assaults that had been so costly. With notable lack of ceremony, the dead men were bundled into GI body bags and dumped in shallow graves. GI crosses were then hammered in to mark the spots.

The US War Department banned the film. To be more precise, they prohibited any showing of it in a place where the families of GIs might see it while there were still American troops in Italy. The reason they gave for the ban was simple: it was not, they said, the business of the War Department to make anti-war movies.

All that, of course, came much later. While we were waiting for Capra's reply, we distanced ourselves from Colonel Gillette by billeting ourselves in the Palace at Caserta. This was easy to do. The place was huge and had contained the entire Italian air force academy with mess halls and spacious dormitories for hundreds of cadets. We were in the place a week before we discovered that it contained, untouched, not only King Ferdinand's vast and hid-eous state apartments but also a small and splendid rococo opera house.

After breakfast one day I ran into the dairy chemist from Wisconsin whom I had met at Troon. We chatted briefly. When I asked him what he was doing at Fifth Army, though, I received a shock.

'I'm one of the planners now,' he said.

Next day a message came from London to Fifth Army Signal Corps (Photographic) requesting my immediate return. I was to report forthwith on arrival to DAK War Office.

In a way I was sorry to leave. We had tried very hard to do what we had been asked and found it impossible. We had been given, albeit by intelligent men, the wrong orders. It happens in all modern wars to all ranks. What we should have been able to do was to devise orders that we could constructively obey and then, democratically, arrange to receive them. That we failed to do this was due largely to our equivocal status. We were wearing army uniforms but working for and owing loyalty to Psychological Warfare, a civilian agency with ill-defined functions and uneven political backing. Still, in spite of these handicaps, we ought to have done better. Together, we ought to have been ingenious enough to succeed. The Nazis and the KGB's predecessors always did that sort of thing better.

Arranging to return to London was difficult. I would have to go to Algiers and, from there, play it by ear. The night before I was to leave from Capodichino there was an entertainment for Fifth Army headquarters troops in the Palace opera house. It had comfortable seating for about three hundred with a number of boxes. As we went in we were all handed little slips of paper by a warrant officer who muttered as he gave out each slip, 'It's sung to the tune of God Bless America, I think. Please give it all you've got.'

As we reached our seats in the circle and began to look at the slips of paper, the generator in the quadrangle failed and all the lights went out. When power was restored the lighting level was lower. Flashlights had to be used to read the words on the paper.

The well-known patriotic folk tune played by the three-piece combo was certainly not 'God Bless America'. I really don't remember now what it was; but these are the words I have on the slip of paper I was given:

THE SONS OF GENERAL CLARK
Stand up and sing the praise of General Clark,
Your hearts and voices raise for General Clark,
Red, White and Blue unfurled upon the field

Its message flaunts Clark's sons will never, never yield.
We'll fight, fight, fight with heart and hand,
As soldiers true embattled staunch will stand,
The Fifth's the best army in the land,
FIGHT, FIGHT, FIGHT!!!

That was all. The lyricist was not mentioned. I like to think that it was General Clark himself.

Getting out of Algiers by then was as difficult as getting out of Italy. Finally, I managed to get a lift to Gibraltar and the RAF flew me back in a Wellesley to Lyneham.

At home the news was much better. Louise, having worked on *Vogue* for some months, had moved to *Harpers Bazaar* and been appointed Knitting Editor.

TWELVE

When the United States came into the war against the Axis powers, the Hollywood film industry had been quick to co-operate with the US armed services in making information films designed to promote good relations between American forces and those of their European allies. Many of these films were what were then called 'compilations' made by combining newsreel, library and documentary footage with specially scripted and shot linking sequences. Typical compilations were the two series of films made under the collective titles of *Know Your Allies* and *Know Your Enemies. Know Your Ally Britain* was supplemented by other films made about the British people for GI consumption. Some were highly entertaining and were enthusiastically received by British troops lucky enough to see them. Where tensions existed between British and American units using the same pubs and dance halls (the 'overpaid, over-sexed and over here' problem) the showing of such films had a beneficial effect; so beneficial, indeed, that the absence of even one comparable film about America made by the British had become embarrassingly noticeable. It became politically desirable to have such a film made. Action this day.

The MoI said that the Crown Film Unit had other commitments and that, anyway, it was the army's business. The Army Film Unit was busy with Burma and the coming invasion of Europe. The job was passed to DAK. The Director sent for Colonel Niven.

David felt at once the heat of the hot potato he was being handed and did his best to drop it.

'Unless this film is going to be absolutely first rate,' he had told the Director, 'it would be better not to make it at all. It could make us look pretty silly. Maybe we should let the MoI stick their necks out.'

'They've already refused,' the Director said. 'We've been ordered to make the film, so that's what we'll do.'

'It's not a straightforward training film, sir. To get a script that will be approved by both us and the Americans, we'll need a writer.'

'What about that fellow Ambler who wangled his way out to Italy? He's a writer isn't he? Get him back here and make him do some work.'

That, at least, was the embellished version of the way things stood that David gave me on my return. The truth was that he was about to leave DAK for a more glamorous D-Day job at SHAEF. He was passing the hot potato to me. But he was always a thoughtful man.

'Tell you what, chum,' he added; 'if you do an absolutely marvellous script and it has a voice-over or a commentary, I'll come down to Wembley and do it for you. I've got an English accent that even Harry Cohn can understand.'

It was a start. The director, too, had encouragement to give, and also a warning.

'How you go about this', he said, 'is up to you. You can go for help to anyone you like, MoI, OWI, even your trick-cyclist friends. If you do manage to write a script that's approved, Colonel Gluckstein thinks we ought to let you take charge of making the film. You'd better remember, though, that it's our political masters that we have to please with this. Don't keep them waiting a day longer than you have to. They'll only get more difficult to please.'

I did go to the psychiatrists for help and it was Tommy Wilson who told me to ask for Professor Brogan as adviser on the film. Herbert Agar and the OWI persuaded Denis Brogan that I needed, and could use, his help.

My idea was to let the audience see America through the mind's eye of a homesick GI stranded in the waiting room of a British railway station. It would not be Hollywood's America of which he was dreaming, but that of Thoreau, Thomas Wolfe and the New Deal documentary film makers such as Pare Lorentz. Mixed with images from *The Plow That Broke the Plains* and *The River* would be library footage about the Chicago stockyards and a suburban landscape such as that of Nutley, New Jersey.

Denis Brogan listened to these vapourings and then asked if I knew why Chicago and its stockyards were where they were and not somewhere else along the shores of Lake Michigan. I didn't. He began to tell me about the early Great Lake portages and the coming of railroads to those parts. He went on to give me a crash

215

course in American history and economic geography. Each morning, on his way to his own work, he would bring me an armful of books flagged at the passages I was to read carefully. Thirty years or so later I happened to see on BBC television one of a resplendent series of films about America made by Alistair Cooke. One or two of the insights seemed familiar. I was not surprised to find that the historical adviser had been Sir Denis Brogan. However, in 1944 *United States* had only a somewhat breathless forty minutes in which to tell its story.

I never had the required script approval. The OWI people in London could give private blessings and encouragement, but they were far too careful of protocol to approve officially the script of what was still technically a British army training film. Besides, the script of that kind of film is difficult to approve. The words were approvable, but who could tell what effect the images and the editing would have on their ultimate meaning? Much would depend on the library footage available to me. First, I had to find it, then get permission from copyright owners to use it, and finally secure fine-grain prints of the pieces I wanted so that we could make our own negatives.

The OWI in London did their best. They could get me UV prints of US Government film just by cabling for it, but they could not get me a clip of a Crosby–Hope gag from a Paramount picture without negotiating by letter. In any case, all the well-catalogued film libraries, such as that of *The March of Time*, were in America. If I knew what I wanted, the quickest way would be to go there and bring it back.

Colonel Gluckstein agreed. I flew to Washington and then went up to New York. The US Army equivalent of AKS had taken over the old studio at Astoria in New York. I was expected and welcomed. In two weeks I had nearly all the film I needed. I flew back via Montreal.

I had ordered some animated map sequences before leaving and these were ready. Reggie Mills was the film editor with whom I worked at Wembley. He was patient and tireless. So was the composer Alan Rawsthorne who kept writing timed music sequences for us only to find that the timings had changed yet again. There came a time, however, when I could ask David Niven, safely back at SHAEF after his adventures in France, to record the voice-over. A week later I was told that we could submit the film for approval. I was given a day and a time. The place was a projection theatre in the old War Office building in Whitehall.

There was an audience of four: a senior personage from the

United States Embassy, a man from the OWI, Sir James Grigg, our Secretary of State for War, and one of his aides. Sir James was known to be under the eye of the Prime Minister. From something said during the preliminary courtesies I gathered that he was seeing the film for the Prime Minister. I found myself wanting to apologize for the quality of the print we were running, but managed instead to keep my mouth shut and pretend that I was just there with the film as its escort.

The first three reels were received, except for a grunt or two, in silence. The linking scenes between the homesick GI (played by a Canadian actor) and the British soldier (Leslie Dwyer) breezily ignorant of America produced most grunts. Then came the fourth reel and America's entry into the war. I had had to be careful. The film was ostensibly for British consumption only; it had, therefore, to take into account some irrational British thinking. This included the suspicion that America had been content to let the British stand alone just a little bit too long. I had tried to deal with this by reminding the audience that America had not been the only civilized nation reluctant to go to war. I had a shot of Neville Chamberlain waving his piece of Munich paper at the newsreel cameras and promising peace followed by a shot of Charles Lindberg at a pro-Nazi rally in Chicago promising that no one could ever attack the United States. Over the last part of Lindberg's speech I had put the whistle of a descending bomb and then cut to a bomb explosion at Pearl Harbor.

The man from the Embassy coughed sharply. 'Oh no,' he said; 'no, no, no. That's out.'

A cloud hung over the rest of the screening. At the end there was a short silence before the Minister turned to the Embassy man.

'Did you mean', he asked coldly, 'that that was not Mr Lindberg or that he did not utter those words?'

'What I meant, Minister, was that we're not having a clip of Lindberg in there making a horse's ass of himself. Not, that is, if you want us to say that in our opinion this little movie makes a contribution to Anglo–American understanding and good relations between our peoples.'

'You're not open to argument on that?'

'No.'

'Then,' said the Minister deliberately, 'we shall take out Neville Chamberlain.'

'I think you're wise, Minister. There are some things better forgotten. We try to be forward-looking.'

'Any other objections?'

'No, I think your people have done a pretty good job.'

The War Office aide was a civilian. As his Minister started being polite again to the Americans he took me aside.

'You're quite clear, Captain?' he asked. 'All references to Charles Lindberg and Mr Chamberlain to be deleted? Is that understood?'

'Yes, though I was hoping that they were not being altogether serious.'

'Captain, if *you* have any thought of not taking those decisions seriously, I would strongly advise you to think again. We shall be minuting DAK, of course.'

Reconstructing the fourth reel was a dreary job and America's entry into the war became, for me, flatfooted. In the end, though, *United States* had quite a big audience. At the Astoria studio I had met Leonard Spigelgass, the comedy writer, who was responsible then for putting out 'GI Movies'. These were the entertainment and information film packages that went out regularly to all US forces worldwide. He had liked the script I had shown him and I asked OWI to send him a print of the finished film. Forty minutes was the standard length of a GI Movie. Prefaced by a title explaining that it was a training film made for showing to British troops, *United States* made a complete GI Movie edition and, as such, was well received. It was shown, in places, to British troops too. I heard of no complaints being made about it.

At about that time the Directorate was reorganized and the Director asked me to take over AK4 and make myself responsible for the production of a programme of education and information films to be made in consultation with Ministries immediately involved with post-war planning. I would have other responsibilities. I could have all the help I needed, but I would be in charge and responsible. The appointment would mean immediate promotion to lieutenant-colonel. How did I feel about all this?

About the responsibility I felt splendid; about the promotion I was dubious. I had never heard of a captain being promoted directly to lieutenant-colonel and doubted if it could be done. But I was wrong. It could be done easily, and quickly too. Demotion, I gathered, could be even quicker.

*   *   *

Gabriel Veraldi, the principal translator of my books into French and himself a novelist, has written of my time as ADAK in the War Office that, '*On peut dire maintenant qu'il profita des moyens mis à sa disposition pour faire de la propagande crypto-communiste.*'*

I really don't think that one can quite say that. The director was a good, thoughtful man who regarded most of us who worked on the production side with the kindly amusement of a police Alsatian watching a Pomeranian tumbling act. However, he was also an Indian Army officer who knew that all men had a bit of the scally-wag in them and always took the necessary precautions before it showed. He also had as his Deputy Colonel Louis Gluckstein, a QC and a most distinguished member of the Conservative Party. Naturally, they put in minders to see that I did not do anything too silly or disastrous to be concealed. The chief minders were my second-in-command Donald Bulmer, promoted from captain to major on appointment, and Jack Clark, up to captain. Don Bulmer was a master at Rugby school. Jack Clark I seem to have mis-understood. I thought of him at the time as a High Tory redeemed by wit. According to our mutual friend Julian Symons, he now says that he was a socialist then, though always a conservative at heart. On the whole, I think, it was our clients, those for whom we made the films, who were the hard-liners. Among the psychiatrists and army education people there used to be talk of a War Office 'briga-dier belt' of radicals who were the *éminences grises* of several of the more influential Directors. I never positively identified any of them, but in some corridors a distinct whiff of political ambition could be detected.

At first our most demanding client was the Army Bureau of Current Affairs whose educationists persistently failed to under-stand why their ABCA bulletins on, say, the Beveridge Plan or full employment and the welfare state could not be used, practically as they stood, as film scripts. At ABCA, the playwright Bridget Boland had the unenviable task of trying to make both parties see reason. We could have been of more help to her. Our difficulty was a shortage of writers capable of doing the kind of work for which we were now being asked. Our request to the Adjutant-General's department for a round-up of professional writers already in the army produced a rum lot. Most of those I interviewed turned out

* Gabriel Veraldi, *Le Roman d'Espionage*, Presses Universitaires de France, 1983. It is a book addressed to graduate students of contemporary literature.

not to be writers at all. One who did write was a private named Willis and he produced a cutting from his wallet to prove it. The cutting was from a local newspaper for which he had written a short article about his life in the army. It was signed 'Ted Willis'. At least he had managed to get into print. I was glad to have him.

In the September after D-Day I had a letter from the senior partner in a City of London firm of surveyors. He had a cousin, a captain in the army, attached to the American Counter-Intelligence Corps in northern France. The cousin had been approached by British naval officers in 'a certain town in France'. The naval officers had requested him to arrange billets for a Mme 'C' until she could return to her home in another part of the country.

Towards the end of August Mme C and her husband had been arrested by the French police with the concurrence of the American CIC on suspicion of espionage and collaboration.

Mme C was Betty Dyson and her husband was poor Yves. They had been picked up by the FFI in a town near Brest.

Betty had asked the British captain to arrange for legal aid and to inform me of her plight. She hoped that I would, if alive and available, speak on her behalf. The surveyor gave me, should I be willing to speak, his cousin's Army PO address.

I tried to do better than just speak. I obtained the name of the American G2CI for the area and wrote direct to him. I explained that Yves was a titled Breton nationalist who would certainly have been of interest to the *Abwehr*. He would, no less certainly, have incurred the displeasure of a militant FFI resistance group.

Betty was harder to explain. I could imagine all too easily the way it might have happened. An attractive German officer had addressed her as *madame la baronne* and she and Yves had been invited to a dinner party. She would have made the remarkable discovery that the German army was not after all an army of monsters. Only a hint of local disapproval would then have been needed to convince her of the essential rightness of her new friendship. She would have been a brazen and indiscreet collaborator. The charge of espionage, I thought, had probably been no more than an expression of spite.

What I said about her in my letter to the CIC man was that she was her father's daughter and that he had been a renowned Australian artist and a committed socialist. Why I should have been simple enough to suppose that this information would cause an

American chicken colonel to defend Betty from her accusers I cannot think. Since, in writing direct to him, I had gone outside channels I did not expect a reply, and I did not get one. Soon, however, Betty and Yves were released and came to England. Yves had been roughly handled by the FFI, but Betty had suffered only a loss of dignity. Neither of them ever displayed any inclination to explain what had really happened. The subject was closed.

Towards the end of 1945 I counted the films we had made that year. It was possible to do so because Don Bulmer had set up elaborate wall charts so that we could keep track of all our productions: those being done on location and those with civilian contractors as well as the studio stuff at Wembley. There were ninety-five on the charts.

During the year we had taken over the original training film branch with some of its personnel so that more than half of these were shorts made to be used in conjunction with the training manuals for new or modified equipment. The education and 'morale' films were more elaborate and, on the whole, more interesting.

We made a series of films describing a variety of civilian jobs and careers.

Even before D-Day, all the arrangements for the eventual, and orderly, demobilization of British forces were already complete. They had been made in compliance with a directive from the Prime Minister who, as Secretary for War under Lloyd George, had had to deal in 1919 with mutinies by undemobilized soldiers confined to camps. Ernest Bevin's Ministry of Labour had also given these matters thought. Some service men and women would return to Civvy Street and take up more or less where they had left off. Others would return with changed ideas about their abilities and revised expectations. In a country in need of replenishment, renewal and reconstruction there would be plenty of room for change. Our task had been to show on film what different worlds of work looked like and to stimulate thought on the subject. We were guided by the Ministry of Labour and we worked in conjunction with the MoI.

We made films for returning prisoners of war of all services. Some men, those in particular who had been POWs since the early days of the war, had difficulty in adjusting to changes that had taken place in the surface of life at home. Trivia could be painfully important: not knowing the way clothing coupons worked, say, or the new basic price of a London bus ticket. A repatriated POW could be reluctant to ask questions for fear of making himself conspicuous. For some, just knowing the news stories that had broken while they had been away was important. We made a very long two-parter called *A British Diary* to supply this and other information. It was shown mostly in the staging camps where freed prisoners were assembled for repatriation.

We made an educational film for surgeons that caused distress at Wembley. It had an awkward title – *Treatment of Maxillo-Facial Injuries in the Field* – but the content was memorable. Much of it was photographed in a forward area field hospital at the time of the Rhine crossings. Men, our own and prisoners, were brought in at the point of death with their jaws shot away. Surgeons of the maxillo-facial unit, using newly-devised tools and methods, were shown quickly wiring the fragmented jaws back into place so that recovery could begin. The filming was supervised by a captain in the Army Medical Corps named James Dyce. The distress was mainly in the film cutting rooms. None of the senior editors could look at the material, even in a movieola, without being taken ill. I had difficulty myself and was tempted to make excuses for not seeing the rushes when they arrived from the lab. The only person, apart from Jimmy Dyce, who viewed them with enthusiasm was an ATS assistant cutter. In the end she took over the editing. She did an excellent job.

When the army captured the main V2 assembly plant near Cuxhaven it was found that there were only enough parts in stock to make up three missiles. At the request of the Scientific Adviser to the Army Council we sent all the AKS camera crews we could muster to cover the test firing that was to take place. A director went too. He made a short documentary showing in detail the assembly processes that were carried out immediately before fuelling and launch. The V2 was an unreliable weapon and it was thought that, even with a co-operative German crew to help, we would be lucky to get even one successful launch out of the three possibles. When a V2 launch sequence went wrong the missile usually collapsed and blew up on or near the launch site. There was relief when the first firing went as planned and we saw the phenomenon of missile 'lift-off' on film for the first time. The Scientific Adviser was pleased. Some of the best footage was supplied through the MoI to the newsreel companies.

*   *   *

The only secrets with which I was ever entrusted were those contained in the Middle East and South-East Asia military censorship reports. From those muddy-brown duplicated sheets it was possible to learn that a lot that one had been told about the behaviour of men in armies at war was true.

It was true, for instance, that a good unit would be at its best soon after a first baptism of fire, and that from then on it was likely to become less and less good, depending on how fast it suffered casualties. It was also true that the most experienced troops were, in the end, the least useful because they had become too knowing. It was also noticeable that units suffering from low morale and high petty crime rates in the ranks were often commanded by officers much decorated for gallantry. Some displays of guts were all right, but experienced troops did not really care for an officer who was too brave. It wasn't just his neck; he could get them killed too.

There was nothing particularly secret about stuff like that, of course. *Disenchantment* had already said most of it. What *was* secret was the fact that soldiers' letters were being read not just for military indiscretions – the kind that could be cut or inked out – but for the expression of private doubts and longings that earlier censors had been instructed to skip.

The secret was that some of us pried.

Both Warner Brothers and RKO had London offices then and their people were kind enough to run for me the movies that had been made of *The Mask of Dimitrios* and *Journey into Fear*.

Orson Welles had master-minded the filming of *Journey into Fear* and he had acted in it, but he had neither written the script nor directed it. I had admired *Citizen Kane* and had hoped to see a thriller of mine rendered on film with some of the same style and skill. I was disappointed, though not greatly surprised, for I knew a little about the film's production history. Welles had been quarrelling with the RKO front office when it was made. Shooting had been started with an incomplete script. On the first day, one of the sound stage crew had fallen from a high rostrum and been killed. There had been other clouds over the picture. In the end, RKO had lost patience, taken the film away from Welles and edited it themselves. The result was scrappy. In places I found it hard to follow the story line. There was some good acting in it but not much else.

I had been puzzled when Warners had bought the rights of

Dimitrios and believed that they would find themselves unable to make a film of it. When we were on our way to Italy, John Huston, always a cheerful bearer of bad news, had disillusioned me. He had seen a rough cut of the film before leaving Hollywood.

'Guess how it opens,' he said, and gave me a moment or two to sweat before going on in the orotund tones he employed for a script exposition. 'We see two children, kids, running towards us along a sea shore washed clean by the tide. They run right up to camera and then stop, wide-eyed. They have seen something on the sand in front of them. They open their mouths to scream. The main titles come up as we see that what they have found is a body. Right?'

Right. I understood. The film opened with a B-picture cliché. A pity. But what I wanted to know about was the solution that had been found for the book's central difficulty as film material. Until nearly the end the reader sees Dimitrios only obliquely, through the eyes of those he has victimized and through the mind of Latimer, the scholarly detective story writer in search of reality. How had Warners managed to lick that problem?

They hadn't licked it, I was told; they had ignored it. There was an unknown actor Zachary Scott, playing Dimitrios, and you saw him from the start the way he was at the end, except for wardrobe changes. An old writer of westerns named Frank Gruber had done the screenplay. The director had been Jean Negulesco who had made band shorts for Warners and was really an art director. He, John, would have done it differently, and better. I believed him. I was of the opinion, possibly heretical, that *The Maltese Falcon* by Dashiell Hammett was better entertainment as a film scripted and directed by Huston than it was as a book.

The Mask of Dimitrios had been made cheaply in standing sets and on the Burbank lot with Warner contract players, and by that time had already been tipped as a 'sleeper'; that is, the kind of small film that goes on making money for years. I had not expected to enjoy myself – *Background to Danger* with George Raft had made me very queasy – but I had not expected a screen Dimitrios to give me stomach cramps. They were quite severe.

Writers who have had anything to do with psychiatrists and psychoanalysts, as I had had, usually know enough to keep quiet about that kind of physical symptom. One can interpret these things for oneself. However, sitting in the projection room with the Warner PR man, I was careless enough to groan aloud. His insights proved to be pre-Kleinian, even pre-Freudian. He thought that I was hating every moment of the picture. He protested that it wasn't that bad.

He was right; it wasn't that bad; and bits of it, those in which Sidney Greenstreet could compel an audience to overlook the miscasting of Peter Lorre, were almost good. And the film did prove to be a sleeper of sorts. Forty years after it was made it was still occasionally to be seen on television. However, on seeing it for the first time that day I felt put down. I tried to tell myself that thriller writers were not entitled to be so uppish, but failed to convince.

Of course, by then I thought that I knew a lot about screenwriting and had, indeed, learned some things about it. I had noticed, for example, that for some directors the script had a stronger affinity with a strip cartoon, or the storyboard used by a team of animators, than with the kind of writing that conveys thought in clauses, sentences and paragraphs. I knew that a highly readable script was not necessarily a good one; readability could conceal grave structural faults. I had perceived that writing for the screen and writing to be read are crafts that have almost nothing to do with one another.

I had been amazed more than once to discover that, although a basic fault in a script may disappear during the shooting of a film, it will always reappear, as deadly as ever and a thousand times more costly to correct, when one sees the rough cut. The script is the heart of a film.

I concluded – as other writers before and since have concluded – that films would probably be better on the whole if the screenwriter retained control of the story material by becoming a writer–producer or a writer–director.

Perhaps this is the moment to recall that, although I eventually became a good screenwriter, the only time I made a complete and amateurish hash of an adaptation for the screen was when the source material was a book of my own.

Shortly after the war Louise and I rented a furnished beach house at St Margaret's Bay near Dover. It was somewhere to take the children at weekends. Our landlord and close neighbour was Noël Coward, and one of the oral conditions of the lease was that I should use the peace of the house and the music of the sea on the shingle to write another book. The admonitory Coward index finger had wagged under my nose.

'Forget all this film nonsense,' he said. 'Write more books. You think that you will always be able to go back to the well. That may be so, but remember this: if you stay away too long, there will come a day when you will go back and find the well drr-y.'

We had had a second martini before lunch and I knew that he was talking as much to himself as to me. He, too, had been having trouble with his work. In his case the main trouble had been an expensive but unsuccessful musical. All the same, his advice to me was thoughtful and kind as well as sound.

I had been one of the 'talents' on whom Filippo Del Giudice of Two Cities Films had been relying to restore his fortunes after the batterings they had received from *The Way Ahead** and *Henry V*. *The October Man*, an original screenplay which I wrote and produced at Denham, did nothing for Del's fortunes or for anyone else's. When the Cineguild team of Anthony Havelock-Allan, David Lean and Ronald Neame asked me to join them at Pinewood I had accepted gladly, though unwisely. Cineguild was a production company originally set up to make films from Noël's plays. When I joined, it was an independent production company working under the aegis of the Rank Organization. The independence we enjoyed was largely illusory. We were counted upon to make pictures that would recover their negative costs on the Odeon and Gaumont circuits and at the same time bring credit to the Rank Organization by becoming big dollar earners in America. A policy of selling British cars to America with their steering wheels on the right would have had the same chance of success.

I had not written a book for ten years and in the army had lost the habit of a concentrated and solitary writing routine. The process of its recovery was slow. Besides, during those ten years the internal world which had so readily produced the early books had been extensively modified and had to be re-explored.

Charles Rodda had returned from Cornwall to live in London and was having a hard time. He had usually written under pseudonyms rather than his own name and had relied on the royalty advances of at least two potboilers a year to provide him with an income. Paper rationing had made that sort of publishing impossible in England and he had never had a regular publisher in America. He thought that what he needed was a new story idea.

---

* The general release of *The Way Ahead* had coincided with the arrival of the buzz-bombs which closed many London cinemas. The film had not earned its cost.

I had a knack then of being able to 'talk' a story from almost nothing into a coherent whole. The trick had been occasionally useful at film story conferences, but practically nowhere else. The thing I had to remember was that talking a story my way was usually a first step towards forgetting it. I once offended an actor whom I liked by telling him at length a film story that was just right for him and then neglecting to write it. He assumed, not unreasonably, that I had changed my mind about him. In fact, I had forgotten most of what I had told him and was bored by the oddments that were left.

The story I told Charles Rodda that evening was not new, but it sounded new because it had some new props and a fresh setting. He liked it, did not forget it and said that he would write the book if I would agree to his doing so under a pseudonym belonging to us jointly.

The pseudonym was Eliot Reed. Of the five books published under it in Britain and America only the first two, *Skytip* and *Tender to Moonlight*, contained substantial contributions from me. They were substantial because I am not a good collaborator.

Our bargain had been that I would supply the story material and that he would do the writing. I could not keep to it. The trouble was not just that I am touchy, pernickety and possessive about work in progress, but that when writing for myself alone I never follow a set story line. I try things out, I rewrite and I change my mind about the characters as I go along. At the end, I make further changes.

So, the moment Charles gave me his typescript to read I reached for a pencil and began editing. Then, I started to rewrite. Charles seemed amused rather than affronted by this high-handed behaviour, but when I showed signs of treating his writing of the second book in the same way, it became clear to both of us that the Eliot Reed understanding would have to be modified. Charles took over the pseudonym and thereafter treated it as his own.

When I began writing again to please myself rather than to further the war effort or to sustain the Rank Organization's American ambitions, I began, as I had begun in the past, with vague story ideas that could be developed on paper rather than through talk.

One of the pleasanter discoveries Louise and I made when we were able to get to Paris again was that Win Harle had survived and was back in the rue Marbeuf. Her account of her arrest by the Gestapo was for me particularly interesting.

She had been informed on by the concierge and the Gestapo men had arrived while she was in the act of running off her BBC news sheet on a duplicating machine. Caught red-handed, her response had been to unleash the dog Bingo and set him on the two intruders. Bingo had attacked with such enthusiasm that the senior Gestapo man had pulled a gun and threatened to shoot the brute.

According to Win, she had at once responded by accusing the man of cruelty to animals, taunting him with being German and then inviting him to look behind the chimney shutter for her secret radio transmitter. The man had raised the shutter and, again according to Win, had been engulfed in soot.

I did not believe a story that had the Gestapo behaving like Keystone Cops. I did feel, though, that the combination of Win's abuse and Bingo's way with a trouser-leg and a male ankle may well have hardened the local Gestapo attitude towards her case. When her death sentence had been commuted to life imprisonment she had at once been removed to a non-political penal authority which had committed her to a criminal prison for women in southern Germany.

She had spent three years there. The work given to her group of prisoners was the washing and darning of woollen socks that had been sent by the German army for renovation. Win had continued to fight the war on the side of the Allies by darning a blister-raising knot into the heel of every German army sock that passed through her hands.

The prison doors were opened in 1945 by American troops who believed at first that they were liberating political prisoners. She stayed there for a week or two, acting as interpreter for the local American commander and helping him to separate the thieves and murderers from the prostitutes and the mentally ill, before going by train back to Paris on a *laissez-passer*. Her offices had long ago been looted and the former concierge had disappeared, but she was ready to start up in business again. She had only one complaint: her lawyer had informed her that it was now necessary to keep two sets of books, one for herself and another for the tax inspector. She had never before in France found that kind of deceit to be necessary.

The post-war Win was a mellower person than the one we had known before. She had come to terms with herself and could talk freely of old times. One of the things she told us about was the search for a missing heir to an American fortune that she had worked on in the thirties. She had been engaged as a trilingual interpreter by an American lawyer named Starr to help him to assess claimants and to make secret inquiries all over Europe. Some of the inquiries had been complicated and had involved official records going back to Napoleonic times. Lawyer Starr had died before a true heir had been found. The Nazis had been after the money she said, and wondered if the search would ever be resumed.

I knew that it would be resumed, but fictionally and by me. Win was amused when I told her this; we had made our peace. She let me ask questions about the search and told me in detail about some of the difficulties.

The book that I wrote about all this was called *The Schirmer Inheritance,* but I did not write it immediately. In the last year of the war our friend Lesley Blanch had met and married the novelist Romain Gary, then an officer in the Free French air force. At war's end, Romain had been invited to join the French foreign service. He and Lesley were *en poste* in Sofia when the Bulgarian show trials ordered by Stalin were staged there. Romain attended the trials as French diplomatic observer. Later, in Paris, he told me of the methods used by the state prosecutor to manipulate and coerce the defendants. One of them was a diabetic and the prosecutor arranged for the prison authorities to withhold insulin from this prisoner during the trial.

The book in which I used this piece of information, *Judgement on Deltchev,* has been described flatteringly as an anti-Stalinist socialist novel. For me it represented a happy return to writing thrillers.

Its reception in America was mixed. Why, it was asked repeatedly, had I not written another *Dimitrios*? The mixture as before? No, of course not; just another book like Dimitrios or maybe *Journey into Fear*. Was this supposed to be a straight novel or a mystery? Was it a triumph or a disaster? I had a letter from one American reader who wished to draw my attention to the work of a New York psychoanalyst specializing in writers' block.

In England, the letters I received about the book were all more or less abusive. I was a traitor in the class war struggle, a Titoist lackey and an American imperialist cat's-paw. One message was a single piece of used toilet paper. The single piece was a delicate touch I thought; it spoke of careful premeditation. The oddest letter came from a man who wanted to know why, if I was so against Soviet Communism, my name was down on the letterhead of the Society for Cultural Relations with the USSR as a member of the Literary Committee. I did not know for certain why, but I could guess. It was probably th ere for the same reason that J.B. Priestley's name was there; because we were both on Mrs Brown's list. Mrs Brown was a friendly soul who went around touching writers who lived in central London for subscriptions to the *Daily Worker*. 'Jack Priestley gave me twenty pounds,' she would say; 'surely you can manage ten. I don't mind taking a cheque.'

I had several fallings-out with Mrs Brown. We fell out over Poland and Czechoslovakia and we fell out over Tito. She was always well briefed and usually I had no answers for the 'facts' with which she assailed my limp misgivings. 'I suppose you've been reading the *News Chronicle* again,' she would say as if it were an addiction to be equated with that of the opium of the people; 'for Pete's sake, let's have a few of the facts.'

After *Judgement on Deltchev* was published, though, she never called on me again.

Among the novels that I can always re-read with pleasure is W.S. Maugham's *Cakes and Ale*. It was first published in 1930 and went into many editions, both here and in America. I was learning then about the business of writing and took an almost professional interest in the publishing progress of a book I so much admired. It was impossible not to notice over the years that almost every new edition of it, English or American, had a graceful preface by Mr Maugham denying the widespread belief that the character of the novelist Alroy Kear in the book was based on the real novelist Hugh Walpole. These denials were so disingenuous and unconvincing that I was sure that, if I ever had the good fortune to meet Mr Maugham, I would be careful to say nothing about them.

I met him eventually through his publisher A.S. Frere, whom most of his friends called Frere, and Pat Wallace, Frere's wife, whom most of her friends call Wallace.

In the post-war forties, when exchange control regulations were at their worst, we shared with the Freres the cost of leasing a villa at St-Jean-Cap-Ferrat for a few weeks in the sun. Mr Maugham's Villa Mauresque was just along the road. We were invited once or twice to lunch or dine.

Much has been written about life at the Villa Mauresque. Not all of it can have been true. An American writer who spent a couple of weekends there managed to inflate the experience into a full-length book of memoirs. The tone was adulatory. Academic biographers, who can only have heard tell, have tended to be bitchier. When I first knew him Mr Maugham was in his seventies and still working hard as a writer. No one was obliged to accept his hospitality. The trouble was that, as well as being an overbearing host, he could also be a very tiresome guest.

In St Jean one year he replied to a note of mine thanking him for dinner with a note telling me not to be so stand-offish and to call him Willie. I replied by asking him to dine with us when he came to London. He accepted.

It was a ghastly evening. He had been to a cocktail party with an Assistant Commissioner (Crime) at Scotland Yard and left there early, bored. We had asked him for eight o'clock and he arrived at seven demanding food. We had ordered the Indian dinner he had wanted, and a special chef to cook it, for eight-thirty. Mr Maugham refused a drink and sulked until the Freres and Alan Searle came. The food was to his liking but he asked for beer instead of wine and then drank wine. When he left he said, with a thin smile, that he had enjoyed himself.

In November of that year, Wallace, who was running the Rank story department then, had to go to New York. While she was away Frere gave a dinner party at their rooms in Albany. The guests were Mr Maugham, J. B. Priestley, Noël Coward, Phillip Jordan of the *News Chronicle* and me.

Willie and I were the early arrivals. More from the need to say something than because I thought it would interest him I mentioned that I had bought a first edition of *The Explorer*, a bad novel of his that had been published in 1908.

He gave me a sharp look. 'How much did you have to pay for it?'

'Three pounds.' Those were still the days of the seven-and-sixpenny novel and before collecting contemporary first editions became fashionable. He may well have gathered that I thought the price excessive.

'Wasn't it worth three pounds?' he asked.

'Well . . .'

He nodded bleakly and went to talk to Frere. He had had enough of me. Noël was the one who knew how to please him. He came bounding in, made straight for Willie, bobbed a curtsey, went down on one knee and said, '*Maître!*'

Willie simpered with pleasure. They began to talk about the theatre.

At dinner, Willie, who was at the head of the table, concentrated on his food until someone, I think it was Priestley, in saying something about the Book Society regretted Hugh Walpole's death. He had often been helpful to promising writers.

Willie put down his knife and fork and looked up. 'I knew Hugh Walpole for a great many years,' he said deliberately. 'I can tell you from my own knowledge that he behaved disgracefully to several talented young writers, one of whom I knew personally. Hugh Walpole ruined his life.'

He glowered at us. His meaning was plain. We all knew perfectly well that what he was really talking about was not a talented writer but a stolen boyfriend, an unrequited love and an old canker of jealously. Only Priestley remained unimpressed.

'You know, Willie,' he said, 'I've always thought that in *Cakes and Ale* you were a little unkind to poor Hugh.'

Willie began to stammer badly. Priestley waited for a moment and then went on: 'There were five men in Hugh Walpole,' he said, 'and one of them was a very nice fellow.'

Phillip Jordan muttered that one nice fellow in five didn't seem much of a percentage, but the remark was lost when Noël tried to introduce a lighter note.

'I once travelled up from Cornwall on a train with Hugh Walpole,' he said. 'I was fifteen at the time. He patted my knee and gave me half-a-crown.'

Willie did not join in the amusement. He began to stammer again, and then suddenly the words came, and his anger with them.

'I have known some odious men in my time,' he said deliberately. 'One of the most odious was Lord Alfred Douglas. But, odious though he was, he always remained a gentleman.' His voice rose. 'Hugh Walpole was a c-c-c-cad.'

There was a silence. We were none of us very young, but I don't think that anyone there remembered hearing the word 'cad' used as such a virulent expression of hatred. Even Noël, who had last used 'cad' back in 1932 to rhyme with 'mad' in the lyric of 'Mad About The Boy', looked startled. The rest of us avoided Willie's eye by looking at our plates.

Later, I thought of all the fun Willie must have had over the years, writing those graceful denials that Alroy Kear was a portrait of Hugh Walpole and knowing all the time that he would never be believed; least of all by Hugh Walpole.

*   *   *

Not long after that I was asked to deliver a lecture at the *Sunday Times* Book Exhibition. The subject of the lecture was to be the relationship between the film industry and those novelists for whom it seemed, at that time, to have become an occupational hazard.

The audience was much bigger than I had expected and I had several minutes of stage fright. Frere, who was acting as chairman and introducing me, had a rough-and-ready way of restoring my confidence.

'Book people', he said, 'are always very decent and polite. They may smother yawns but they won't walk out. In my introduction I'm going to mention that you were decorated for bravery in the war. That's all right, isn't it?'

'No, Frere. I wasn't decorated for bravery.'

'You're sure? Oh well, it doesn't matter.' He crossed out a paragraph of his notes. 'You'll be all right. I'll tell you something. The best person at this kind of thing was Hugh Walpole. He could do it off the cuff, without a note.'

'I've got a complete script.' I showed him the thing.

'As long as you don't let them see that you're reading it, that's all right. Make it seem like a few notes. Book people are very tolerant.'

And so they were. I was asked by the Director of the British Film Academy, Roger Manvell, to give the lecture again, and on the Academy's behalf, at the Edinburgh Festival. For that occasion, I elaborated the lecture a little and took the precaution of learning it by heart.

In order to dramatize my theme I invented a case history. The writer in it was a young novelist whom I called Jerome Anders. He sold his first novel to a film producer, was asked to work on the script and suffered the usual bouts of euphoria and disillusionment. He learned that writing to be read and writing for the screen were different crafts. He arrived at a moment of decision. I went on:

'It is not everyone who can fertilize the sacred cow, and he may find the experience deeply satisfying. If he does, then, as a novelist, his goose is cooked. But if, and this is possible, all that he experiences is a sense of anti-climax, a feeling of irritation because his work must now be handed over to others, yet not sufficient irritation to make him want to do the rest of the work himself, there is hope. It will not be long before he is back

233

working in a medium in which he can be fully creative; in which he can forget for a while the sacred cow and its attendant male nurses, and function again not only as a father to the child, but as mother, doctor and midwife also.

'Is this, then, after all, a simple dilemma – fulfilment or frustration? Fulfilled he stays, frustrated he leaves? I think that for some writers it proves to be so. For others, however, the issue is not so clear cut.'

Quite so. I was, of course, speaking for and about myself.